ART IN PSYCHOANALYSIS

PSYCHOANALYTIC IDEAS AND APPLICATIONS SERIES

IPA Publications Committee

Gennaro Saragnano (Rome), Chair; Leticia Glocer Fiorini (Buenos Aires), Consultant; Samuel Arbiser (Buenos Aires); Catalina Bronstein (London); Paulo Cesar Sandler (São Paulo); Christian Seulin (Lyon); Mary Kay O'Neil (Montreal); Gail S. Reed (New York); Rhoda Bawdekar (London), Ex-officio as Publications Officer

Other titles in the Series

The Art of Interpretation: Deconstruction and New Beginning in the Psychoanalytic Process
  Wolfgang Loch
    edited and commentary by Peter Wegner

The Unconscious: Further Reflections
    edited by José Carlos Calich & Helmut Hinz

Escape from Selfhood: Breaking Boundaries and Craving for Oneness
  Ilany Kogan

The Unconscious in Psychoanalysis
  Antonio Alberti Semi

From Impression to Inquiry: A Tribute to the Work of Robert Wallerstein
    edited by Wilma Bucci & Norbert Freedman; associate editor Ethan A. Graham

Talking About Supervision: 10 Questions, 10 Analysts = 100 Answers
    edited by Laura Elliot Rubinstein

Envy and Gratitude Revisited
    edited by Priscilla Roth and Alessandra Lemma

The Work of Confluence: Listening and Interpreting in the Psychoanalytic Field
  Madeleine & Willy Baranger
    edited and commentary by Leticia Glocer Fiorini
  Foreword by Cláudio Laks Eizink

Good Feelings: Psychoanalytic Reflections in Positive Emotions and Attitudes
    edited by Salman Akhtar

Psychosomatics Today: A Psychoanalytical Perspective
    edited by Marilia Aisenstein & Elsa Rappoport de Aisemberg

Unrepresented States and the Construction of Meaning: Clinical and Theoretical Contributions
    edited by Howard B. Levine, Gail S. Reed, & Dominique Scarfone

ART IN PSYCHOANALYSIS

A Contemporary Approach to Creativity and Analytic Practice

Edited by

Gabriela Goldstein

Preface by
Harold P. Blum

General Editor
Gennaro Saragnano

Psychoanalytic Ideas and Applications Series

KARNAC

First published in 2013 by
Karnac Books Ltd
118 Finchley Road, London NW3 5HT

Copyright © 2013 to The International Psychoanalytical Association for the edited collection, and to the individual authors for their contributions.

The rights of the contributors to be identified as the authors of this work have been asserted in accordance with §§ 77 and 78 of the Copyright Design and Patents Act 1988.

All rights reserved. No part of this publication may be reproduced, stored in a retrieval system, or transmitted, in any form or by any means, electronic, mechanical, photocopying, recording, or otherwise, without the prior written permission of the publisher.

British Library Cataloguing in Publication Data

A C.I.P. for this book is available from the British Library

ISBN 978 1 78220 003 1

Edited, designed and produced by The Studio Publishing Services Ltd
www.publishingservicesuk.co.uk
e-mail: studio@publishingservicesuk.co.uk

Printed in Great Britain

www.karnacbooks.com

CONTENTS

PSYCHOANALYTIC IDEAS AND APPLICATIONS SERIES   vii
   IPA Publications Committee

ABOUT THE EDITOR AND CONTRIBUTORS   ix

PREFACE: Psychoanalysis and the arts   xv
   Harold P. Blum

INTRODUCTION   xix
   Gabriela Goldstein

CHAPTER ONE
Form and content in the visual arts: a psychoanalytic perspective   1
   Charles Hanly

CHAPTER TWO
Implicit "motion" in non-verbal art: transmission and transformation of affect   21
   Gilbert J. Rose

CHAPTER THREE
Picasso's prolonged adolescence, his Blue Period, and blind figures 39
Harold P. Blum

CHAPTER FOUR
Psychoanalysis and art: from applied analysis to interdisciplinary dialogue 57
Adela Abella

CHAPTER FIVE
From a source to a fountain, or from the sublime to the uncanny 79
Carlos Weisse

CHAPTER SIX
Creative processes in art and psychoanalysis: moving towards an expanded metapsychology 97
Hector Fiorini

CHAPTER SEVEN
In between and across 109
Andrea Sabbadini

CHAPTER EIGHT
A fragment of the complex world: resorting to creation in the midst of negation, disavowal, and working through 123
Dominique Suchet

CHAPTER NINE
Living creatively: the concept of a sound-minded individual and the healing phenomena 139
José Outeiral

CHAPTER TEN
To heal or create, to create and heal: in search of their author 151
Murielle Gagnebin

CHAPTER ELEVEN
The greatest love of all 171
Gabriela Goldstein

INDEX 189

PSYCHOANALYTIC IDEAS AND APPLICATIONS SERIES

IPA Publications Committee

The Publications Committee of the International Psychoanalytical Association continues, with this volume, the series "Psychoanalytic Ideas and Applications".

The aim of this series is to focus on the scientific production of significant authors whose works are outstanding contributions to the develolpment of the psychoanalytic field and to set out relevant ideas and themes, generated during the history of psychoanalysis, that deserve to be known and discussed by present psychoanalysts.

The relationship between psychoanalytic ideas and their applications has to be put forward from the perspective of theory, clinical practice, technique, and research in order to maintain their validity for contemporary psychoanalysis.

The Publication Committee's objective is to share these ideas with the psychoanalytic community and with professionals in other related disciplines, in order to expand their knowledge and generate a productive interchange between the text and the reader.

Art in Psychoanalysis: A Contemporary Approach to Creativity and Analytic Practice, edited by Gabriela Goldstein, is a book that fits perfectly with our series' aim and provides one beautiful example of a valid interdisciplinary approach to themes that have always been in the interest and in the passion of psychoanalysts worldwide. The relation between art and psychoanalysis, the problem of form and the creativity processes, are all viewed and explored from different theoretical frames, which, at the same time, highlight the main issues and allow for new and interesting hypotheses. What, in my opinion, gives this book a particular value is its constant reference to clinical work and to the possibility of improving—by studying art and the creativity processes—our understanding of the psychoanalytical phenomena.

I am, therefore, sure that this book will encounter the appreciation of both psychoanalysts and students of the relationship between art and psychoanalysis. I think that very special thanks are due to the editor and to all the distinguished contributors to this volume, which enriches the IPA "Psychoanalytic Ideas and Applications" series.

Gennaro Saragnano
Series Editor
Chair, IPA Publications Committee

ABOUT THE EDITOR AND CONTRIBUTORS

Adela Abella is a medical doctor and a child, adolescent, and adult psychiatrist. She is a training analyst for children and adolescents (COCAP), and of the Swiss Psychoanalytical Society. President of the Centre de Psychanalyse de la Suisse Romande, she is a Full Member of the International Psychoanalytic Association and a Member of the IPA's Culture Committee. She has published papers in several issues of the *International Journal*, among others, with a special interest in the interface between psychoanalysis and contemporary art.

Harold P. Blum is Clinical Professor of Psychiatry and Supervising and Training Analyst at the Psychoanalytic Institute of the New York University Medical Center. He is also the Executive Director of the Sigmund Freud Archives. His service as editor of the *Journal of the American Psychoanalytic Association* inspired readers and contributors alike, as well as those fortunate to serve on editorial board during his tenure. Dr Blum is recognised as a true Freud scholar and the author of significant and varied articles. His books include *Defense and Resistance: Historical Perspectives and Current Concepts* (1985), *Female Psychology: Contemporary Psychoanalytic Views* (1977), and *Reconstruction in Psychoanalysis: Childhood Revisited and Recreated* (1994). He has been highly influential in psychoanalytic thought both in the USA and abroad. He is the founder and chair of the "Art and Psychoanalysis Symposium", held in Florence, Italy since 1997, and he has written and presented contributions and books on the field.

Hector Fiorini is a medical psychiatrist and psychoanalyst, and Professor of Psychoanalytic Clinic and Psychotherapies at the University of Buenos Aires for graduate and postgraduate studies. He is a postgraduate professor at Universidad Complutense de Madrid, Universidad de Salamanca, Aalborg University, Denmark, and Campinhas University of Sao Paulo, guest professor of the Institute of Psychoanalysis of New York (colloquy with foreign authors), and guest lecturer on creative processes in clinical work at Anglia Ruskin University, Cambridge. His books, *The Creating Psyche*; *Theory and Technique of Psychotherapies*; *The Theoretical and Clinical Field of Psychoanalytic Psychotherapies*; *Structures and Approaches in Psychoanalytic Psychotherapies*, are published in Spanish, English, and Portuguese, and have reached seventy editions. He is the Director in Buenos Aires of the Training Center in Psychotherapies, a psychoanalytic institution of clinical assistance and training.

Murielle Gagnebin is a Full Member of the SPP and the IPA, and a professor at the Paris-III Universities (New Sorbonne). She holds a State Doctorate in Letters and Human Sciences, with very honorable mention and the unanimous congratulations of the jury on her thesis, "Philosophical and psychoanalytic interpretation of artistic creation" at the University of Paris-I; DESS in Clinical Psychology at the University of Lyon-II, 1988; State Doctorate in Letters, University of Geneva, with very honorable mention and the unanimous congratulations of the jury on her thesis, "Essay on ugliness". She also holds a Doctorate Honoris Causa from the State University of Moscow (Lomonosov), 2008. Some of her books are: *The Living Buried. Some Psychic Mechanisms of Creation* (Seyssel, Champ Vallon, PUF, 1987); *For Psychoanalytic Aesthetics. The Artist, Strategist of the Unconscious* (Paris, PUF, coll. "The Red Thread", 1994); *From the Couch to the Screen. Cinematic Montages and Interpretative Montages* (Paris, PUF, coll. "The Red Thread", 1999); *Authenticity of the False. Psychoanalytic Readings* (Paris, PUF, coll. "The Red Thread", 2004); *The Work and its Artist* (Paris, PUF, coll. "The Red Thread", 2011). She is also the author of several articles and contributions to journals throughout the world, has been Director of a Research Centre on images and their relations since 1997, at the University of Paris III, a Member of the French Society of Aesthetics since 1980, and a Member of the French Society of Poetics since 1994.

Gabriela Goldstein graduated in Psychology and Architecture and is a psychoanalyst in private practice in Buenos Aires. She is also a training analyst and member of the board of the Asociacion Psicoanalitica Argentina (APA) (2008–2012), a full member IPA, and member of the Psychoanalysis and Culture Committee, in addition to being a Member of the Library and Publications Committee, and secretary of the Visual Arts Committee in the APA. She has published, and presented, lectures in Congress and Symposia, written papers and collaborations on art and psychoanalysis, "Aesthetic post-impressions", "The violence of creativity", "Et in Arcadia Ego ...", "On love and sexuality in middle-aged men", "*La vida de los otros*, o la vida propia", (over the film *The Life of the Others*), and other presentations, and the book *The Aesthetic Experience: Writings on Art and Psychoanalysis*, Editorial del Estante, 2005. She is also a painter, showing in galleries in America and Europe since 1987..

Charles Hanly is a psychoanalyst in private practice, a training analyst at the Toronto Institute of Psychoanalysis and a Professor Emeritus at the University of Toronto. He studied at the University of Toronto and at Oxford University. He has been in part-time practice in psychoanalysis since 1974, when he completed his training and became a member of the Canadian Psychoanalytic Society. Since 1995, he has been in full-time private practice of psychoanalysis. He is the author of more than seventy clinical and scientific papers and four books in the field of psychoanalysis. He is invited to give lectures and panel presentations at conferences in North America, Europe, and Latin America. Professor Hanly's clinical skills and scientific contributions were recognised internationally in 2007 when he was elected President-elect of the International Psychoanalytic Association. He took office as President of the IPA in 2009.

José O. Outeiral is a medical doctor, psychiatrist, and psychoanalyst. He is a Full Member of the International Psychoanalytical Association, a training analyst of the Society Psicanalítica de Pelotas, and Guest Member of the Brazilian Society of Psychoanalysis of Rio De Janeiro. He is a former professor of the College of Medicine of the Pontifical University Catholic of Porto Alegre, and the author of books and articles published in Brazil and abroad. He is a Member of the Board of "Encontros Latinoamericanaos sobre o Pensamento de Donald Winnicott", and a Collaborator of the *Brazilian Magazine of Psychoanalysis*.

Gilbert J. Rose is a graduate of Harvard College (with Honors in Psychology), Boston University Medical School, and Downstate Psychoanalytic Institute in New York. A former faculty member of Yale University Medical School and The Western New England Psychoanalytic Institute, he is a Member of Muriel Gardiner Program in Psychoanalysis and the Humanities at Yale and the author of four books: *The Power of Form, Trauma and Mastery in Life and Art, Necessary Illusion,* and *Between Couch and Piano.* He is in private practice of psychiatry and psychoanalysis in Norwalk, Connecticut.

Andrea Sabbadini is a Fellow of the British Psychoanalytical Society and its current Director of Publications. He works in private practice in London, is a Senior Lecturer at UCL, a trustee of the Freud Museum, a member of the IPA Committee on Psychoanalysis and Culture, the director of the European Psychoanalytic Film Festival, and the chairman of a programme of films and discussions at the Institute of Contemporary Arts (ICA). He is the founder editor of *Psychoanalysis and History* and the Film Section editor of *The International Journal of Psychoanalysis*. He has published in the major psychoanalytic journals, and has edited *Il tempo in psicoanalisi* (1979), *Even Paranoids Have Enemies* (1998), *The Couch and the Silver Screen* (2003), *Projected Shadows* (2007) and *Psychoanalytic Visions of Cinema/Cinematic Visions of Psychoanalysis* (2007).

Dominique Suchet was born in Paris in 1955, and practises psychoanalysis at Lyon, where she resides. A Member of the Psychoanalytic Association of France, she publishes in diverse psychoanalytic journals and contributes to collective works: "Incarnation", in *The Intermediate Kingdom. Psychoanalysis, Literature, about J. B. Pontalis* (Gallimard, Paris, 2007); "Torn places in evenly suspended attention", in *The Object, Reality, the Rule and Tact* (APF/*Annuary*, 2008, PUF); "Making latent in the work of the session", in *The A Posteriori* (RFP, 2009); "The invisible object", in *Lacan* (2010).

Carlos Weisse is a medical doctor, training analyst in Asociación Psicoanalítica Argentina (APA, member of the Scientific Committee and Center of Studies of Psychoanalysis of APA. He is a full member of the International Psychoanalytical Association, a psychiatrist, full member of FEFAL, a training analyst of the IPA, and a specialist and resident in psychiatry at Hospital Nacional "Dr. José T. Borda". Some of his published papers are: "Vacío y pulsión en la obra de arte"; "El objeto y el concepto en el arte contemporáneo"; "Los mitos populares argentinos y su relación con el sacrificio"; "Discurso y representación"; "Arte y discurso"; "Angustia, duelo y sublimación"; "Clínica de la Angustia"; "Certeza y psicosis"; "Duelo y sublimación: el surgimiento de un nuevo lenguaje"; among others. He is the founder of the Editorial Board of the magazine *Caracu*, on art and psychoanalysis.

PREFACE

Psychoanalysis and the arts

Harold P. Blum

Psychoanalysis and art have had a relationship that is both complementary and controversial, with cross-fertilisation and isolation of the two fields. Although Freud stated that analysis must lay down its arms before the problem of the creative artist, he did not do so himself. Following Freud's application of psychoanalytic thought to the understanding of art, there has been an increasing number of psychoanalytic contributions to the comprehension of art and the artist, taking into account his/her history and personality as well as the artistic productions. Aesthetics and the creative process have been considered, as well as the responses of spectators both outside and within the psychoanalytic setting. When an analysand refers to a work of art, analytic work might lead to further exploration of their own conflicts and/or creative interests. Interdisciplinary studies attempt to link psychoanalysis, art, and, more recently, neuroscience, lending the excitement of new perspectives and connections. These contributions, however, are vulnerable to over-simplification and wild analysis. The history of homo sapiens is remarkable in its revelations of the universality of artistic production, its value through the ages, and mankind's capacity for innovation and creativity.

This book brings together a group of papers by distinguished, scholarly analysts, representing a wide range of views about the psychoanalytic interpretation of art as well as the relation to the clinical analytic process. An overview of some of the salient issues addressed by these authors, as well as by some earlier contributors, is interwoven with some of my own thoughts.

These papers illustrate the evolution of psychoanalytic thought concerning the productive interplay of psychoanalysis and art in the contemporary context of theoretical pluralism. Psychoanalysis is a scientific discipline which has advanced and been enriched by artists and their art. Clinical interpretation and the interpretation of art are, in themselves, creative endeavours. Psychoanalytically orientated biography and pathography do not have distinct boundaries and now focus on both the creative and the conflictual or regressive aspects of the artist's personality.

Analyst and artist are open to latent meanings behind manifest façades and are able to restore connections, make new connections and discoveries, to create what had not existed before. Psychoanalytic considerations of art no longer simply reduce its creation to a form of sublimation; the concept of drive sublimation without repression has lost its lustre. The concept of sublimation was overextended to apply to many issues, such as curiosity. However, when sexual curiosity was displaced on to intellectual curiosity, there was a transformation not only of drive aims, but also of object relations, values, and structural organisation. In clinical work, voyeurism of the psychoanalyst is modified and transmuted in psychoanalytic enquiry and the pursuit of insight. Curiosity is over-determined and does not fundamentally derive from sublimation, but from the innate endowment of primates. In addition to sublimation, the early analysts noted and emphasised the Oedipal conflicts of the artist expressed in their art. Art reveals universal fantasies as well as the individual variations of the Oedipal fantasies of the artist. Art is also understood as attempted mastery and working through of real traumatic experience and object loss.

With the introduction of pre-Oedipal, narcissistic, and self and object relations perspectives, the interpretation of art was greatly enriched, but became far more complex. Novelty, a fundamental precursor to art, begins in the earliest playful transactions of infant and mother. The infant creates the breast/part object within the reciprocal affecto–motor dialogue with the mother, who becomes the primary object. Transitional objects and transitional space bridge fantasy and reality, and transitional space becomes the initial locus of creativity. Art may partake of pre-verbal archaic communication and incomplete self-object differentiation in empathic response, and in the patterning, rhythm, and harmony or disharmony of the dialogue. This form of knowing and feeling, inchoate and ineffable, might be evoked in the spectator, and in the analytic transference–countertransference relationship. The affective communication could involve the endowment of humans with mirror neurons, which might also contribute to capacities for empathy and trial identification. In later development, the good object is invested with primordial love, survives hostile aggression, and is preserved in art. Form is only artificially separated from content, and form might not only defend against content, but also defines and informs content. Art might not only defend against reality, but might also interpret and inform aspects of reality. Every interpretation has subjective elements and there is no immaculate perception without the distorting influence of the unconscious. In every work of art, the artist has unconsciously and/or consciously recreated the self. The spectator completes the artwork, analagous to the concept of co-creation of an analytic narrative.

While a work of art may be studied without any knowledge of the artist or of the historical, cultural context of the art, these severe restrictions will limit analytic enquiry and interpretation. In contradistinction to interpreting a work of art in isolation, an analyst has far more certainty regarding interpretations of the work when the artist's biography and cultural–historical background can be integrated with perceptions of the work itself. While analogies may be drawn between clinical analysis and the analysis of art, the analyst has far more data about his/her patient on which to base interpretations than are available to understand an artist and his/her work. Moreover, the mute work of art does not respond and cannot confirm or modify interpretation. Analysts employ symbolic interpretation, but cannot confidently extend analytic interpretation and genetic reconstruction without the type of information and associations they have when working with patients. The psychoanalytic understanding of symbol and metaphor in art was incorporated by many art historians in their own interpretations of art. Prior emphasis on the artist's utilisation of regression is a generalisation which might not hold true for all artists or all types of art.

Currently, analyst and art historian take into account the age and development of artists and their art through the life cycle. Art could be linked to a particular developmental phase, such as adolescence, with its burgeoning originality and creativity. An artist's work might change during the various phases of the life cycle.

Despite Freud's pessimism regarding a psychoanalytic approach to aesthetics, aesthetic propositions are now ubiquitous in applied psychoanalysis. Most art is pleasurable, and what is considered beautiful is usually highly pleasurable. When art is designed to shock, frighten, or intimidate the spectator, a sense of beauty might still prevail in the colour, composition, or formal harmony of the art. Metabolising aggression, hostility, and trauma might also provide aesthetic rewards. Love, Eros, is necessary for the unifying and binding integration in a work of art, as opposed to chaotic destruction. The love of art might derive from bodily pleasure, narcissistic self-love, and from its connection to the idealised, beloved object. If beauty conveys a feeling of unalterable perfection, when not a dot or line need be changed, beauty is rooted in the unconscious narcissistic object representation, modified by development and culture.

Uncertainty abounds concerning a psychoanalytic approach to aesthetics and the sense and meaning of beauty. There are many significant, yet very different, propositions about these deeply perplexing topics. It is not known whether infants have an anlage of beauty, and any infantile experience could hardly be the same as the sense of beauty in later development. The later sense of beauty, or what is regarded as ugly, is powerfully influenced by culture and by the impact of the artist or a community of artists on what will, in time, be regarded as beautiful. There are many examples of art that were unrecognised or disparaged by spectators and art critics, only to be subsequently acclaimed. The excitement of first encounter with great art might evoke an experience of beauty, especially if it does not arouse opposing affects of envy and rivalry with the artist and work of art. To be delighted or dismayed by a work of art suggests the impassioned revival of unconscious love or hate, which might be associated with a conscious feeling of the uncanny. A lovely beauty, a mysterious beauty, or a terrible beauty might provide an aesthetic experience, highly dependent on the individual. Although "beauty is in the eye of the beholder", there is frequently consensus in a historical social context about a work of art being beautiful. However, the complex concepts of beauty remain ill-defined and enigmatic.

Introduction

Gabriela Goldstein

This book explores recent contributions to the status of psychoanalytic thought in relation to art and creativity and the implications of these investigations for contemporary analytic practice. New interdisciplinary developments have shed light on the great topic of "the essence of artistic function", which Freud (1910c) characterised as *psychoanalytically inaccessible*. The authors who participate in this book took up Freud's challenge and based their essays on various frames of reference in the fields of art and psychoanalysis. Addressing the inaccessibility of art might open paths to understanding the elusive aspects of subjectivity.

When French philosopher Didi-Huberman states that "a painting thinks, perhaps, what is unapproachable to thought" (2007), not only does he reopen the historical debate concerning the opposition between feeling and thought, but also introduces a different approach to art that supersedes the idea of the aesthetic in art as pure pleasure. Although art and painting certainly involve emotion and the deciphering of a meaning, they also promote a discourse inherent in art that reformulates a question: what is it that lies beyond the figurable and sayable that uncovers the creative potential of aesthetic experience? In a new twist, this discourse also gives a certain degree of *autonomy* to the object of art, which is, in a way, a subject.

The title, *Art in Psychoanalysis: Contemporary Approaches to Creativity and Analytic Practice*, reflects a dual perspective: that of art and its contributions to theory and clinical practice on the one hand, and the response from psychoanalysis, the "interpretation" of art, on the other. *Art in Psychoanalysis* opens the way for reflections on the relevance of art and discovers the "aesthetic value of analytic work when it is able to create something new in the relation with the patient" (Saragnano, 2011).

Deeply committed to the subject of art and its research through psychoanalysis, all the authors breathe the air surrounding the phenomenon of art and inhabit and explore its folds and filigrees. Thus, experience with art and creation emanates a psychic atmosphere, or *Seele Stimmung*, that advances the work of fantasmatic subjectivisation. These contributions to a "psychoanalytic aesthetics" introduce us to the idea put forth by Didi-Huberman (2007) that art thinks.

Aesthetics (*Aesthetis*) emerges as a specific discipline with Baumgarten (1750) in philosophy. It transcends the value assigned to the sensible, the area to which it seemed to have been reduced, and connects the notion of thought to art. The historical dichotomy between the sensible and the knowable, a Platonic legacy, also brings to light other oppositions—reason and sentiment and the beautiful and the sublime (negative pleasure in Kant). This theoretical debate posits an eternal *disjunction*. However, Jauss (1972), a theoretician of the aesthetics of reception, and others propose a *conjunction* in the historical controversy between aesthetic pleasure and reason as knowledge. For Jauss (1982), *aesthetic pleasure already involves a theoretical condition*, which he understands as a pleasure that thinks. The latter occurs when a kind of "discomfort" is added to aesthetic pleasure that questions us, contributing to the enigmatic character of the work of art. In this way, new orders of discourse emerge, as well as the shudder of symbolic continuity.

The question of *the enigmatic condition of art* recognises something inaccessible in it that exceeds all that is thinkable, felt or symbolisable. This riddle has no solution. It may only be decoded or encoded, since "in each genuine artwork something appears that does not exist" (Adorno, 1997, p. 82), which raises the question of truth in art. This truth can be neither wholly revealed nor said, and originates in forbidden unconscious desire and, in another sense, in the impossible encounter with "the thing"—the lost object, a trace of that unforgettable prehistoric Other (Freud, 1896). The truth of the artwork involves a traumatic encounter with *das Ding* and is also, paradoxically, a pleasurable encounter mediated by a veiling of form in the work.

It is perhaps because the condition of possibility of this type of encounter is a veiling that Hegel states that Kant is "too tender with things" (quoted in Eagleton, 1990). The creation of a veil is part both of the aesthetic experience and of the *poiesis* of making works of art. In contemporary art, this encounter with the Other, which appears to be more immediate, was described by Foster (1996) as "the return of the real". Such return of the traumatic appears in a specific guise in repetition (*Wiederholung*), which reconnects art and life in a different way.

For Warburg, this issue finds its place in *Pathosformeln* or emotional formulae, the expression of an essential, or we could say primal (in Aulagnier's (2001) sense of the term), movement that explains the tension between the Dionysian and the Apollonian (Burucúa, 2003). From a psychoanalytic perspective, this tension is the confrontation between desire and the forbidden, where the encounter with the other reveals the tension of alterity. When this tension is mediated by the work of art, it has the power to move us.

The Freudian text recovers its density with the developments of contemporary psychoanalysis in its intersection with aesthetics, an intersection that inaugurates a new regime of the visible and the legible that Rancière describes as "a specific regime of the sensible" (Rancière, 2004, p. 23). This aesthetic regime configures a place where art's distinct tensions find meaning in psychoanalysis. The conscious of the unconscious is able to unfold on this common ground, bridging the experience with art and analytic experience. It is here where unresolved tensions emerge between thought and non-thought, the said and the unsaid. For this reason, works of art have occupied a privileged place in psychoanalysis since its origins.

The authors' investigations in the field that straddles psychoanalysis and art show the inversion demanded by Heidegger (1950) when he says that we should be prepared in advance to see how everything turns towards us in a new way. We could say, as Goethe did, "My purpose in making this wonderful journey is not to delude myself but to discover myself in the objects I see" (Goethe, 1962, p. 57).

This book unfolds as a narrative in which, chapter by chapter, readers may discover different aspects of, and approaches to, the question of form in art and creative processes, and their respective relations with psychoanalysis. The first chapter will immediately stimulate their curiosity, raising questions that will be taken up again later and offer answers or new questions. It is a matter of finding and weaving together one's own "connections and correspondences", as Benjamin (1968) would say, between chapters. Each opens up a world and invites readers to explore it.

Although all essays intersect and share some themes and areas, each may be read independently. We are, thus, invited to read both transversally and longitudinally. A transversal reading builds a new written discourse depending on the choice of chapters; a comprehensive successive reading might discover the core of a more intimate discourse. The book reveals its sources and dialogues with culture and illuminates new ways of thinking about psychoanalysis and clinical practice. This quality constitutes its vitality. Convergences and divergences emerge at the different crossroads of psychoanalysis and art. However, the reader might find a "red thread" linking the authors' ideas that explains a paradox or creative ambiguity intertwining three lines of thought present in the different chapters, and their discussions and openings.

The first is the perspective of the intermediate area, a concept formulated as a space of interrelation between art and psychoanalysis. In this space, heir to Winnicott's (1971) "intermediate zone-area of creativity", metaphorical bridges are built that skirt the edge of the void (Winnicott, 1971). This space that circulates between primary and secondary processes configures a peculiar and complex interweaving with the Other of culture. Considered in relation to this intermediate zone, the concept of "tertiary process" (A. Green and others) acquires a status of its own and unfolds a metapsychology of creativity.

The second line establishes the state of the art of conceptual instruments that have been used up to now in the "interpretation" of art. These instruments are pushed to the limit in order to expand the boundaries of psychoanalysis's thinking about art. Conceptualisations in relation to art, particularly contemporary art, are proposed, such as the picture function, the veil, Lacan's Real, and Bion's thought provoking. These notions resonate with issues such as the enigmatic in art, the encounter with "the thing", and what emerges from a primal instance that is so remote and is the drive. The "movement" that marks the body in art and the artist's emotions explains another path in the category of the non-figurable.

Finally, and in the same move, this enquiry is reversed; the tension of the encounter between art and psychoanalysis opens up new territories and strategies in analytic practice. What appears as resistance might become working-through and the incorporation of a hint of something dispersed, lost, or disavowed. The alter ego constructed in the analytic situation finds its counterpart in the construction of the artwork. In the duplication of opposites, the paradox emerges and constitutes an Other, an "ego alter", giving the work of art the autonomy demanded by Adorno (1997).

Curative phenomena show both the distance and the proximity between health and pathology, at whose edges and in whose paradoxes we find the potential for creativity in life. "If there is anything – other than love and friendship – that may give meaning to life, it is the beauty of art" (Riemen, 2004, p. 30). The love of art as a "new" paradigm of love puts a classical metapsychological concept in words: Eros is not diluted in processes of symbolisation and sublimation. Rather, it might reappear in the highest products of culture and art and provide keys to the cure.

In the manner of a fresco or a symphony, this book includes chapters that are very strong conceptually as well as others that are more open-ended and interpretative. The first chapter, by Charles Hanly, situates us psychoanalytically at the philosophical origins of the issue of form and content. From this point of view, form emerges coloured by the culture and subjectivity of its time, and, in a nuanced dialogue with literature, reveals something more than a defensive condition. Expanding on this reflection, the author interprets works by Monet, Cézanne, and Michelangelo.

The essay by Gilbert Rose (Chapter Two) discusses the place of subtle movement both in art in general and in non-verbal art, and in the artist. The latter uncovers secrets of the production of the image in that to and fro between primary and secondary processes when venturing beyond words and the affects aroused by art. The dialogue created by Rose between form, non-verbal art, and music touches the innermost motivations stirred by the artwork.

Harold Blum's approach in Chapter Three might be considered classical when he discusses the relation between some paintings by Picasso and "eternal adolescence". He also poses the question of the singularity of artists and the ways in which they transmute and refine their personal history in their work.

Considering the influence of the artist's background and based on her study of Duchamp, Adela Abella, in Chapter Four, enquires into the limits of "interpreting" this background and of "applied" psychoanalysis in relation to the paradigms of contemporary art. She proposes various frames of reference, such as Freud's, Segal's, and Bion's, with their contributions and sometimes their slips, as well as the potential openings offered by other ways to access artworks in an appeal for interdisciplinary thought.

With a different theoretical framework, Chapter Five, by Carlos Weisse, opts for the Freudian–Lacanian perspective. Theorisations on art and sublimation take the form of a dialogue between Ingres and Duchamp that shows an exchange between extremes in art. The great themes of the sublime and the sinister, pleasure and the uncanny, are opened for discussion at this juncture.

As an articulating and meeting point for the book's major topics, creativity and art's contributions to analytic practice, Hector Fiorini develops an "extended metapsychology" in Chapter Six. Not only does he discuss great contributions in relation to art, but he also expounds on them in relation to contemporary thought (from Deleuze to Steiner, from Beuys to Borges). In this way, the new conceptualisations he creates, such as the relevance of tertiary processes (Green and others), reformulate ways of understanding both art and psychoanalytic practice.

In Chapter Seven, Andrea Sabbadini examines the concept of "transitional time". Thereby, he lends continuity to previous developments, such as the intermediate zone (a "transitional space" characteristic of art), and reviews diverse artistic expressions in painting, cinema, and literature, as well as clinical experiences that illustrate borderline zones and meeting points.

Another group of chapters centres more specifically on the issue of creativity. Each is unique, and yet all are interrelated and also connected with clinical practice, thus contributing diverse conceptualisations of art. The chapter by Dominique Suchet (Chapter Eight) discusses how some artistic manifestations appear in the analytic situation as a form of "resistance", but might, at the same time, provide an introduction to a "fragment of a complex world" in subjectivity.

Nearly at the other end of the spectrum, we find the chapter by José Outeiral (Chapter Nine), who, building on ideas of British thinkers (e.g., A. Phillips, Masud Khan), discusses the expansion of "curative phenomena beyond the analytic field". The difference between health and madness is again brought into question within creative processes. So-called healing phenomena are the ones at work in creativity and in experiences with art, culture, love, and friendship.

In Chapter Ten, Murielle Gagnebin discusses strangeness as the point of departure for a new subjective construction that functions as an alter ego in both art and clinical practice. The relation between artists and their work entails alternation, inversion, and innovative creation, like the "chimera" (De M'Uzan, 1994) in clinical practice. Gagnebin's assertions are supported by thorough interdisciplinary enquiries that define a specific status of the ego as the ego alter of the work of art.

In the final chapter, I take up the dialogue between the artwork, the artist, and the riddles of creation. As for the experience with art, I discuss phenomena that lie between strangeness and alienation and bring into question the borders between agencies, as well as those between the subject and the work of art. I find a specific place for love in my notion of "the greatest love", essential for creation and the cure. This reappearance of Eros, with its deep, primary desires, together with prohibition and defences, makes aesthetic pleasure a transcendental pleasure that might transform subjectivity.

The book in itself forms a corpus that introduces founding concepts. In its various chapters, psychoanalysis and art engage in fruitful dialogue. The authors develop their main hypotheses regarding the interrelation between these fields by means of a deep exploration of the creative process in art and in analytic experience. This text aims to show how the interplay of psychoanalysis and art implicit in analysts' know-how promotes the realisation of the subject's creative potential within the analytic process in the context of the complexity of present-day practice.

The world's increasing complexity demands greater semantic precision in our everyday work. Psychoanalytic practice poses challenges that, if explored in their interweaving with art, might give rise to new approaches to treating contemporary modes of presentation of psychopathology, such as addiction, borderline states, and feelings of emptiness. For this reason, I consider *Psychoanalysis and Art* a significant contribution to our field in terms of both the enrichment of psychoanalytic theory through interdisciplinary approaches, and the application of these ideas to tackle new modes of psychopathology faced by psychoanalysts today.

References

Adorno, T. W. (1997)[1970]. *Aesthetic Theory.* London: Routledge and Kegan Paul.
Aulagnier, P. (2001). *The Violence of Interpretation: From Pictogram to Statement.* Philadelphia, PA: Brunner-Routledge.
Benjamin, W. (1968). The work of art in the age of mechanical reproduction. In: *Illuminations: Essays and Reflections* (pp. 217–251). New York: Schocken Books.
Burucúa, J. E. (2003). *Historia, Arte, Cultura, de Aby Warburg a Carlo Ginzburg.* Buenos Aires: Fondo de Cultura Económica.
De M'Uzan, M. (1994). *La bouche de l'inconscient.* Paris: Gallimard.
Didi-Huberman, G. (2007). *La Pintura Encarnada y La Obra Maestra Desconocida de Honoré de Balzac.* Valencia: Edición Pre-textos (co-edition with the Polytechnic University of Valencia).
Eagleton, T. (1990). *The Ideology of the Aesthetic.* Oxford: Blackwell.
Foster, H. (1996). *The Return of the Real: The Avant-Garde at the End of the Century.* Cambridge, MA: MIT Press.
Freud, S. (1896). Letter 52. S.E., *1*: 233–239. London: Hogarth.
Freud, S. (1910c). Leonardo da Vinci and a Memory of his Childhood. S.E., *11*: 59–137. London: Hogarth.
Goethe, J. W. (1962)[1816–1817]. *The Italian Journey.* London: Penguin.
Heidegger, M. (1950). *Off the Beaten Track.* Cambridge: Cambridge University Press, 2002.
Jauss, H. R. (1972). *Pequeña Apología de la Experiencia Estética.* Buenos Aires: Paidós, 2002.
Jauss, H. R. (1982). *Aesthetic Experience and Literary Hermeneutics*, Minnesota, MN: University of Minnesota Press.
Rancière, J. (2004)[2000]. *The Politics of Aesthetics: The Distribution of the Sensible.* London: Continuum.
Riemen, R. (2004). Introduction. In: G. Steiner, *The Idea of Europe* (p. 30). Nexus Library Volume IV. Tillburg: Nexus Institute.
Saragnano, G. (2011). Personal communication.
Winnicott, D. W. (1971). *Playing and Reality.* London: Tavistock.

CHAPTER ONE

Form and content in the visual arts: a psychoanalytic perspective

Charles Hanly

This chapter advances the hypothesis that identifiable defensive processes give meaning to the formal qualities of the visual arts. These reflections are limited primarily, although not entirely, to painting. The foundational distinction between form and content can be traced back to the ancient Greek aesthetics of Plato and Aristotle. It is often enough assumed that the descriptive elements of art constitute its thematic content and that they are the source of the meaning of the work, whereas form refers to the purely geometrical structural arrangement of the subject, its dimensions, colours, lighting, and other technical aspects of a work. It has been argued by certain philosophical aestheticians that the beauty of a painting is to be found exclusively in these formal qualities. From this perspective, questions of verisimilitude, likeness, or correspondence have nothing to do with questions of the artistic beauty of a work. Or, to state it differently, the descriptive, thematic features of a painting are but the means through which the pure formal beauty of the work, which some philosophers consider to be the essence of aesthetic appreciation and pleasure, is expressed. I shall argue that the formal beauty of a work is not pure and that it can powerfully convey values and ideals held by the artist (and which are indicative of his/her time and world). These values and ideals are materially and psychologically meaningful, as well as being integrally related to the descriptive elements of visual works of art.

A much abbreviated history of the idea of form

Form was given a profound and powerful place in Plato and Aristotle's ancient theories of the cosmos. Plato named the organising Ideas of the cosmos Forms. These animistically conceived, impersonal, unchanging psychic entities were thought by Plato to be the organising principles of nature. The difference between Plato and Aristotle was largely a difference of ontological geography. Plato held that the Ideas (or Forms) were located outside of nature and that they exercised a teleological attraction upon matter to shape it into the animate and inanimate species that make up the world. Aristotle held that the Forms, or Essences, as he named them, inhere in the totality of the individuals that make up the diverse species of animals, vegetables, and minerals. The Forms remain the same for Aristotle as for Plato, that is, they exercise their creative teleological influence in nature to sustain the cosmos in its order and grades of being in space and time.

This animistic understanding of the creation of nature, which gives rise to a universal idea of causality, was built up upon a metaphor with artistic creativity. These ideas, which were systematised by Aristotle (*Physics*, 1947), were already in varying degrees implicit or explicit in Plato's Dialogues. According to this idea, there are four causes at work in any natural process: a *material* cause (that from or out of which anything is made), an *efficient* cause (that by which it is made), a *formal* cause (that according to which it is made), and a *teleological* cause (that for which it is made). This analysis of natural causality was anthropomorphically modelled on and generalised from the creativity of the artists and artisans of ancient Greece. The material cause of a statue by Phidias is the marble out of which it is formed, but the marble cannot form itself into an inanimate duplicate of a man; in itself, it provides only a potentiality to be formed into a statue. It is Phidias and his assistants who must provide the work (the efficient causality) that transforms a shapeless piece of marble into a replica of an object. This work, in turn, is guided by the form (or idea) according to which the stone is chiselled by the sculptor for the purpose of making a statue that will represent the character and quality of a real person. The efficient and formal causes were thought to be guided and rendered effective by the teleology of higher orders of being which lower orders imitate. In Aristotle's cosmos, a supremely narcissistic Unmoved Mover (engaged in eternal self-contemplation) is the perfect being that the various species seek to emulate in their own ways according to their forms.

Although medieval thinkers were divided over whether Plato or Aristotle's philosophy was more suited to Christian beliefs and theology, the anthropomorphic causal metaphor shared by Plato and Aristotle largely dominated medieval thought. This domination nourished the profoundly mistaken idea that nature works in the same way as the human psyche. Modern humankind is slowly coming to terms with the idea, formulated initially and with only rudimentary knowledge by the Epicureans in ancient times and by Hobbes at the beginning of our age, that it is the human psyche that works in the same way as nature; the medieval experience of nature facilitated a blindly ecstatic encounter with the world that made it at once benignly (but unknowably) familiar and fundamentally vulnerable to superstitious dread (as Epicurus, Hobbes, and Hume all understood). The animistic idea of causality seemed self-evident to most ancient and medieval thinkers because of the way that it appears to describe human creativity in all of its manifestations, as well as our experience of the causality at work in our own lives involving attraction and aversion, love and hate, and desire and frustration. The projection of the human psyche on to nature seems natural and revealing. Human experience makes the animistic idea of causality appear to be self-evident, just as it makes it appear self-evident that the sun rotates around the earth, but the one is not less illusory than the other. Copernicus released us from the solar illusion; Freud released us from the illusion that we rule and form ourselves by purposes we choose to pursue. But not a few psychoanalytic theorists still need to deny the scientific and philosophical import of psychoanalysis by placing their confidence in narcissistically motivated introspection rather than on the findings and logical implications of psychoanalytic enquiry. What follows is a study of the question of secularised animistic retention in the field of aesthetics through a consideration of Bloomsbury (and other) aestheticians' revival of the belief in the purity (and irreducibility) of artistic form.

The revival of form in modern aesthetics

The aesthetics of form revived the classical idea of formal causation in its account of aesthetic pleasure. According to this approach, it is the formal, as opposed to the pictorially descriptive, elements of the visual arts that arouse in us the highest, most intense experience of aesthetic beauty. Imbedded in this idea of the primacy of form is the notion that the purpose of the visual arts, their *telos*, is to arouse (to cause) in us the aesthetic experience of the beauty of form. Thus, we can see that the metaphor of causation from the classical theory was revived in the field of aesthetics. The formal and teleological causes dominate over the material cause (the materials out of which the artistic object is created) and the efficient cause (the work of creation by the artist). In aesthetics, representation becomes the descriptive subject matter of the visual arts, while the form is embodied in the arrangements of colours, shapes, perspectives, and their relationships that organise that representation, whether of objects, scenes, or actions (as well as the abandonment of these types of elements in abstract art). In the aesthetics of form, representational and thematic elements of the visual arts are reduced to means for the articulation and expression of form. Form becomes the *telos* of representation. Form transcends content. From this vantage point, it is easily seen that abstract art merely takes the aesthetics of form to its logical conclusion by removing representational elements in favour of the exhibition of formal elements.

Members of the Bloomsbury group, such as Clive Bell (1914) and Roger Fry (1924), as well as Veron (1878), Hirn (1900), Carpenter (1921), and Parker (1924), were advocates of formalism in aesthetics. Bell makes the distinction between form and thematic content a first premise of aesthetics:

> If a representative form has value, it is as form, not as representation. The representative element in a work of art may or may not be harmful, it is always irrelevant. For to appreciate a work of art we need bring with us nothing from life, no knowledge of its ideas and affairs, no familiarity with its emotions. Art transports us from the world of man's activity to a world of aesthetic exaltation. (Bell, 1914, p. 25)

Bell makes it clear that a second premise of his aesthetics is the derogation of description, of the evocation of life experience or imagination, and of representation, in a word, content, along with the idealisation of form as the *telos* of aesthetic experience. He who cannot forgo life experience cannot enter into what is sublime in aesthetic experience. Bell states the ontological implications of his aesthetics as follows,

> ... he who contemplates a work of art, inhabit[s] a world with an intense and peculiar significance of its own: that significance is unrelated to the significance of life. In this world the emotions of life find no place. It is a world with emotions of its own. (Bell, 1914, p. 26)

Cleansed of the wants and affects that bind us to life and the world, aesthetic appreciation of form provides us with a passport to a world of emotion that is an end in itself. Bell's "world of aesthetic exultation" appears to have much in common with Plato's (*Symposium*, 1997b) account of the sublimations that lead from the physical beauty of youths to their character, to the laws that form their character, and then to the experience of the origin of all beautiful things in the "vast sea of beauty". Bell's aesthetics also revives Plato's epistemological and ontological derogation of the value of life and the natural world. Plato (*Symposium*) treats heterosexuality and the love of offspring as inferior substitutes for the homosexual love of beautiful boys that is the first step in the ascent to the vast sea of beauty. In the allegory of the cave, Plato (*Republic*, 1997c) treats curiosity about nature as a deceptive substitute for the knowledge of the forms (or ideas) of things which natural objects merely imitate.

During the first half of the twentieth century, the Paleolithic cave drawings of Northern Spain and the Dordogne valley of South West France were of great interest as they provided evidence of an early burgeoning of creativity in the visual arts. It was speculated that the animal drawings had been part of magical hunting rituals, whereby our Ice-Age ancestors aroused in themselves the courage and co-operation required to hunt for large, dangerous animals. Aesthetic formalists argued that just as later artists who sought to represent heroic, tragic, or religious events transcended their own representational, descriptive and celebratory intentions in their creation of formally beautiful paintings that arouse an aesthetic experience, so, too, the formal beauty of the Ice-Age cave drawings transcends any magical utilitarian use that might have occasioned them.

In this respect, aesthetic formalists have revived the teleological idealisations of the metaphysics of Aristotle and, especially, due to his transcendentalism, of Plato. Plato sought to purify thought by rejecting its origins in sensual experience, just as aesthetic formalists sought to reduce representation in painting to a means for revealing the end on which aesthetic experience depends—that is, the formal elements of the work of art. I want to argue that a reduction of the cave drawings of our Ice-Age ancestors derogates their creativity, as well as the psychological utility of their art, because it detaches the expression of the sinuous power of the animals from the lines that instantiate their shape, motion, strength, and danger, as well as value, to the carnivorous hunters. In doing so, this reduction artificially dissolves an ingeniously simple and unified synthesis. In the formalist's abstract purification of the drawings, there is a denial of our ancestors' hunger and fear, and of their struggle for existence.

Freud's aesthetics

Freud's (1908e) aesthetic theory is diametrically opposed to formalism. For Freud, form is a means to the aesthetic end of an insight-laden experience of life. Like the formalists, Freud differentiated the formal elements of works of art from their thematic content. However, he took these elements to be pleasurable bribes that worked to relax our defences ("this is true but I can experience it without its happening", or "life can be beautiful despite its darkness, peaceful despite conflict, etc.") against deeper affective responses. This can open up for us an aesthetic experience of what we share with many others—the universals of human experience. Freud valued the formal elements of works of art because they are means to a more personal and profound aesthetic experience of the content: for example, the themes represented in a painting. I have argued elsewhere (Hanly, 1992a) that Freud's hypotheses about the nature and function of form in art and about the play of children are correct as far as they go, but that they are incomplete. In fundamental agreement with Freud, and against the formalist aestheticians, I shall argue that form is an integral part of the thematic meaning of works of visual art and of the aesthetic experiences that deepen our affective understanding of what it is to be human.

Two clarifications

At this stage of the argument, let me pause briefly to clarify two points. First, it should be noted that there are rich, valued, pleasing works of art that do not seek the high seriousness of the visual works of art of which I write here. These works are often decorative. They do not aim at a deeper understanding of life; they aim only at giving incidental visual pleasure in the conduct of our daily domestic and public lives by combining formal aesthetic values (colours, shapes, and the patterns of their arrangement) with usefulness. A Persian rug may be hung on a wall to be seen or it may be placed on the floor, where it can be seen, but where it also provides warmth and enables more comfortable walking. Similarly, we can often experience the same painting as simply decorative or as thematically demanding, based on our variable moods, purposes, and circumstances. Art critics and art lovers can always disagree about where works of art should be located on the spectrum that runs from decoration to thematically significant. The reader is asked to take these considerations into account even though they cannot be elaborated here. One such consideration would be to ask to what extent abstract art is primarily decorative. Suffice it to say, for the purposes of this argument, that the author does not hold such a view. At its best, abstract art arouses affects, moods, and the reflections that might accompany them (just as music does). Neither pure abstract visual art, nor music, is descriptive. And neither are they merely decorative, because of the emotions they can arouse.

The argument that guides this enquiry into psychoanalytic aesthetics turns on whether or not the formal properties of art are themselves thematic and meaningful (i.e., that they contribute to the thematic significance of the work). I argue that they do. This is the primary hypothesis of this chapter. The secondary hypothesis concerns the mechanism of this integration in works of art of high seriousness. The meaningfulness of the formal properties derives, at least in part, from the influence of defensive psychic activities. I shall pursue this possibility by way of some brief interpretative studies that follow.

Form and content in Monet's Gare Saint-Lazare

Monet's *Gare Saint-Lazare* (1877, oil on canvas, Musee d'Orsay) brilliantly expresses the formal elements of impressionism in its capture of the steam from the locomotive, mingling with mist, in the diffuse sunlight streaming through the glass panes that form the high roof of the railway station that is reflected in the shadows cast upon the platform. In these formal elements, there is a specific abstraction occurring that involves a reversal of background and foreground, which gives to the painting a unique expressiveness. A more typical experience of the Gare Saint-Lazare would have been more homocentric and physical. The engine, as a machine with a boiler fired by coal (or wood), has been displaced into the steam of its emissions; people "disappear" in the sunlight rather than being illuminated by it, despite the steaming engine suggesting recent arrival and/or imminent departure. These displacements create metonymy as a crucial element in the form of the painting. Although the engine is there, it is, as it were, represented by the steam it emits, producing a visual "softening" of its physical mechanical nature, as, in language, the expression "the masts in the harbour" uses a part of a sailing ship to refer to the whole ship while, by implication, conveying its state of rest (as would "the sails on the lake" convey the impression of boats in motion). (Lacan mistakenly connected displacement with metonymy and condensation with metaphor when he traced these elemental tropes to their origins in primary process thought.) We are familiar with metonymy and condensation in literature, but it also occurs in painting, sometimes within the painting itself, and sometimes in the associations and reflections of the aesthetic experience stimulated by the painting. An example of this visual metonymy is the steam that represents the engine that emits it in a way similar to the literary use of "mast" to represent "ship".

The use of metonymy by Monet in *Gare Saint-Lazare* precisely embodies key elements of formalist aesthetics. Monet painted the Saint-Lazare railway station numerous times. In this painting, the description of the actual railway station is treated as being mildly irrelevant to the purifying dissolution of its substantive physical and social reality into a scene of luminous beauty fabricated of mist, steam, light, shadow, and reflection. Gone are the carbon particles of the smoke belching from the engine; gone are their tenacious creosote deposits on the glass panes in the roof. These potential descriptive elements lie hidden (and unacknowledged) in their transformation into the radiance of softly illuminated mist. There is no indication of hurrying porters struggling with the luggage of the bourgeois travellers walking unencumbered before them, only the figures who seem to be looking expectantly down the platform, perhaps at an approaching train. The hurly-burly of the station and its cacophony of sounds is discreetly hidden by the tranquil muting mist, as in Sandberg's poem, *Fog*. Formalism authenticates this disregard of life, and the experience of life, in favour of the experience of a world of refined, elegant, gently ecstatic beauty into which the reality of the railway station has been transformed. A formalist aesthetic validates the extent to which impressionism, as a school of painting, promoted the paradoxical idea that surface is depth. This is not meant as a disparagement of impressionism or of the aesthetic pleasure caused by the specific formal elements of impressionist painting (which this author happens to greatly enjoy). The argument is, rather, that the aesthetic experience is extended to irony, for example, by experiencing the painting in its larger descriptive and referential context.

For, surely, this very transformation acquires further meaning once we dare, contrary to formalism, to allow the painting to refer beyond itself to the railway station and allow it to place itself in the context of life in the industrial age of nineteenth-century France. After all, the coal that powered the locomotive of Monet's painting was mined under physical and social conditions described by Zola (1888) in *Germinal*. Metonymy in Monet's painting introduces a psychological denial of morally difficult social and economic realities by providing an idealised representation of the excitingly rapid, for the times, and comfortable new means of travel made possible by technical, industrial, and engineering invention and the exploitation of dehumanising labour. Through this idealising, defensive use of visual metonymy, the railway station has become, in its way, more pleasantly pastoral than it was. The sublimation involved gives rise to the "purified", mildly ecstatic, aesthetic emotion prized by formalism. It yields an idealising vision of the object that is reminiscent of the idealisations of Platonic/Aristotelian metaphysics. As I have implied elsewhere (Hanly, 1992a), it is architectural, mechanical, and natural reality rendered more sublime than they are in order to disregard social reality and render us, for a tranquil moment, oblivious to the human and social realities that mundane experience obliges us to acknowledge and which is acknowledged, as it were, in the negative hallucination of the metonymy of the work. However, it would be unfair to the formalism of impressionism to say that it expresses a certain *haut bourgeois* attitude of superiority and disdain toward social reality because of the Epicurean tranquillity and harmony into which the harshness and injustices of social life, the indifference of nature, and the clutter and clatter of physical reality, are dissolved.

Surely, though, it can be said that the price is high. Impressionistic formalism abstracts from the industrial, economic, social, and political conflicts that soon enough were to devastate Europe, as well as from a sense of the damage to nature that modern viewers bring to the contemplation of the *Gare Saint-Lazare*. Yet, the critic of this argument can always retort that, first, it is beauty rather than truth that is the value proper to the visual arts and, second, it is just because art is an end in itself, and without social utility, that it is able to contribute aesthetic experience to human well-being.

Form and content in Cézanne

Cézanne found a new formal element: geometry. By selecting the geometry of objects in the space of landscapes and buildings, Cézanne painted natural scenes as though, according to one critic (Bernard, 1920), he sought "to join the erring hands of nature". In these paintings, there is the impression that Cézanne is revealing spatial structures inherent in nature. It would be interesting to speculate that Cézanne was exploring the implications of the non-Euclidean geometries that had been discovered by Riemann and others. Although our experience discloses objects located in rectilinear space, we now know that the space of nature, although not the space of our ordinary experience, curves in the vicinity of mass. One could speculate that Cézanne's joining of the erring hands of nature revealed a spatial order in nature that is not evident in ordinary experience. However, disappointingly for this line of interpretation, Cézanne's spatial "correction" of our experience of nature is, for the most part at least, rectilinear, as is our everyday experience of natural space because of its finitude. Nevertheless, even if this speculation does not work, it is evident that Cézanne continued and enriched the use of impressionistic idealisation, specifically, by means of a geometrical idealisation of nature that promises, beyond the casual, accidental, mutable, conflicted, yet fateful indifference of nature, a deeper geometrical order that is harmonious, peaceful, reliable, and congenial to what is best in life and worthy of our aesthetic contemplation. The antithesis of Cézanne's vision of a deeper geometry of nature is the nausea attributed to Roquentin, the existential hero of Sartre's (1938) novel, aroused in him by the facticity and contingency of things—the radical erring of the being of things leaving them without a stable nature, explanation, order, or reason for existing. The geometrical form of Cézanne's work is a gentle transformation of artefacts and nature on behalf of a more secular, Platonic abstraction from their haphazard, accidental, and unpredictable nature. This transformation offers a mildly ecstatic relief from the reality left behind, but which is associatively present, in the negative hallucination of the form that, to be appreciated, must refer, beyond itself, to that from which it escapes. He who would pause to relish his escape from a danger must revive the memory of the danger from which he has escaped. In general, the formal elements of painting express, by means of "correcting" or "revealing" abstractions what we (artists and viewers alike) seek to avoid and deny in our experience because of the defensive processes that are at work in the expression of what we would prefer reality to be. The defence expresses, in a more or less disguised way, that against which it defends.

Form and content in Picasso

I now turn to a different example of this ambiguous unity. Elsewhere, I have argued (Hanly, 1992a), following Golding (1958), that in *Les Demoiselles d'Avignon* (1907, oil on canvas, Museum of Modern Art, New York), Picasso used Iberian and African masks to begin a new development in the formal aspect of painting that led directly to the geometric anonymity of cubism. Picasso's treatment of two of the prostitutes uses the forms of Iberian sculpted heads, and the forms of African masks are used in his representation of the faces of the other three, as well as in the drapery in which they are swathed. These devices create a dramatic tension between modesty and exhibitionism and, at the same time, take a step toward the anonymity of cubism (Golding, 1968). Earlier during this period of exceptional creativity, Picasso had painted his *Self-portrait* (1906, oil on canvas, Philadelphia Museum of Art, Philadelphia) under the influence of the form of two primitive Iberian sculpted heads. This self-portrait bears, because of the formal distortions derived from the heads, an undeniable similarity to the figure of the prostitute second from the viewer's left (and which is echoed in the taller central figure). It is as though Picasso was ironically repeating the formal device frequently practised by Renaissance painters of including themselves in the painting as a playful means of attesting to its ownership. By means of the formal device of the Iberian sculptures, Picasso is able to unconsciously (or pre-consciously) convey his feminine identity and his attitude toward it. One conjecture is that Picasso expressed a wish to be as attractive as women are and his embarrassment for having such a wish. Early in his thinking about the work, this figure (the prostitute who is second from the viewer's left) was to have been a sailor whose presence would have accounted for the startled ambiguity of the exhibitionism and modesty of the painting's drama. If so, from this we can surmise that a negative Oedipal attachment to his father found its way into Picasso's use of the Iberian heads, giving rise to the expression of sexual ambiguity. This interpretation is confirmed by Picasso's portrait of Gertrude Stein (1906, oil on canvas, Metropolitan Museum of Art, New York), which conveys the same impression of gender ambiguity.

To be sure, Picasso had two Iberian sculptures for inspiration, one feminine and one masculine, but it is the formal similarities inspired by these heads that appear in the self-portrait, in the portrait of Gertrude Stein, and in the portrait of the prostitute in the *Demoiselles* that suggest gender ambiguity, independently of the sculptures that are their source. If so, the formal device of the Iberian mask is not pure shape and colour detached from psychic reality, as the formalists would have it. Furthermore, if so, form is rather a means for expressing and exploring the unconscious psychic reality of the artist by the artist. In doing so, an important formal aspect of the work (the use of distortion modelled on an Iberian mask) challenges us to a similar exploration of our own psychic reality, for example, in the sexual ambiguities of latency and early puberty. One is reminded, by the ubiquity of Picasso's use of the Iberian heads, of Leonardo's use of the enigmatic Mona Lisa smile.

The form of *Les Demoiselles d'Avignon* was soon developed into the geometric anonymity of the multi-perspectival disintegration of objects characteristic of cubism, which makes the visual identity of the object uncertain and, therefore, anonymous and ambiguous due to the abandonment of its commonsense description. To give a particular example, we need the title of *La Femme aux Poires* (1909, oil on canvas, Museum of Modern Art, New York) to resolve the gender ambiguity of the object, as well as to recognise the species of the fruit. Cubism is challenging in the extent to which it literally meets the requirements of aesthetic formalism by taking everyday objects and resolving them into a descriptive ambiguity and a statuesque immobility. This invites us to enjoy the tranquillity of a geometric ordering of objects that releases us, for a time, from their ordinary usefulness and demands. A differently ordered world is created that suspends our ordinary reactions to things and, by means of this abstraction, the paintings generate a world of their own. A parallel in literature is Fry's dictum that the words of a poem refer to the words of other poems, an idea that posits a world of literature beyond, and cleansed of, the world of experience. If we consider this idea empirically, we do come upon poetry that uses this device. For example, in Eliot's *The Waste Land* (2001), the line that refers to the barge she sat in reminds us (and is intended to remind us) of the arrival of Cleopatra by barge in Shakespeare's play *Anthony and Cleopatra* (1606). The meaning of Eliot's reference to Cleopatra would be lost on anyone who was not familiar with Shakespeare, but, of course, so would it be lost on anyone who does not connect it with what Eliot took to be the wasteland of the 1920s (as evidenced by J. Alfred Prufrock's timid pondering about whether or not he dare to wear his pant legs rolled if he should walk upon a beach, and with the aimless, politely cultured and bored women who distract themselves from living by talking about Michelangelo). Yet, while this and similar uses of this formal device occur often in poetry, it does not follow, and there is no evidence to suggest, that Shakespeare's description of Cleopatra also refers to yet an earlier poetic incarnation of the ancient Egyptian queen in a literary world rather than to the historical Egyptian queen. Similarly, cubistic form in painting is constructed out of the parts and perspectives on the objects that it geometrically deconstructs; the human face is rendered metonymical by spatial displacement of its parts and by unusual or multiple perspectives on them. In order to grasp the metonymy or appreciate the aesthetics of the reconstruction, the canvas must refer us to the mundane original that continues to haunt it. It seems to me that what might be called extreme Cubism, when a work is completely purified of description, when real objects cease to haunt it, can produce a decorative babel of coloured or monochromatic shapes. However, it can also be used to generate ironical, satirical, or comic visual impressions, as when Picasso's playing with perspectives invites us to look up the nostrils of a female figure (which is not a usual perspective for the appreciation of female attractiveness), or when his massive plunging women simultaneously reveal their inability to ever reach the water (as if captivated in a Zenoian paradox of motion). When the ideal loses all connection with the real, it ceases to be ideal, but it may still generate affects, although scarcely affects deemed appropriate by the aestheticians of form.

Form and content in Michelangelo's The Last Judgement

Let us turn to an example of "signing" a painting in Renaissance art. Michelangelo painted himself into *The Last Judgement* (1536–1541, fresco, Sistine Chapel, Vatican City) in two places: once on the right side of the serenely righteous Jesus and once on the left side, precariously near those being sentenced to eternal damnation in hell. On the right side, Michelangelo is among those rising from their graves looking hopefully toward heaven; on the left side, he appears skinned alive and being held up to be seen by a powerful, handsomely muscular St Bartholomew, who gained sainthood and a passage to heaven by such a martyrdom himself. St Bartholomew appears to sanction Michelangelo's appalling living agony without pity or concern. This agony is expressed by distortions of his face that are not unlike the emotionally expressive facial distortions employed by Picasso in his painting *Weeping Woman* (1937, oil on canvas, Tate Gallery, London).

Freud's (1910c) account of Leonardo da Vinci's asexual, austere character as the result of a radically sublimated homosexuality would seem also to apply largely to the underlying dynamic of Michelangelo's character and sexuality. It has been said of Michelangelo, who appears to have been of a depressed, abstemious, and solitary disposition, that he "withdrew himself from the company of men" (Condivi, 1999, p. 106). However, the sublimation of sexuality does not seem to have been as complete (or austere) in Michelangelo as in Leonardo. Michelangelo expressed his love for Cecchino dei Bracci in elegiac poetry after his untimely death and, later, when Michelangelo was in his late fifties, he wrote love poetry to Tommaso dei Cavalieri, a young man in his early twenties. Cavalieri remained devoted to Michelangelo to the end of his life. There is no evidence that Michelangelo had a sexual relationship with Bracci or with the poet Vittoria Colonna, whose friendship, late in his life, inspired him to write poems to her. Interpretations of the little that is known of Michelangelo's relationships over his lifetime are speculative. What is more certain is his passionate, irrepressible (but sublimated) sensual love of the idealised, muscular, and powerful nude male body (including the body of the Christ figure in *The Last Judgement*). This love can be characterised as passionate and irrepressible because it introduces an erotic element into a religious, apocalyptic scene, sublimated but, nevertheless, sensual because of the muscular idealisation of the nude male body. On Plato's (*Symposium*) ladder of sublimation, these figures can best be located between the lowest rung, sexual love for a particular physically handsome youth, and the second rung of ascent, love of the character of a youth. *The Last Judgement* as a whole is at the third level of sublimation, the love of the law, obedience to which is the source of beauty of character, for it is on behalf of retributive justice that the division of the beautiful good and the ugly evil is being made by the central figure of the Christ. Thus, there is a tension in the work between the meaning of the depicted scene of the Last Judgement as a whole and the powerful partially sublimated sensuality of the details—the figures of which it is composed. This tension is deepened by the depiction of figures consigned to Hell, for example that of Cesena, despite the donkey's ears and the snake, in which Michelangelo appears to have invested no less idealising affectionate attention to the representation of male physical power and beauty than he invested in the figures of saints, aerial attendants, and the awakened dead bound for heaven. The tension is deepened yet further by the distortions of the skinned body and agonised face of the painter.

There is courage, defiance, and confident self-assertion, as well as trust in his patron, Pope Paul III, behind Michelangelo's depiction of his sublimated homosexual masculine ideal. Even before it was completed, the mural was attacked by Biagio Cesena as a desecration of the chapel, with nudity fit for public baths and taverns. Michelangelo's Dantesque revenge was to paint Cesena in Hell with a serpent coiled about him biting on his penis, but, shortly before Michelangelo's death in 1564, the Council of Trent prohibited nudity in sacred painting and commissioned a pupil of Michelangelo, Daniele de Volterra, to clothe the unholy genital shame, although the castration of Cesena was left uncovered. Although subsequent efforts at purification by clothing the sexuality of Michelangelo's vision were later removed, the correction did not go so far as to expose the original genitalia, which remain discreetly covered with underwear or drapery painted by Michelangelo's pupil. It is also true that Michelangelo had the covering excuse of ancient Greek sculpture and painting, but his nude male figures convey a passion beyond imitation.

What, then, are we to make of the agonising self-portrait by means of which Michelangelo "signed" his great mural, acknowledging it to be his handiwork? In the first place, Michelangelo's sublimated homoerotic and sensual idealisation of the male body could not be erased by making genitals invisible, not, one might say, by their visual castration. Neither did Michelangelo realistically need to have any fear of persecution from the religiously motivated condemnation of his work. Upon completing the murals of the Sistine Chapel, his reputation for divine genius as sculptor, painter, and architect remained intact and was confirmed by his being appointed architect of St Peter's Basilica, for which he designed the dome in his old age. However, Michelangelo must surely have known the motivations and phantasies about masculinity that inspired and guided his work despite the extreme abstemiousness of his life. Self-esteem is not governed only by the admiration of others, not even when that admiration is justified by the most extraordinary works of genius. Self-esteem is also, and perhaps primarily, governed by the life motivations and experiences that caused Michelangelo's need to idealise sensual masculinity and, as far as one can tell, to live a life of abstemious self-denial. Perhaps the agony he suffered from the privations of a self-inflicted, cruelly abstemious sexual life, an agony proportional to being flayed alive, still left him guilty and uncertain about what his last judgement might bring, and perhaps it is this that is expressed by his location in purgatory at the edge of the descent into hell.

Michelangelo was, philosophically, a Neo-Platonist. There is a pattern in Plato's attitude to homosexuality that might have similarities with Michelangelo. In Plato's early dialogue, *Charmides* (1997a), there is a frank description of Socrates being aroused sexually by catching a glimpse of the genitals of the handsome youth Charmides that evidently motivates his desire to be his tutor. In the *Symposium*,

Plato locates homosexual physical love at the lowest level on the ascension to the love of Beauty, although he denied heterosexual physical love any place at all. In the *Republic*, Plato gave homosexual and heterosexual soldiers who had fought bravely for the city in war their choice of youths or women as a reward for their risk taking. And in the *Laws* (1997d), probably his latest dialogue, Plato criminalised homosexuality, declaring that it is unnatural. Was Plato's condemnation of homosexuality in the *Laws* a recantation motivated by an unresolved anxiety that had inhibited and derogated his love for women? If so, was Michelangelo's signature on *The Last Judgement* a similarly motivated attack on the delight he took in masculine beauty everywhere to be found in the painting itself? Was this signature a kind of Pauline moral equivalent of Galileo's recantation of his Ptolemaic heresy and a reference to the privation and suffering inflicted on him by the austerity of his life, despite his magnificent capacity for sublimation made possible by his exceptional genius and ego strengths?

Whatever one might think of this interpretation, and there is no claim that this interpretation is the whole story, any improvement on it would surely have to reject the formalist aesthetic that would "elevate" Michelangelo's self-portrait "signature" in *The Last Judgement* to a coloured set of shapes uprooted from his life and his time. Elevating Michelangelo's achievement to such a rarefied aesthetic is surely to impoverish, rather than to deepen, its meaning. Michelangelo has transformed a conventional way for an artist to "sign" his painting into an evocation of his anguished anticipation of judgement and death. Despite his magnificent achievements, despite the high regard in which he was held, and despite his austere self-denial, there appears to have been in his soul a profound guilt demanding an appalling expiation of doubtful efficacy.

Conclusions

In an earlier paper (Hanly, 1992a), I argued that, while the purely formal aspects of painting can be studied and appreciated on their own, in doing so a richer unity of form and content in art is lost. The present chapter follows up that argument by tracing the origins of formalism in art interpretation to the "rational animism" of Plato and Aristotle. However, when it came to aesthetics, Aristotle would not have agreed with the aesthetic formalist's thesis that the content is merely the vehicle for the form, a means to a higher end, as the potentiality of matter is to form. To revert briefly to theatre, Aristotle would not have considered the story of Oedipus to be a means by which Sophocles was able to instantiate the three formal unities of time, place and action. Aristotle considered *Oedipus Rex* to be exemplary of what is best in tragedy, not only because of its observance of the three unities, but also because it expressed, in action, a fundamental truth about the human condition. For Aristotle, the end is the truth conveyed and the form is the means by which it is best conveyed. Aristotle would have appreciated the greatness of Shakespearean tragedy with its sub-plots because they enrich the action of the main plot as, for example, in *King Lear* (Shakespeare, 1610; Hanly, 1992b). I have argued previously that psychoanalysis can help us understand how form can enter into the fabric of the expressiveness and meaning of works of art by appreciating the influence of defensive processes such as idealisation and sublimation (Hanly, 1992a). This study has provided further evidence of this view by considering the work of Monet, Cézanne, Picasso, and Michelangelo. Form must do more than offer a "bribe of pleasure"; it must provide an order that "allows the ego to tolerate the exploration of identities and experiences that might otherwise be denied to it" (Hanly, 1992, p. 96). I would now add that when art holds a mirror up to human nature, or when art transforms nature to make it appear as we would have it be rather than as it is, the form of an artistic work becomes itself expressive, and enriches the meaning of the content, as well as making its meaning accessible to consciousness, even, and perhaps especially, when this unity encompasses conflict.

Finally, there are certain ontological and epistemological issues at stake here. Formalist aesthetics are premised on the Platonic and Aristotelian metaphysical ideas of the primacy of form. According to formalist aesthetics, form in art is more refined, more ideal, more intrinsically ordered, and of a higher order of being than the mundane natural, social, historical, and mythological descriptive or abstract representations that make possible its instantiation. The formal in art expresses a yearning for an order of being more exalted and more fundamental than the restless becoming and transience of human and natural events. In this respect, a formalist aesthetic is Platonic in its epistemological disparagement of the descriptive in art, which must be reduced to a secondary position of being a means to a higher end. And formalism in art is Aristotelian in so far as the form of the work must be abstracted from its content, just as the form (or essence) of anything must be abstracted from the sense experience of its physical exemplar(s) in nature. In contrast, a psychoanalytic aesthetic is stoical in its acceptance of what cannot be changed, Epicurean in the consolation of whatever pleasure life and human creativity can provide. A psychoanalytic aesthetic celebrates the artistic representation of what sense-experience reveals to us about our nature and the natural world in which we live and die, including our dissatisfaction with it and our longing for how we would prefer it to be. In this, there is no Platonic or Aristotelian derogation of sense experience as the source (and end) of such knowledge of ourselves and of the world as we are able, by means of sense experience, to acquire. Ontologically, despite the intensity of our hopes, there is no evidence provided by our sense experience that there is anything beyond nature that corresponds with what we seek when we try to "join the erring hands of nature".

References

Aristotle (1947). *Physics*. In: *Introduction to Aristotle* (pp. 112–139), R. McKeon (Ed.). New York: Modern Library.
Bell, C. (1914). *Art*. London: Chatto & Windus.
Bernard, E. (1920). *La méthode de Cézanne*. Paris: Mercure de France.
Carpenter, R. (1921). *The Aesthetic Basis of Greek Art of the Fifth and Fourth Centuries B.C.*, revised edition. Bloomington: Indiana University Press, 1962.
Condivi, A. (1999). *The Life of Michelangelo* (2nd edn), A. S. Wohl (Trans.), H. Wohl (Ed.). University Park, PA: The Pennsylvania State University Press.
Eliot, T. S. (2001). *The Waste Land*. New York: W. W. Norton.
Freud, S. (1908e). Creative writers and day-dreaming. *S.E., 9*: 143–153. London: Hogarth.
Freud, S. (1910c). *Leonardo da Vinci and a Memory of his Childhood. S.E., 11*: 63–137. London: Hogarth.
Fry, R. (1924). *The Artist and Psychoanalysis*. London: Hogarth.
Golding, J. (1958). *Cubism: A History and an Analysis*. Boston: Boston Book and Art Shop.

Hanly, C. (1992a). Psychoanalysis and aesthetics. In: *The Problem of Truth in Applied Psychoanalysis* (pp. 86–102). New York: Guilford Press.
Hanly, C. (1992b). Lear and his daughters. In: *The Problem of Truth in Applied Psychoanalysis*, (pp. 103–120). New York: Guilford Press.
Hirn, Y. (1900). *The Origins of Art: A Psychological and Sociological Inquiry.* London: Macmillan.
Parker, D. H. (1924). *The Analysis of Art.* New Haven, CT: Yale University Press.
Plato (1997a). *Charmides.* In: *Plato: Complete Works* (pp. 639–663), J. M. Cooper (Ed.). Indianapolis, IN: Hackett.
Plato (1997b). *Symposium.* In: *Plato: Complete Works* (pp. 457–505), J. M. Cooper (Ed.). Indianapolis, IN: Hackett.
Plato (1997c). *Republic.* In: *Plato: Complete Works* (pp. 971–1224), J. M. Cooper (Ed.). Indianapolis, IN: Hackett.
Plato (1997d). *Laws.* In: *Plato: Complete Works* (pp. 1318–1617), J. M. Cooper (Ed.). Indianapolis, IN: Hackett.
Sartre, J.-P. (1938). *La Nausée.* Paris: Gallimard.
Shakespeare, W. (1606). *The Tragedy of Antony and Cleopatra.* In: *The Oxford Shakespeare: The Complete Works* (2nd edn) (pp. 995–1030), S. Wells & G. Taylor (Eds.). Oxford: Oxford University Press, 2005.
Shakespeare, W. (1610). *The Tragedy of King Lear.* In: *The Oxford Shakespeare: The Complete Works*, (2nd edn) (pp. 1153–1184), S. Wells & G. Taylor (Eds.). Oxford: Oxford University Press, 2005.
Veron, E. (1878). *Aesthetics*, W. H. Armstrong (Trans.). London: Library of Contemporary Science.
Zola, E. (2011). *Germinal*, R. N. MacKenzie (Trans.). Indianapolis, IN: Hackett.

CHAPTER TWO

Implicit "motion" in non-verbal art: transmission and transformation of affect[1]

Gilbert J. Rose

"The arts reflect the motion of mind"

(Leonardo da Vinci)

Introduction

Although language is considered to represent the highest stage of thought and ego development, this overlooks the significance of non-verbal art in relation to affect transmission, transformation and the refinement of experience.

"Word-presentations" were, for Freud (1923b), the main route by which affects could find their way into consciousness. He did, however, allow that affects might also become partially conscious by an earlier way, closer to unconscious processes, namely, thinking through pictures. "Thinking in pictures is ... a very incomplete form of becoming conscious ... In some way ... it stands nearer to unconscious processes than does thinking in words, and it is unquestionably older than the latter" (p. 21).

This proximity to the unconscious might indeed account for the significance of thinking in pictures, but does not address the non-verbal realm in general as a possible source for creative thought. Yet, Einstein (1934), for example, noted that words played no role in his productive thought. Rather, he pointed to "psychical entities" consisting of visual images and muscular elements engaged in a "combinatory" or "associative play". Only then, when these were sufficiently established that he could reproduce them at will, would he struggle to discover how to communicate his thinking by means of words or signs.

It is worth noting that the primacy of words was not always taken for granted. There is a long history of struggle between image and word for dominance (Belting, 1994). During the Reformation, the Roman church decreed the primacy of the Word as God's instrument over the significance of the Image. This enabled the preacher to exert control over the congregation. The members of the congregation were expected to live by the pure word as conveyed in the letter of the text rather than the imprecision and ambiguity of the image with its potential for conveying alternative interpretations and danger of straying into "error" and subversion.

Words remain, of course, the main tools-in-trade of psychoanalysis. They make possible the interpretation of latent meanings of *content*. However, they tell us too little about the significance of a world of non-verbal art and musical masterpieces of *form*—especially in relation to feeling.

This justifies an attempt to expand the subject of affect transformation to include the role of abstract art, that is, non-representational art and music without narrative, programmatic or illustrative intent—affect-stimulating forms considered, as far as possible, apart from any discursive, cognitive meaning.

Affect and motion

Among the names cited below whose work influenced this paper, William James and Paul Schilder are paramount in their insistence on the normal close relationship between affect (referred to as emotion) and motion. This, it must be mentioned, is a sharp contrast to the psychoanalytic recommendation of supine immobility in the formal arrangement of a therapy session to facilitate uncovering latent affect which might otherwise be overlooked or discharged in acting out, enacting, etc.

James insisted that, primarily, affects are of the body. "A disembodied human emotion is a sheer nonentity", he wrote (James, 1892, p. 380). He linked motion to emotion. "Movement is the natural immediate effect . . . of feeling, irrespective of what the quality of the feeling may be . . ." (James, 1892, p. 426).

Theodor Lipps (1851–1914), in the tradition of Vico (1668–1744, cf. Berlin, 1980), emphasised the importance of empathy and feelings rather than pure intellect as a basis of knowledge of other minds. "Feeling into" another's mind is based on the imperceptible mirroring of another's movement patterns. Such "motoric empathy" draws on one's body memories and feelings as it bridges between Self and Other.

Rappaport, Gill, and Schafer (1945) found that the implicit movement involved in the human movement (M) response on the Rorschach test makes it the most important and informative aspect of the protocol. It is the only Rorschach determinant that brings something to the card that is not inherent in the inkblot and, therefore, indicates the potential for creativity.[2]

Schilder's (1950) concept of the body image elaborated on the link between motion and emotion. For Schilder, action was the essence of the body image. Sensations and perceptions give rise to the body images. These, in turn, influence perception and a constant building up and dissolution of body images. He thought it probable that a vertical line is perceived by the vestibular and equilibrial apparatus as well as by the eye. Every mental picture is connected with a set of motor attitudes and small movements, thus continuing the process of experimentation that takes place in perception and action.

Kris's *Psychoanalytic Explorations in Art* (1952) noted that on looking at an image of the human figure one experiences a slight muscular reaction. He suggested that this signifies that we "imitate" the artist's strokes and lines that produced the image (p. 56). While he considered that this was a key to one's response to pictorial art being a "regression in the service of the ego", he emphasised the motor element in art to the neglect of feelings, affects, or emotions.

My own view (Rose, 1980, 1987, 1996, 2004) is that creativity is not a privileged regression to primary process. It belongs, rather, in a more normative and progressive context than an aberrant one. Studying the structure of aesthetic form, it becomes evident that art does not follow the psychoanalytic mantra that secondary process replaces primary process. The primary process can undergo development as a result of feedback, interplay, and recombination with the secondary process (Noy, 1969). Thus, the dynamics of feeling and imagination are embodied in mental activity not only in art, but also in the "creativity of everyday life"—where, for example, each instant of perception may be viewed as part of an essentially dynamic "creative" process in that the elements of perception are subliminally rearranged and recomposed as they enter fully conscious awareness (Fisher, 1954, 1956).

The writings of Noshpitz in the 1980s, never published until recently (Sklarew & Sklarew, 2010), are most congenial to my own. He emphasised that motion, rooted in rhythm, is a biological basis of all works of art, that aesthetic expression requires a coherent sense of self within one's body musculature to experience affect and agency, and that aesthetic forms capture the intensity and rhythmic coherence of early child–mother engagements.

Implicit "motion"

The ancient question of how creative art transmits its emotional impact becomes less daunting if we reduce it to more down-to-earth pieces that link together. (1) An artist's personal expressive affective patterns while creating abstract aesthetic forms; (2) these forms carry an affect-evoking potential that we name implicit "motion"—the main focus of this chapter; (3) implicit "motion" stimulates expressive affect in a responsive person; this is the disparate counterpart of the affective motor patterns that accompanied the artist's own expressive feelings while working.

What is implicit "motion"? This invented term instantiates Dewey's statement (1934, p. 207): an artwork seeks out, develops, and accentuates the expressive properties of perception "to elicit [the] quality of all things we experience and express it more energetically and clearly" than the original from which it was extracted.

Thus, implicit "motion" is intended to denote these dynamic qualities of normal perception, abstracted, intensified, and transformed into aesthetic forms; they have the potential to trigger the experience of motion in its actual absence; they serve, thus, as a hypothetical "hinge" between the affects of the creator and responder.

Implicit "motion" stimulates an immediate, active, physical affective response. The response is so unthinking and spontaneous in the receiving subject that it is projected and attributed to the creative work—as though *it* were alive, which of course, it is not. Thus, "motion" is bracketed in quotation marks.[3]

How does implicit "motion" work? Seeing and hearing, in art and music, become dynamic phenomena. A (western) musical scale is, itself, a dynamic system where tones seem to "strive" towards the tonic in an imaginative field of force. Tones have resonance, amplitude, thrust, and other dynamic qualities of seeming to move within balance and unbalance in contrast to mere inert acoustic sounds (Zuckerkandl, 1956, 1973). Composition and performance transform tones into the "living" shapes of affect.

Likewise in painting, an ordinary visual line becomes a stroke, described by Matisse as "a certain disequilibrium ... within the indifference of the white paper" (quoted in Merleau-Ponty, 1961, p. 184). In painting, he reminded his students to see directions in colours and lines, to "... search for the desire of the line, where it wishes to enter and where to die away" (quoted in Spurling, 1998, p. 408).

Rilke (1985[1952]) described implicit "motion" in Cézanne's *oeuvre*:

> It's as if every place were aware of all the other places— ... each daub plays its part in maintaining equilibrium and in producing it ... Everything ... has become an affair that's settled among the colors themselves: a color will come into its own in response to another, or assert itself, or recollect itself. ... In this hither and back of mutual and manifold influence, the interior of the picture vibrates, rises and falls back into itself, and does not have a single unmoving part. (pp. 80–82)

Both visual and musical implicit "motion" is related to the body. Music might involve an intimate relation especially to respiration, in that each musical phrase is that portion of music that must be performed in a single breath. Moreover, when we hear music, what we hear above all is a sense of forces moving. (Perhaps that was behind the remark attributed to Nietzsche that one listens to music with one's muscles.) The subjective sense of right or wrong is less a matter of pitch than pitch in relation to the direction of motion. Thus, in jazz, it is said a note may be acoustically wrong in its pitch yet musically right if the deviation is correct in the sense of its movement.

These statements of the significance of motion in music receive support in a musical analysis (Epstein, 1993) of samples of music of Mendelssohn, Mozart, and Wagner. It concluded that "affect [in music] is deeply and intrinsically wed to structure, and structure inseparably tied to [musical] motion" (p. 119) and that "tension/ release may indeed be the essential factor conveying the sensation of movement, of motion" (p. 99). Again:

> It is motion, with its correlated affect, that makes ultimate sense of the music, that ultimately guides, indeed dictates, the direction of the music, the nature of its flow—in brief, how it will 'go.' . . . In the [musical] examples [cited above] motion is found to be the clue. Within the sense of motion—a sense that can be delineated, refined, grasped with precision—there seems to be a liaison of form, structure, and affect. (p. 101)[4]

It is not unusual for an art instructor inspecting students' work to be able instantly to point to an area where the work seems to "move", where it is dead, or where it is being "quoted" from a known work. He or she might scarcely touch the beginner's sketch and, in a leap of sublimation, it suddenly springs to life. This can be so striking that, like a key in a lock, one is left to suspect that it may have something to do with a hidden concordance between the seemingly trivial intervention and some as yet unknown harmonic in the brain.

Let us be clear and unmystical. Implicit "motion", undoubtedly drawing on the activity of mirror neurons, encompasses the perceptual wherewithal to move an observer into active, affective response. Moreover, it is precise. In the language of Zen Buddhism, "A tenth of an inch's difference and heaven and earth are set apart" (Seng-ts' an, as translated by D. T. Suzuki, cited in Ross, 1966, p. 137).

As Tolstoy (1951, pp. 127–128) wrote, "There is no way to teach . . . those infinitesimal elements which make up [an artist's] work. These . . . can be achieved only by feeling".

Implicit "motion" might spark the observer or listener into greater aliveness because, lacking the precision of words, it perks the mind to search for meanings. It stimulates perception and ambiguity to interplay to the limits of each person's imagination. Thus, its wide-angle openness to unforeseeable new meanings serves as an entry code to the *mind.* This marks it as a not-so-secret sharer in the spirit of exploratory psychotherapies.

Artist and body

The expressive motor aspects of affect are significant aspects of both art-making and the aesthetic experience.

In poetry, as many poets testify, the physical experience comes first in both making poetry and enjoying it. Cognitive meanings come last. When they do arise, a reader's interpretation might well be different from the poet's intention—and equally valid or better (Eliot, 1957, p. 23).

Mandelstam was the greatest Russian poet of the modern period. His wife relates,

> When he was 'composing' he always had a great need of movement. He either paced the room . . . or he kept going outside to walk the streets . . . I only once saw [him] composing verse without moving around . . . Restlessness was the first sign that he was working on something, and the second was the moving of his lips . . . In the first stage the lips move soundlessly, then they begin to whisper and at last the *inner music* resolves itself into units of meaning. (Mandelstam, 1970, pp. 184–187, my italics)

Consider now the artist engaged in the active to-and-fro "dance" of making a painting.

Many painters work with music in the background. They might describe their motions, posturing, advances to, and retreats from, the canvas as a kind of ballet. Whether pacing, sitting, or even paralysed like the quadriplegic painter, Chuck Close, neural maps of muscle tonus changes reflect the projection of kinaesthetic impulses and the body as a whole. One keeps projecting one's body image. Muscles, tendons, and joints contribute to the knowledge of whether the work "feels right" and what the artist should do to make it "work" and "grow". And breathe. Rhythm, respiration, equilibrium (vestibular and proprioceptive) could all be involved in the projection of body images. What one sees or hears is supplemented by what the body as a whole indicates. In case of contradiction, priority rests with the projected body image. It is intimately reliable.[5]

A special word is reserved for the hand of a painter. A friend asked Matisse, in his studio surrounded with a litter of drawings, "'How do you know the really good ones?' Matisse answered. 'Well, one feels that in the hand'" (Gilson, 1959, pp. 52–53).

The hand of the artist is not just an obedient servant. The artist and art philosopher, Gilson (1959), insists that the hand is an active collaborator and full of surprises.

> The knowledge that an artist has of his own art is not abstract ... it is the concrete cognition of the very acts and motions whereby a certain patterns of lines, surfaces and colors can actually be produced ... It is impossible to distinguish between art itself and execution ... A painter could entertain no thought about his own art if his hand were not there to give to the word 'art' a concrete meaning ... (p. 28)

One might add, "including body rhythms and breathing". In short, if it "moves", "works", "breathes", it has become "living art", taking its place among the "life of forms in art" (Focillon, 1948).

Art as craft

The knowledge of art as a physical craft provides the artist with tools to draw on personal affects in order to shape expressive bodily patterns into aesthetic forms. This includes what has been absorbed from immersion in art as well as knowledge of its history and traditions.

The principle of isomorphism (Arnheim, 1949; Langer, 1953; Pratt, 1952) holds that every affect has a specific bodily contour and any shape that is similar in form may activate that affect. Different contours can be reliably identified with different affects (Clynes & Nettheim, 1982; Tomkins, 1962–1963).

For example, certain shapes in art increase tension; others reduce it (Arnheim, 1954). Increase tension: oblique, rectangle, oval, parabola, shade, blur, wedge, inequality, particular admixtures of colour, etc.

Painters may also employ optical tricks like "equiluminance" to disrupt one's sense of dimension, motion, and volume. For example, the stream in Monet's *Water Lilies* is composed of contrasting dashes of equal value colours that appear to glimmer and undulate due to the brain's inability to distinguish which colours are "closer". Other examples are the swaying leaves in Klimt's *Rosiers Sous Les Arbres*, or the dancing red and yellow blocks in Mondrian's *Broadway Boogie Woogie*. It is as if the visual cortex has to struggle to discern the priority of elements and the struggle is perceived as motion (Livingstone, 2002).[6]

Aside from the tools provided by the craft of art, the countless personal expressive actions that go into making art deserve special mention. Since experiments have shown that affects and kinaesthesia are intertwined (Sheets-Johnstone, 1999), it would be plausible to assume that even these random accompanying movements also carry affect.

Turning to music, it has "depended for centuries on tension and resolution" (Rosen, 1971, p. 24). Some of its tools: sharp keys imply increase of tension, flat keys, reduction of tension; delayed closure, modulating in different keys, the minor mode, elaboration and dissonance increase tension (Meyer, 1956, 1967).

"Motion of mind" in neuroscience and in psychoanalysis

Leonardo's "motion of the mind" is so well illustrated in contemporary neuroscience that it merits a brief digression.

Neural maps are generated at any given moment, representing the state of the body in both its internal (visceral) and external (musculoskeletal) aspects. They are the foundation on which all our more complex self–body images (in Schilder's sense) are built. They include the current state of affects in their two aspects of inner experience and motor expression. Finally, in addition to these neural maps of Self there are maps of any Other with whom one is interacting, and of the interaction itself.

Every map of self, other, and the interaction between them is constantly altering in response to every change in each of the others.

Initially, these neural maps are in the form of wordless mental images that can be converted secondarily into language (Damasio, 1999, 2003). Therefore, any single "snap-shot" constitutes a decontextualised single frame of the mind's continuously running silent "movie" without words.

Changing our framework, we turn from neuroscience to psychoanalysis, where two basic modes of thinking and of energy discharge might be considered to be "movements of mind": primary and secondary processes.

They describe different types of thought, affect, and modes of discharge. Primary process corresponds roughly to passionate,

Dionysian mind styles, secondary process to reasoning, Apollonian mind-sets. In aesthetics, these correspond, respectively, to romantic and classic styles. They have been said to alternate through art history like the systole and diastole of the human heart.

Specifically, primary process is mostly unconscious, strives for quick discharge of tension or energy, and is characterised by labile shifts of focus such as condensation and displacement. Primitive affects and wishful, irrational thoughts and perceptions appear in holistic, undifferentiated forms. Secondary process is mostly conscious, builds tension with slow, delayed discharge and tamed or signal affects. Forms are delineated within realistic boundaries and rational rules.

The original theory held that, in the course of growth and development, an open-ended process of (mostly) conscious secondary process tends to replace (unconscious) primary process; later, that there is a continuum between them, so that feedback and interplay between them permits the primary process to undergo development (Noy, 1969).[7]

All this has significant implications for our subject. First, it offers us the possibility of moving beyond an impressionistic description of implicit "motion". We can now conceptualise implicit "motion" as a heightened degree of interplay between primary and secondary processes.

Further, it offers a rationale for connecting implicit "motion" with affect, in that faster (primary process) or slower (secondary process) rates of energy discharge determine the type and quality of affect, from explosive rage to tender love. It also explicates imagination as being a mixture of rational (secondary process) thought and unrealistic (primary process) fantasising.

Most apposite to our subject, the interplay of primary and secondary process is a key to the structure and awareness of aesthetic forms. Aesthetic forms represent a recombination of primary process forms (condensation and displacement, for example) with the slow discharge of secondary process. It is the latter that allows them entry to perceptual consciousness.

Examples in modern art: Picasso and other artists play with space and light in primary process figure–ground reversals, fusions and condensations, multiplications, displacements, rotations, fragmentations (Ehrenzweig, 1953). Music, too, embodies all the perceptual configurations associated with the primary process (Fisher, 1954, 1956; Friedman, 1960).

These primary process forms are usually buried in the fast, subliminal pre-stages of perception (Fisher, 1954). Intermixing them with the slow secondary process discharge of energy in the explicit structure of aesthetic forms enables us to see them in the light of expanded perceptual awareness. An open-ended interplay between primary and secondary processes entails a recharge of energy and increased range of affect now safely contained, that is, regulated and transformed.

It is important to specify the unique quality that the experience of aesthetic forms conveys. As often noted, it might take a paradoxical form, such as a blend of logical opposites. Tranquil vitality might be an approximation of one kind of aesthetic experience that has brought more than one listener to tears. It is the motion superimposed on stasis in some music, like that of late Beethoven. The paradoxical combination, blurring the distinction between motion and stasis, might be described as otherworldly.[8]

In a technical (secondary process) musical manoeuvre, a listener is presented with primary process perceptual properties that are normally preconscious and evade full attention. The primary process coexistence of motion and stasis is now seen in the light of full secondary process consciousness as each and both. Such fertile ambiguity demands actively shifting attention and comparison with existing norms of reality. Reflection demands increased mental activity, stimulating a mixture of tension and gradual release, resulting in further affect and expansion of our perception of time.

Rhythm deserves special mention as a particularly intense and ubiquitous form by which implicit "motion" is expressed. Born of the interplay and recombination of primary and secondary processes, it embodies degrees of tension and discharge, change and constancy, time flow and timelessness.

Its unchanging recurrence is a primary process holistic form. It stands for unity, sameness, and constancy, all of which tend to reduce tension, but its ever-changing variety is a display of secondary process detail and contrast, all of which heighten tension.

With each change, tension mounts, but with the constancy of the pattern of change, tension falls. The sequential nature of rhythm embodies waves of seemingly simultaneous rising and falling tension, beguiling the senses into reconciling the paradox of time: forever changing while remaining constant.

Above all, rhythm contributes significantly to an aesthetic experience wherein one re-finds oneself more alive in a field of motion and emotion. This appears to be independent of whatever cognitive meanings are construed in the course of time. As in poetry, the experience might come to mean different things, all independent of their creator's intention and each expressive of the reader.

Affective responsiveness: resonance and "unity"

What happens when one is exposed to a new aesthetic experience? A biologically based primary function of perception is to alert the organism to the dynamic aspects of reality that indicate potential danger or friendliness (Arnheim, 1954). After an initial shock at losing the safety of the familiar, one may begin to resonate to the concordance between the implicit "motion" of aesthetic forms and one's own responsive affects. Then, contained in the safety of that frame, one might re-find oneself affectively on levels of deepening re-signification.

In infant terms, brief loss and re-finding oneself reflected in mother's eyes and responsive facial expression represents early tension, validation, and reassurance. Such peek-a-boo, to the accompaniment (universally) of the music of baby-talk, involves many sensory modes "orchestrated" to enliven baby's experience with graded tension and relief. Surprise, recognition, and embrace might, thus, be an infantile precursor of empathic capacity and a subjective model of early affect regulation and its never-ending higher-level transformations.[9]

This is a model for understanding the enhanced affect regulation and transformation that ultimately accrues to the aesthetic experience, itself. Indeed, increased range and modulation of affect might constitute the ongoing psycho-biological contribution of the experience of aesthetic sublimation, increasingly through life. This is to suggest that a person might value and seek out an aesthetic experience as a temporal/rhythmic holding environment within which to feel stimulated as well as protected from transience.

Drawing on early unconscious recognition and sense of primal unity, this might even extend to the point of restful *and* stimulating experiences of at-oneness with what had been initially strange. It is a not altogether uncommon discovery during exotic travel to experience the thrill and comfort of Nature. During meditation, it is said, such "unity" extends to classical states of mystical fusion between external and internal—like those that James (1902) might ascribe to relief from "the solitude of individuation" (p. 386). And, too, in the abiding inner presence or recall of old love: "She was a music I no longer heard, that rang in my mind, itself and nothing else, lost to all sense, but not perished, not perished" (Robinson, 1980, p. 160).

Transmission and transformation of affect in art and therapy

We have traced an artist's subjective affective expressiveness to its initial transformation into objective aesthetic forms. These forms have the potential to transmit the experience of implicit "motion" to an affectively responsive person. In this process, our argument goes, affect has been transmitted from the subjective realm of the artist into the objective one of aesthetic forms, and then transmitted again into the subjectivity of an Other.

In summary, affects have been twice transmitted and transformed. During the process, affects have been regulated—potentially to be transformed eventually into "sublimated" new experience—in the old-fashioned sense of elevated and refined.

One may reasonably suppose that the progressively new experience resulting from the radical creativity of art exceeds the regulation and transformation of affect that occurs "naturally" in everyday life, including humour—such a valuable lubricant. In contrast, the transformation of affect that occurs through art comprises qualities of life such as enhanced sensibility and sensitivity: (a) sensibility to nuances of feeling, as distinguished from intellect, and (b) emotional sensitivity, discernment, and responsiveness to sensory stimuli.

There are non-verbal moments in therapy, too, where "things come together" in a way that warrants mention in the context of aesthetic experience. They seem to have as much to do with silence as speech and are sufficiently evocative to warrant inclusion in the context of implicit "motion".

As any therapist knows, one listens with mind and body, one's self one's own instrument, for the verbal manifest and latent content, of course, plus the non-verbal "musical" forms of feeling: rests and rhythms; what was been left out yet implicit—or absent—or empty. One's own affective tuning in—or out. One's breathing. A tune—which tune?—in one's head.

The quality of silence: heavy, light, pregnant, sexy, dead, menacing. Silence in relation to music and especially its rests. Debussy held that music is the space between the notes. Beckett wrote that the function of music is to restore a silence.

The way one listens to music informs how to listen in therapy. Musical listening in therapy involves an oscillating attention, between global and focused. It interweaves cognitive and sentient-aesthetic modes of perception. It involves a continuous oscillation between global and focused attention. It recalls Robert Frost's "sound of sense", pre-reflective, primarily bodily, sensuous experience of sound, not looking for ideas. Meanings-unsought—emerge from the corporeal, sentient experience (Frank-Schwebel, 2010).

Rarely, musical listening in therapy evokes a special form of silence, attuned, bringing with it the warm chill of instant recognition and unity, tacit partners of the moment, carried by implicit "motion", shared by an unspoken duo.

Notes

1. Exclusions and definitions: the concept of sublimation is avoided because it remains obstinately undeveloped. Affect transmission and transformation are considered to be constituents of affect regulation. Dance, mirror neurons, and embodied simulation theory lie beyond the scope of this paper. Music refers to western tonal music. Affect is used to comprise the full array of physiological constituents that accompany and underlie the subjective experience of feelings; emotions refer to the manifestations by which feelings are recognised by others.
2. I am grateful to Professor Sidney Blatt for this reference. (See also Allison, Blatt, & Zimet, 1988.)
3. Cognitive meanings also necessarily unfold for each person in the course of time and contribute their affective thrust to one's aesthetic experience. They are non-linear and continue to elaborate in the context of a favouring cultural climate.
4. There is now, too, some neuroscientific basis for the relation between music, motion, and affect: neural projections from the ear include some

to the cerebellum, where motion and emotion are regulated. Also, raising tension in music, as by altering the sense of motion, triggers the brain's non-specific pleasure–reward system of opioids and dopamine (Levitin, 2006).
5. One's own gait is the key factor in recognising oneself when all other cues are blocked out (W. Wolff, cited in Allport, 1937).
6. I am indebted to Alex Rose for this reference.
7. Related to, but in a radical departure from, Freud, Bion's (1962) "alpha-function" unites primary and secondary processes into a collaborative and oppositional but not conflictual function—more like binocular vision (Grotstein, 2009).
8. It has been ascribed to a particular musical structure—accelerated motion (speed) along with rhythmic diminution (smaller and smaller values of notes) and minimal harmonic action (Solomon, 2003).
9. Neuroscience holds that the primary care-giver acts as a "hidden" regulator of chemical agents that influence the maturation of centres in the temporal and orbital cortices (Hofer, 1984, 1990; Schore, 1996, 1997).

References

Allison, J., Blatt, S. W., & Zimet, C. (1988). *The Interpretation of Psychological Tests*. Boca Raton, FL: Taylor & Francis.

Allport, G. W. (1937). *Personality*. New York: Holt.

Arnheim, R. (1949). The Gestalt Theory of Expression. *Psychiatry Review*, 56: 156–171.

Arnheim, R. (1954). *Art and Visual Perception: A Psychology of the Creative Eye*. Berkeley, CA: University of California Press, 1957.

Belting, H. (1994). *Likeness and Presence. A History of the Image before the Era of Art*, E. Jephcott (Trans.). Chicago, IL: University of Chicago Press.

Berlin, I. (1980). *Against The Current: Essays in the History of Ideas*. New York: Viking Press.

Bion, W. R. (1962). *Learning From Experience*. London: Heinemann.

Clynes, M., & Nettheim, N. (1982). The Living Quality of Music, in *Music, Mind, and Brain. The Neuropsychology of Music*. New York: Plenum.

Damasio, A. (1999). *The Feeling of What Happens*. New York: Harcourt Brace.

Damasio, A. (2003). *Looking for Spinoza*. Orlando, FL: Harcourt.

Dewey, J. (1934). *Art as Experience*. New York: Minton, Balch.

Ehrenzweig, A. (1953). *The Psa of Artistic Vision and Hearing*. New York: Julian Press.

Einstein, A. (1934). *Essays in Science*. New York: Philosophical Library.
Eliot, T. S. (1957). The music of poetry. In: *On Poets and Poetry* (pp. 17–33). New York: Farrar, Straus and Cudahy.
Epstein, D. (1993). On affect in musical motion. In: S. Feder, R. L. Karmel, & G. H. Pollock (Eds.), *Psychoanalytic Explorations in Music* (pp. 91–123). Madison, CT: International Universities Press.
Fisher, C. (1954). Dreams and perception. *Journal of the American Psychoanalytic Association*, 2: 389–445.
Fisher, C. (1956). Dreams, images, and perception. *Journal of the American Psychoanalytic Association*, 4: 5–48.
Focillon, H. (1948). *The Life of Forms in Art*. New York: Wittenborn, Schultz.
Frank-Schwebel, A. (2010). The sonic dimension of the psychoanalytic encounter: an interdisciplinary study integrating psychoanalysis, music theory and developmental research. Unpublished.
Freud, S. (1923b). *The Ego and the Id*. *S.E.*, *19*: 12–66. London: Hogarth Press.
Friedman, S. M. (1960). One aspect of the structure of music: a study of regressive transformations of musical themes. *Journal of the American Psychoanalytic Association*, 8: 427–449.
Gilson, E. (1959). *Painting and Reality*. New York: Meridian Books.
Grotstein, J. S. (2009). Dreaming as a 'curtain of illusion': revisiting the 'royal road' with Bion as our guide. *International Journal of Psychoanalysis*, 90: 733–752.
Hofer, M. A. (1984). Relationships as regulators—a psychobiological 'perspective on bereavement'. *Psychosomatic Medicine*, 46: 183–197.
Hofer, M. A. (1990). Early symbiotic processes: hard evidence from a soft place. In: R. A. Glick & S. Bone (Eds.), *Pleasure Beyond the Pleasure Principle* (pp. 55–78). New Haven, CT: Yale University Press.
James, W. (1892). *Psychology*. New York: Holt.
James, W. (1902). *The Varieties of Religious Experience*. New York: Random House.
Kris, E. (1952). *Psychoanalytic Explorations in Art*. New York: International Universities Press.
Langer, S. (1953). *Feeling and Form*. New York: Scribner's.
Levitin, J. D. (2006). *This Is Your Brain On Music*. New York: Dutton.
Livingstone, M. (2002). *Vision and Art: The Biology of Mind*. New York: Abrams
Mandelstam, N. (1970). *Hope Against Hope*. New York: Atheneum.
Merleau-Ponty, M. (1961). *Eye and Mind, in The Primacy of Perception*. Chicago, IL: University of Chicago Press.

Meyer, L. B. (1956). *Emotion and Meaning in Music*. Chicago, IL: University of Chicago Press.
Meyer, L. B. (1967). *Music, the Arts, and Idea*. Chicago, IL: University of Chicago Press.
Noy, P. (1969). A Revision of the Psychoanalytic Theory of the Primary Process. *International Journal of Psychoanalysis, 50*: 155–178.
Pratt, C. C. (1952). *Music and the Language of Emotion*. Washington, DC: US Library of Congress.
Rappaport, D., Gill, M., & Schafer, R. (1945). *Diagnostic Psychological Testing*. Chicago, IL: Year Book Medical.
Rilke, R. M. (Ed.) (1985)[1952]. *Letters on Cézanne*, J. Agee (Trans.). New York: Fromm International.
Robinson, M. (1980). *Housekeeping*. New York: Picador.
Rose, G. J. (1980). *The Power of Form. A Psychoanalytic Approach to Aesthetic Form* (expanded edn), 1992. Madison, CT: International Universities Press.
Rose, G. J. (1987). *Trauma and Mastery in Life and Art*. Madison, CT: International Universities Press.
Rose, G. J. (1996). *Necessary Illusion: Art As Witness*. Madison, CT: International Universities Press.
Rose, G. J. (2004). *Between Couch and Piano. Neuroscience, Music, Art and Neuroscience*. Hove: Brunner-Routledge.
Rosen, C. (1971). *The Classical Style*. New York: Viking Press.
Ross, N. W. (1966). *Three Ways of Asian Wisdom*. New York:Simon & Schuster.
Schilder, P. (1950). *The Image and Appearance of the Human Body*. New York: International Universities Press.
Schore, A. N. (1996). The experience-dependent maturation of a regulatory system in the orbital prefrontal cortex and the origin of developmental psychopathology. *Development and Psychopathology, 8*: 59–87.
Schore, A. N. (1997). Early organization of the nonlinear right brain and the development of a predisposition to psychiatric disorders. *Development and Psychopathology, 9*: 595–630.
Sheets-Johnstone, M. (1999). *The Primacy of Movement. Advances in Consciousness Reseach* (Vol. 14). Amsterdam, PA: John Benjamins.
Sklarew, B., & Sklarew, M. (Eds.) (2010). *The Journey of Child Development, Selected Papers of Joseph D. Noshpitz*. New York: Routledge.
Solomon, M. (2003). *Late Beethoven. Music, Thought, Imagination*. Los Angeles, CA: University of California Press.
Spurling, H. (1998). *The Unknown Matisse: A Life of Henri Matisse: The Early Years, 1869–1908*. New York: Knopf.

Tolstoy, L. N. (1951). *Collected Works*, Vol. 30. New York: Walter J. Black.
Tomkins, S. (1962–1963). *Affect, Imagery, Consciousness* (2 vols). New York: Springer.
Zuckerkandl, V. (1956). *Sound and Symbol. Music and the External World.* Princeton, NJ: Princeton University Press.
Zuckerkandl, V. (1973). *Man the Musician. Sound and Symbol* (Vol. 2). Princeton, NJ: Princeton University Press.

CHAPTER THREE

Picasso's prolonged adolescence, his Blue Period, and blind figures

Harold P. Blum

Introduction

Pablo Picasso journeyed between his Barcelona home and Paris four times between the ages of nineteen and twenty-three. He went to Paris in October, 1900, May, 1901, and January, 1902, staying for varying lengths of time. He settled permanently in Paris in April 1904, after having moved many times within the city. This chapter explores Picasso's prolonged adolescent separation and individuation process, his developmental challenges, unconscious conflicts, and traumas as represented in the art of his Blue Period. Sometimes considered overly sentimental in the past, the Blue Period paintings are now recognised as an important innovative phase in the evolution of his art. Particular attention, from a psychoanalytic perspective, is paid to the intriguing enigmatic paintings of the Blue Period, which include blind subjects.

Picasso was born in Malaga in 1881. With his family, he moved several times, to Corunna, Barcelona, and Madrid, finally settling in Barcelona in 1899. Reportedly always drawing with pencils from age two onwards, he later claimed that as a child he could draw like Raphael. His sister, Lola, three years younger, challenged him to create drawings, requesting, for example, that he draw a dog or a donkey, beginning from any body part such as an ear or a paw. Precocious and versatile, he complied; he could easily compose and rearrange form and figure in space. At the Royal Academy of Art in Madrid, the youthful Picasso was recognised as a prodigy, a potentially great artist. His artwork was nurtured by his father, a mediocre artist who recognised his son's talent as far exceeding his own competence. He reportedly gave his adolescent son his paints and brushes and resigned himself to modest work as an art teacher. An alternative explanation is that his father's vision had become progressively impaired, so he relinquished his work as an artist.

Adolescence

Picasso's adolescence was hardly a moratorium, a time-out in the transition to adulthood. Rather, it was a turbulent period with intra-psychic disturbance involving issues of self-realisation, separation, loyalty, rivalry, and rebellion. Childhood difficulty was antecedent to these adolescent conflicts around separation (Mahler, Pine, & Bergman, 1975). He had a childhood school phobia, and demanded that the maid or his father take him to school, keeping one of his father's painted pigeons in class. Gedo (1980) traced his separation conflicts to the birth of his sister, Lola, and the experience of a severe, virtually simultaneous earthquake in Malaga, when Picasso was three years old. The sequellae of these double childhood traumas and the subsequent death of his sister, Conchita, at age seven, when he was thirteen, unconsciously infiltrated Picasso's later art (Blum, 2010). Picasso had vowed to renounce being an artist if her life were spared.

Picasso's departure from his family and homeland to a foreign city and country meant learning a new language and culture, as well as consolidating his identity and integrating new friends into his object world. Picasso wavered between separation and connection, detachment and attachment, leaving and returning, being independent and remaining dependent. Departing was an adolescent disengagement from past and present object relationships while anticipating a different and exciting future in his life and art.

It is not clear how much Picasso's parents contributed to his adolescent dilemmas. Picasso's narcissistic omnipotence and entitlement were probably anchored in his parents' narcissistic needs and expectations. At the time, Picasso and his parents needed material, social, and psychological support. According to Gilot (1964), his mother had told him that if he became a soldier, he would become a general; if he became a priest, he would become pope. Picasso asserted that he wanted to be an artist and so he became "Picasso". Although Picasso had quarrelled with his mother, who objected to his behaviour, sloppy dress, and lifestyle (not unusual in adolescence), family documents have indicated a close relationship between Picasso and his mother. His mother considered him a divine gift, bestowing on him the names of numerous saints. His own narcissistic needs encompassed a desire to gratify his mother's narcissistic wishes and impress her by achieving fame and fortune. His short stature (5'3") has been overlooked in its impact on his adolescent conflicts and his compensatory grandiosity. To be so short is likely to be experienced as a narcissistic and castrating wound for an adolescent youth. Ever concerned about his prominence in art history Picasso dated his art from the very beginning.

Picasso seems to have been less conflicted about his sister Lola than about his parents. She had been his favourite model in early adolescence and they maintained a separate intimacy. Continuing after he was a celebrity, he would telephone her daily, or delegate the regular sibling connection to his Catalan poet/secretary, Sabartes. In this way, he would "touch base" with her and with home, though his return visits to Spain were rare. Picasso's guilt over his hostility and death wishes, for example, toward his father and siblings, might be related to the theme in his art of the watchful guardian during sleep. Picasso, usually in disguise, protects the sleeping woman with whom he is also identified. Possibly connected to his witnessing his sister Conchita's slow suffocation from diphtheria, this theme could also be a disguised variant of a primal scene with sexual and aggressive implications. Picasso was awake and watchful, working at night while his partners slept. He slept during the day, having to be coaxed out of bed (Gilot, 1964).

The Blue Period

There is no distinct demarcation between late adolescence and adulthood (Arnett, 2004) and aspects of adolescence remained apparent throughout Picasso's life. His gradual transformation from adolescent to adult was manifested in change in his personal and artistic identity. The period of transition of his move to Paris was a time of experimentation with a new self and new art. His ambivalent polarity of departure and return indicated both his adolescent vulnerability and his adult resilience. During this transitional phase of life, he began characteristically, though not exclusively, to paint in monochromatic blue (especially cobalt blue and indigo). Occasional irregular dabs of green and grey were also evident. The blue paintings were actually concurrent with lesser known erotic art in other colours, such as sepia, as well as some multi-coloured paintings. Some predominantly blue paintings had appeared in Barcelona even prior to Picasso's first trip to Paris. Much of the Blue Period work was produced in Barcelona, as well as during Picasso's stays in Paris, tableaux of two cities, as he moved back and forth. While Picasso pursued his unique artistic path, he assimilated the work of other masters, such as Cézanne, Gauguin, Lautrec, Van Gogh, Munch, etc. The emaciated, elongated figures of the Blue Period, with gaunt long faces and hands, were heavily influenced by El Greco and Spanish art. The paintings of these artists, however, are multi-coloured, not monochromatic blue. Picasso's ambivalent travel would have resonated with the existential questions of Gauguin's (1897) great painting, *Where Do We Come From, What Are We, Where Are We Going?*, which Picasso admired. One of the figures in the Gauguin painting was probably a model for one of the women in Picasso's (1907) landmark painting, *Les Demoiselles d'Avignon*.

Achieving emancipation and independence was accompanied by emotional upheaval. His inner reactions of grief, loss, and loneliness were expressed in his melancholic blue compositions. Identifying with social outcasts, Picasso painted the depressed, deprived, and downtrodden. He depicted downcast mothers burdened with needy babies, prisoners and prostitutes, beggars and derelicts, the starved and emaciated. A number of these figures are definitely poignantly identifiable as blind or half blind, to be further discussed. Gauguin's thin brush strokes and flattened perspective, rather than the earlier influence of Van Gogh, were incorporated into much of the Blue Period style.

While blue was always associated with sea and sky, the connection of blue with melancholia had long been present in both art and verbal idiom. In art and literature, blue was symbolic of grave illness and death. Galle had produced a famed glasswork, designated as *Blue Melancholia* (1892). While Picasso's monochromatic blue might represent cognitive or affective rigidity, there was no evidence of rigidity in his compositions, nor in the fluidity of line and brushstroke. The tradition of representing renegades, prostitutes, and beggars derived from Goya and other Spanish artists, but without monochromatic blue colour. Although the predominance of blue was possibly related to blue lamplight and blue-tinted photos of the time, such remote connections fail to elucidate the Blue Period. The blues of his paintings became darker in hue and dark blue outlines became more prominent during the course of the Blue Period.

I regard Picasso's Blue Period art partly as his projection on canvas, and attempts to master, his own mourning and melancholia, alienation, and bitterness during his stressful protracted late adolescence. He alternated between regression and progression in response to developmental challenge. If there were times of inner desperation, there were also powerful motivation, determination, and sublimation. His artwork might have had a therapeutic function, and might also have facilitated his adolescent development. How would Picasso have developed in life and art without his Blue Period?

Physical and psychological travel and increasing separateness from his original objects involved major modification in Picasso's self and identity. This alteration was evident in his change of name. On his first trip to Paris at his nineteenth birthday, he used Ruiz, his father's name, inconsistently. He signed his art P. Ruiz Picasso. (It was traditional in Spain to use the names of both parents.) By the age of twenty and his second trip to Paris in 1901, his father's name was permanently deleted from Picasso's signature, leaving only his mother's name. Suppositions that Ruiz was too common a name, or that the alliteration of "Pablo Picasso" promoted his recognition as an artist, do not consider deeper psychological meaning.

Like Picasso, Freud changed his name and identity during adolescence. It was his first name that he changed, however, from Sigismund to Sigmund. The adolescent name changes for both Picasso and Freud were initially inconsistent, indicative of inner conflict. Arguing with Jung about the pharaoh Akhenaten erasing his father's name from Egyptian temples, Freud interpreted the name erasure as symbolic of parricide. Freud then fainted, and later gave additional interpretations of guilt over the death of his infant brother Julius, and latent homosexual conflicts with Jung. Confirming Freud's interpretation of parricidal fantasy in erasing a father's name, Picasso later stated, "In art, one has to kill one's father" (Richardson, 1991, p. 330). Picasso had ambivalently portrayed his father as Degas in a brothel, and had visited the same brothel as his father. The brothel was located on the Calle d'Avignon, a street of prostitution in Barcelona which related to the title of Picasso's painting, *Les Demoiselles d'Avignon*. For Picasso, eliminating his father's name coincided with his creation of the Blue Period paintings. Repudiating his father's influence and mediocre art was an Oedipal victory, a prelude to his becoming "Picasso". He unconsciously possessed his mother and identified with her creative functions, though not without unconscious guilt.

Picasso's Blue Period was sometimes ascribed to the tragic suicide of his close friend, Carlos Casagemas. Picasso had shared a studio with Casagemas in Barcelona and they were together on Picasso's first Paris sojourn. After they returned to Barcelona, Picasso left his friend and went briefly to Madrid. Casagemas went back to Paris alone. There he committed suicide in 1901, after first threatening to murder his girlfriend, Germaine. He had been obsessed with Germaine, who rejected his hopes for her love and marriage. Picasso, still in Spain, did not attend Casagemas's funeral. His mourning his friend did not deter him from having a brief affair with Germaine while staying in his deceased friend's Paris studio. (Germaine might have wanted to heap scorn and contempt on the man who almost killed her.) This prompt affair with Casagemas's girlfriend in his friend's quarters is strongly suggestive of victorious triumph over Oedipal and sibling rivals. Picasso might simultaneously have symbolically expressed unconscious homosexual love for Casagemas through his sexual relationship with Germaine.

The affair with Germaine, as well as the long delay before Picasso's portrayals of Casagemas, painted many months after his suicide, indicate that the death of Casagemas was not a major determinant of the onset and extent of the Blue Period. However, Casagemas's death might have contributed to and/or exacerbated in some small measure Picasso's late adolescent depression. Casagemas appears as a disguised representation of Picasso in the enigmatic painting *La Vie* (1903) (Figure 1). Scientific studies of the painting have revealed that Picasso covered a self-portrait with that of Casagemas. In *La Vie*, a barely clothed Casagemas stares at a barefoot mother holding an

Figure 3.1. Pablo Picasso, *La Vie*, 1903.

infant. *La Vie* might represent Picasso's disguised need to maintain separation and dissociation from his longing for maternal incest and nurturance. Picasso is himself the baby, and possibly the mother as well, with the father eliminated. The paintings of the deceased

Casagemas and the parricidal fantasy enacted in deleting his father's name from his signed art were chronologically convergent. The painting can also be seen as an undoing of Casagemas's suicide, portraying him next to a nude woman who leans against him, perhaps a way of assuaging his guilt. Picasso might have projected his own melancholy on to Casagemas's suicidal depression in *La Vie*, as well as in other Blue Period art. Picasso's adolescent conflicts and past traumas are expressed in *La Vie*. It might also represent the traumatic experiences of the birth of his sister, Lola, and the death of Conchita.

The blind of the Blue Period

Blindness is a special subject of the Blue Period paintings (Ravin & Perkins, 2004). The blind figures are recurrent and usually predominant in Blue Period paintings such as *The Old Guitarist* (1903), *The Blind Man's Meal* (Figure 2) (1903), *La Celestina* (Figure 3) (1904),

Figure 3.2. Pablo Picasso, *The Blind Man's Meal*, 1903.

Figure 3.3. Pablo Picasso, *La Celestina*, 1904.

and *The Old Jew and the Boy* (1903). *The Frugal Repast*, the first etching produced in Paris (1904), is now a black and white icon of Picasso's Blue Period. In a number of paintings, drawings, and graphic works, one or both eyes are clouded or closed, that is, blind. How mysterious, paradoxical, and disturbing that a visual artist virtually dependent on sight chooses to depict blind subjects.

In his choice of portraying the blind, however, Picasso followed past models: representations of Cupid as blind, and in the art of Rembrandt and Goya (Penrose, 1981): Goya, in particular, had painted blind guitar players; Rembrandt had repeatedly contrasted light and darkness, and had painted the famed portrait of *Aristotle Contemplating a Bust of Homer*. While artists may also have been stimulated by literature, for example, the blind poets, Homer and Milton, the blind

Tiresias in *Oedipus Rex*, we have no definite information that such literature or the Bible influenced Picasso. There are literary stereotypes of the blind seer whose blindness is compensated with foresight or insight. La Celestina , the subject of Picasso's (1904) painting, was a one-eyed procuress in the famous drama by de Rojas (1499); Picasso would have known of her history. Derrida (1993), in a seminar at the Louvre, discussed the subject of blindness in art, from the perspectives of artist and observer, as looking but not seeing beyond biased observation. Using the defence of denial, "there are none so blind as those who will not see".

The blind figures tend to evoke compassion, pity, sadness, and, perhaps, reassure the spectators that they do not share in this misfortune. Yet, all art has elements of ambiguity, and each spectator has a personal perception and response that might change with each exposure to the work of art. Picasso's blue paintings did not sell during the Blue Period, prolonging his indigence, which, in turn, very probably contributed to his depressed mood.

If Picasso fantasised himself as blind, he could reassure himself that it was only a fantasy, that his talion fears need not become reality. Painting the blind could be counter-phobic against the fear of becoming blind and losing the most valued aspect of the artist's self. In his dialogue with the objects on the canvas, as well as with the unseen spectators of his painting, he could be reassured of his capacity to see. *The Blind Man's Meal* depicts a solitary blind man. In *The Old Jew and the Boy*, the boy has seeing eyes for the blind, downcast old Jew. In *The Frugal Repast* the man is blind, and his similarly bony, emaciated female companion is sighted. In a variation on the theme, *La Celestina* (1903) has one sighted eye, and one highly visible, opaque blind eye. Pertinent to Picasso's theme of blindness, Freud's (1900a) first dream in his magnum opus was associated with his father's funeral. He dreamt he was requested to close the eyes, or close one eye of his dead father. Oedipal conflict and denial surface in the dream's manifest content.

Picasso provided subtle compensation and/or vicarious gratification for some of his blind figures. "La Celestina" has one seeing eye, and the "Old Jew" has a companion with a substitute pair of eyes. Compensation for blindness is also offered through alternate modes of sensory perception in the music of the guitarist and the touching contact of the dyadic partners. The old guitarist is bent over his instrument, immersed in the auditory sphere of music, "a rhapsody in blue", so important for the blind. The provision of the brownish guitar is his companion, his sole support and consolation. Homer, the blind poet, sang his verses to the ancient Greeks. Picasso is reported to have said, "They should pull out the eyes of painters as they do to goldfinches to make them sing better" (Penrose, 1981, p. 91)

Was Picasso blinding rival artists to the accompaniment of their singing mournful music as in *The Guitarist*? *The Blind Man's Meal* suggests the scarcity of nurturance and narcissistic supplies of the forlorn figures who connect through touch. At the time of the Blue Period, Picasso could be considered a social critic of blind indifference to poverty, and infirmity, just as he later inveighed against the atrocities of Franco s fascism in his painting *Guernica* (1937). These works of art were both self-referential and searing studies of social tragedy. Although much of Picasso's art was deeply personal and quasi-autobiographical, his multiple frames of reference encompassed social, cultural, and historical perspectives.

Picasso himself did not comment about the meaning of his depiction of the blind in his Blue Period. He did, however, refer to one of his Blue Period paintings which portrayed a blind subject (1903, letter in Barnes Museum, Philadelphia): "I am painting a blind man at the table. He holds some bread in his left hand and grasps with his right hand for a jug of wine". A religious interpretation of the painting invokes the Eucharist; the bread and the wine are symbolic of Christ's body and blood, and his concern for the poor and the needy to whom society turned a blind eye. Christ healed the blind and fed the hungry. As a former altar boy instructed in Catholicism, Picasso would probably have known about cures of the blind mentioned in the Bible. There is no evidence that Picasso made any other comment about his blind figures. In painting the blind of the Blue Period, Picasso regularly framed the ocular orbit in a dark blue shadow. With their affectively charged, simplified figures and background, the paintings comprise sensuous, emotionally interrelated compositions.

For a visual artist, loss of sight would be supremely self-destructive, precluding creation and enjoyment of visual art. During the Blue Period, Picasso often wore blue clothes; he identified with both the blind and the sighted figures, the damaged and the intact eye. He might have felt guilty about deserting his parents, surpassing and devaluing his father and dreaming of surpassing revered Spanish artists of the past. Although searching for mentors is typical of adolescence, "stealing" from other artists, as he told Gilot (1964), could well have been accompanied by guilt and by the "anxiety of influence" (Bloom, 2011). Picasso acquired and psychologically possessed the art of these masters through visual incorporation, emulation, and identification. As in *Oedipus Rex*, Oedipal victory over his masters could be unconsciously punished by blindness, representing castration, and the talion principle of "an eye for an eye". The fear of retaliation is a major psychological determinant of the superstition of the "evil eye". Picasso's adolescent sexual activity and his erotic art might also have been associated with fears of punitive blindness. (His clandestine erotic art included lovers merged in sexual union, eliminating separateness.) Masturbation, at that time, was considered noxious behaviour, which could lead to visual and mental impairment; prostitutes could transmit venereal disease leading to blindness and, ultimately, death. His voyeurism–exhibitionism, also expressed in his art, was a source of both gratification and guilt.

Picasso's blind figures might represent the artist as blind, his internalised self and object relationships, and spectators. He could have erotic and artistic gratification while avoiding the inhibiting and prohibiting gaze of parental authority. If the spectator were blind, he would not be subject to their disapproval or devaluation, fostering artistic freedom. However, if they were blind, he would also suffer the narcissistic mortification of not gaining recognition and respect. Blindness, thus, could be protection against the envy and jealousy of collectors and rival artists, as well as their punishment for their lack of recognition and admiration.

Picasso's figures who had one good eye or a sighted companion could reassure him that he retained sufficient vision, that his worst fears had not materialised. Picasso's own penetrating gaze was repeatedly noted by friends, artists, and dealers. Claiming he could look straight into the sun, he could proclaim victory over blinding light. If the sun represented a father figure, as in Freud's (1911c) Schreber case, Picasso would be more powerful than the paternal masters of art with whom he competed. However, if Picasso failed as an artist in his adolescent "rite of passage", he would be humiliated and might be cast among "the blind leading the blind" (Bible: Matthew, 15:14). In his dialogue with his object relationships and spectators, he could magically control the scene, having always been superstitious and interested in magic. He could safely protect them from his blind rage by dissociation and displacement on to prostitutes and derelicts. While his sometimes savage portrayals of prostitutes in Barcelona gave way to more sympathetic depictions in Paris during the Blue Period, empathy and sympathy for them were often followed by re-emergence of hostility, for example, in the fearsome, primitive harlots of *Demoiselles d'Avignon*. Women in Picasso's erotic art were sometimes depicted as devouring, engulfing, or castrating, dissociated from women as nurturing, alluring, or a muse.

The brooding, embittered aspects of the Blue Period were doubtless exacerbated by his frequently indigent circumstances. He was desperately short of funds, beginning with his second trip to Paris in May 1901. He had to return empty-handed to Barcelona at Christmas, having been unable to sell his paintings for more than a pittance. Picasso was, in essence, one of the beggars in blue, accepting meagre meals on credit. Creature comforts and public recognition of his art were in very short supply during the Blue Period, threatening his self-confidence and self-esteem. Nevertheless, with his perseverance and talent, he gradually succeeded in situating himself in the centre of the international *avant garde* art community in Paris.

From adolescence to young adulthood

Picasso emerged into adulthood after his prolonged adolescence. Enduring aspects of adolescence remained embedded in his adult personality. His adolescent characteristics, probably with a perceptually and artistically gifted neurobiological endowment, might have facilitated his elastic changes of style and form. The adolescent brain undergoes a second pruning of neurons and the personality undergoes varying change while childhood conflicts and trauma are revived, transformed, and reorganised. Adolescence, with its psychic and psychological changes, cannot merely be the past repeated. Striving towards independence in life and art converged in Picasso's Blue Period, with intermittent mourning and melancholia for his largely relinquished original objects. The art of the Blue Period cannot simply be explained by depression as the sole determinant. As in later phases of life, Picasso was prolific, highly innovative, and socially involved. He did not display withdrawal, anhedonia, nihilism, lack of communication, or complain of lack of meaning in life. In his affair with Germaine and ongoing contacts with prostitutes, Picasso did not display the loss of interest in sexual activity characteristic of severe depression.

During the Blue Period, Picasso also produced erotic art in other colors. His late adolescence was a time of further integration and consolidation of his sexual identity and unconscious bisexuality. In his erotic art there are female figures with a phallus, and females with testicles within female genitals. It is not known whether Picasso experimented with overt homosexuality, not uncommon during adolescence. He had camped out and slept beside his close friend, Manuel Pallares, in rural Spain. Several years later, when Picasso, Pallares, and Casagemas were staying with three women in the same apartment in Paris in late 1900, the intimacy of their heterosexual activity also suggested their latent homosexuality (Mailer, 1995). His friend, Max Jacob, was a tormented twenty-five-year-old homosexual French poet–painter when he met Picasso in 1901. Jacob admired Picasso's art at first sight, and provided much needed emotional and material support. They soon shared bed and board, initially communicating in sign language, having no common spoken language. Jacob taught Picasso French language and literature, and remained a close friend. Picasso was always avidly, overtly heterosexual, and his late adolescent challenges were not primarily related to problems of sexual identity. During this transitional period, Picasso sought both old Spanish friends and new French friends. Claims that the Blue Period was precipitated by Picasso's blue portrait of his slavish friend Jaime Sabartes (later his ever devoted secretary) do take into account the complex determinants of the Blue Period. Sabartes presence in Paris during the Blue Period was particularly valuable for his lavish adulation and his subjugated responses to Picasso's moods and requests.

Did Picasso's prolific artistic activity defend against depression and unacceptable sexual and aggressive impulses? His high level of artistic activity and social activity, such as carousing with friends, frequently attending the circus with them, could suggest hypomania. Were there also cyclothymic tendencies in Picasso's juxtaposition or alternation of depressive and erotic art, as well as reversal of day and night activities. Consistent with possible cyclothymia, the Blue Period was succeeded by the Rose Period. Cyclothymic tendencies might have been an inherent feature of his personality.

Discussion

Prolonged adolescence might be considered as contributing to creativity in many gifted persons. Having an enduring adolescent openness to exploration, experimentation, and risk taking may be a frequent, though not necessarily universal, characteristic of creative individuals. Adolescent separation and rebellion against conventional parental authority might foster departure from tradition towards new directions and imaginative innovation. Freud (1905d) referred to the detachment of adolescence as

> one of the most significant, but also one of the most painful psychical accomplishments of the pubertal period – a process that alone makes possible the opposition, which is so important for the progress of civilisation, between the new generation and the old. (p. 227)

Picasso and those rare persons who have transformed the history of art and science might often be permanent adolescents, at least in the creative dimension of their personalities.

Fostering creative potential, the oppositional attitude of many adolescents favours the further development of self-definition and identity. Picasso's adolescent phase struggle over independence might have promoted new creative compromise solutions in the artistic development of the youthful Picasso.

The Blue Period ended with Picasso finding new love, a live-in girlfriend, Fernande Olivier (la Belle Fernande), his own studio, and a group of admiring, devoted French friends. The "band à Picasso", who were not rival visual artists, provided mirroring, companionship, helpful acculturation and enthusiastic support. These friends, especially Max Jacob, Apollinaire, and Andre Salmon achieved literary recognition, parallel to their artist hero becoming prominent. In the context of this group, Picasso was free to work and play. From a negative perspective, Picasso's narcissistic needs were over-gratified. This was a persistent character issue evident throughout his life, accentuated by his relatively early recognition and a lifetime of fame and acclaim.

Picasso remained in France, but never became a French citizen. Nevertheless, his deep Spanish roots were apparent as he continued to enjoy Spanish music, dance, and bullfights in France, donated a treasure trove of his art to the Picasso museum, Barcelona, and *Guernica* to the Prado museum, Madrid. He remained attached to his former home at an optimal distance, with infrequent direct contact with Spanish family and friends.

In terms of psychological development, the Blue Period marked Picasso's transition from adolescence to adulthood, although aspects of adolescence persisted throughout his life, with both positive and negative effects. His artistic genius was becoming apparent during this period as he supplanted more conventional works with art that became increasingly original. Both his personal and artistic identities achieved new integration.

References

Arnett, J. (2004). *Emerging Adulthood: The Winding Road from the late Teens Through the Twenties*. Oxford: Oxford University Press.

Bloom, H. (2011). *The Anatomy of Influence*. New Haven, CT: Yale University Press.

Blum, H. (2010). Adolescent trauma and the Oedipus complex. *Psychoanalytic Inquiry*, 30: 548–556.

Derrida, J. (1993). *Memoirs of the Blind; The Self Portrait and Other Ruins*. Chicago, IL: University of Chicago Press.

Freud, S. (1900a). *The Interpretation of Dreams*. S.E., 4–5. London: Hogarth.

Freud, S. (1905d). *Three Essays on the Theory of Sexuality*. S.E., 7: 125–245. London: Hogarth.

Freud, S. (1911c). *Psycho-analytic Notes on an Autobiographical Account of a Case of Paranoia*. S.E., 12: 1–82. London: Hogarth.

Gedo, M. (1980). *Picasso—Art as Autobiography*. Chicago, IL: University of Chicago Press.

Gilot, F., with Lake, C. (1964). *Life with Picasso*. New York: McGraw-Hill.

Mahler, M., Pine, F., & Bergman, A. (1975). *The Psychological Birth of the Human Infant*. New York: Basic Books.

Mailer, N. (1995). *Portrait of Picasso as a Young Man*. New York: Atlantic Monthly Press.

Penrose, R. (1981). Picasso, perception, and blindness. *Paris Museum*, 33: 193.

Ravin, J., & Perkins, J. (2004). Representation of blindness in Picasso's Blue Period. *Archives of Opthalmology, 122*(4): 636–639.

Richardson, J. (1991). *A Life of Picasso* (Vol. 1). New York: Random House.

CHAPTER FOUR

Psychoanalysis and art: from applied analysis to interdisciplinary dialogue

Adela Abella

On 7 February 1921, Freud wrote to Ernest Jones, "Yet it is evident that there is much slippery ground in many of our applications from psychoanalysis to biography and literature" (Paskaukas, 1993). Coming from a man who had published, during the previous decade, a number of essays on art and culture (among which are some outstanding papers on Jensen's *Gradiva*, Leonardo, and the Moses of Michelangelo), this statement sounds rather like a confession. These kinds of auto-critical and field-labouring comments were usual to Freud. They stand not only as signs of his intellectual honesty but also, still more importantly, they highlight important points of debate which remain vital to present day psychoanalysis.

In this chapter, I will try to discuss the different means through which analysts attempt to deal with art, weighing the contributions and the shortcomings of the various psychoanalytical approaches to art. This issue can be considered at two levels, which can be clearly differentiated. First, we can examine the psychological value and mechanisms involved both in artistic creativity and in the audience's aesthetic experience. Second, we may observe the different approaches taken by psychoanalysts, from Freud to the present day, in order to understand a work of art.

Artistic creativity and the audience's aesthetic experience

At this level, we are dealing with three major paradigms: art as sublimation, art as reparation, and art as thought provoking.

Art as sublimation

Freud's basic proposition suggests considering art mainly as the result of the sublimation of repressed sexual desires. "Sexual curiosity", says Freud, "can be diverted ('sublimated') in the direction of art" (1905d, p. 156), and again, ". . . what an artist creates provides at the same time an outlet for his sexual desire" (1910c, p.132). Nevertheless, as early as 1912, Freud adds narcissistic components to that which can be sublimated through art:

> Thus art constitutes a region half-way between a reality which frustrates wishes and the wish fulfilment world of the imagination – a region in which, as it were, primitive man's strivings for omnipotence are still in full force. (1912–1913, p. 188)

The audience's aesthetic experience is considered under the same vertex. The spectators' pleasure derives from the disguised realisation of repressed wishes through the work of art via an identification with "the mental constellation . . . that in [the artist] produced the impetus to create" (Freud, 1914b, p. 212). In fact, formal aesthetic aspects are given a defensive value: the artist, posits Freud, "bribes us with the formal and aesthetic pleasures" (1908e, p. 153). In consequence, art is lined up with dreams, children's play, hysterical fantasies, neurotic symptoms, daydreaming, and masturbation.

To sum up, at a societal level, art is considered by Freud among "the greatest monuments of civilization" and a precursor of psychoanalysis in that it allows a direct grasp of deep psychological truths. However, at an individual level (both for the artist and the audience) it is equated with a pathological functioning in that it carries out a defence against reality.

Art as reparation

Hanna Segal's thinking proceeds along a very different path (Abella, 2010). Following Klein, Segal suggests considering art in relation to depressive anxieties and reparation. Artistic activity is seen as an attempt "to restore and re-create the loved object outside and inside the ego" (Segal, 1952, p. 197), which implies a successful work of mourning accompanied by symbol formation. The result of this process is, on the outside, the "creation of an entirely new reality" taking the form of a work of art, whereas, at the same time, the ego is enriched, reintegrated, and enlivened.

This radically different point of view carries three major intertwined consequences. First, the intervention of aggression is considered as central to artistic endeavour: "There can be no art without aggression" (Segal, 1991, p. 92). Second, reparation is achieved precisely through formal beauty: "There can be no aesthetic pleasure without formal perfection" (Segal, 1952, p. 204). The basic idea is the following: the destruction, the death, the ugliness, and the horror expressed in the content of a work of art are compensated and repaired through the beauty, the wholeness, and the harmony conveyed though formal perfection, and that is *within* the same work of art.

Third, the defensive value ascribed by Freud to artistic activity is refuted. The artist does not withdraw from reality, posits Segal. On the contrary, a good artist needs to have "an extremely high reality sense", both in order to be in contact with his internal world and to master the material and technical aspects of his work. A similar phenomenon is thought to operate in the audience. The audience's aesthetic pleasure lies in the identification with the reparative processes conveyed by the work of art. Therefore, far from a trivial enjoyment or a flight away from reality, art brings pain relief, integration, and mental growth—all of which imply a sound contact with reality.

Art as thought provoking

Nevertheless, and this is a fundamental point, both these paradigms prove to be unsatisfactory when it comes to a large part of today's artistic activity. Despite the multiplicity and eclecticism of contemporary art, with no hegemonic ideology or formal unity, two particular trends are currently widely accepted in the artistic field. Both are at odds with the presuppositions on which these two main classical paradigms rest. On the one hand, there is a general rejection of the idea of classical beauty, defined in terms of simplicity, equilibrium, rhythm, and harmony, as an appropriate criterion for artistic value. Indeed, contemporary artists often aim at the most powerful, innovative, and efficient impact through a variety of formal means, which includes the ugly, the raw, the shocking, as well as the trivial, the accidental, and the ephemeral.

On the other hand, the communicative intention of art is put into question (Abella, 2008, 2010, 2012). The artist, it is said, must restrain the expression of personal ideas in order to allow the possibility of multiple, highly personal, and often creative interpretations by the public. The underpinning idea is that the wish to communicate runs the major risk of containing the wish of influencing and alienating. Hence, art should propose not so much a beautiful finished object, but a beautiful opened-up experience, one that stimulates the audience to perceive and experience reality in a new way.

Therefore, if the public is to identify with the artist, as both Freud and Segal suggested, this identification should rest on the artist's personal freedom to see and experience the world in a new way, instead of resting on a certain fantasy conveyed by the work of art or on the experience of sensual aesthetic pleasure, however integrative it might be.

It is significant to note that, in this line of thought, Bion's thinking converges with contemporary art's aspirations. Some of the similarities lie in the following areas: Bion's insistence on the value of thinking for oneself and of finding one's O, in the sense of one's deepest truth; his advocacy of a "pro(e)-vocative attitude" pursuing the deconstruction of stereotyped reactions in order to allow the achievement of more authentic experiences and personal truth; the accent Bion gives to psychoanalysis as a transformative process aimed not so much at reconstructing the past or unconscious fantasies, but at fostering mental growth; his warnings against a seductive collusion between the analyst and the patient (we might add, the artist and her public), which has the value of a lie (Abella, 2012).

To sum up, contemporary art, like contemporary psychoanalysis, is concerned mainly with the search for the deepest personal truth. What matters is not formal beauty, but truth. Thus, a third paradigm might be proposed, which is more in attunement with both contemporary art and contemporary psychoanalysis. This paradigm draws from Bion's thinking and emphasises several particular considerations: the deconstructive power of artistic activity; its capacity to allow perceiving and experiencing in a new way and, therefore, its transformative potential; the multiplicity of personal re-creations of a given work of art; the function of art as a stimulus to fresh thinking (mainly fresh unconscious thinking).

It should be noted that any one of these three paradigms might prove to be the most useful, depending on the work of art we are considering. Thus, a love or an adventure story might be understood best as a wish fulfilment attempt, whereas classical Greek tragedies beautifully illustrate the interplay between the horror of the content and the formal perfection. In the case of many contemporary works, where there is neither an identifiable fantasy nor any claim to formal beauty, the thought-provoking paradigm might turn out to be more appropriate.

Different kinds of "slippery ground"

Freud approached artistic activity following two main approaches: we can see them in his essays on Jensen's *Gradiva* and on Leonardo. A third major approach, based on countertransference, might be connected to some anticipatory comments made by Freud, but appears mainly as a post-Freudian development. Finally, I shall discuss a more recent approach centred in interdisciplinary dialogue.

The Leonardo approach

The basic idea is to look for "the connection between the impressions of the artist's childhood and his life history on the one hand and his works, as reactions to those impressions, on the other" (1913j, p. 187).

Freud was aware of the debatable nature of what he called "a psychoanalytical novel", the certainty of whose results he was "far from overestimating". In fact, with the passage of time, psychoanalysts have more and more abandoned the Leonardo approach, mostly because of the highly speculative nature of this type of exercise, which has been severely criticised (Baudry, 1984; Esman, 1998).

The *Gradiva* approach

Freud's comments on *Gradiva* run parallel to the textual approach in literary criticism. The basic idea is that the clues for the understanding of a work of art lie inside the work itself. Thus, its interpretation does not need to draw on any external element, such as the life and (supposed) unconscious conflicts of the author.

Freud's choice in *Gradiva* was to consider the literary characters as though they were a living person. He was, though, equally aware of the pitfalls of the "case study" approach. In fact, assuming equivalence between a constructed character and a living person is highly problematic and has been also put into question (Baudry, 1984; Esman, 1998).

However, Freud's major concern is far more serious and lies in the risk of "tendentious interpretations" (Freud, 1907a, p. 43), that is, in the possibility of "produc[ing] a complete caricature of an interpretation" because it is so "easy . . . to find what one is looking for and what is occupying one's own mind" (p. 91). In other words, the risk is "that what we pretended was the author's meaning was in fact only our own" (p. 83).

The countertransference approach

This approach highlights the intervention of the interpreter's fantasies, expectations, and emotions in the act of understanding a work of art.

Often, the experience of reading/beholding a work of culture is compared to an analytical session. What the analyst feels and thinks is considered to reflect the content and the intentions of a work of art. However, it is highly debatable whether one can equate listening to a patient and interpreting a piece of culture. What is lacking in the second instance is very precisely that which is considered to be central for psychoanalytical understanding: the guiding, refining, and transformative effect of the response of the patient. This is, in my opinion, a dramatic difference.

In fact, the interpreter does not only project his fantasies and feelings on to the work of art. He also injects his theories. Often, the work of art is used either as a source of inspiration, allowing the commentator to develop a previous formless intuition, or as a prop which allows the validity of a given construct to be proved (as Freud deliberately did in the essay on *Gradiva*). In any case, my sense is that the understanding of a work of art is often sacrificed in favour of a theoretical demonstration.

The interdisciplinary dialogue approach

This final approach draws on the idea that, in these times, we do not need to demonstrate the validity of psychoanalysis in the same way that Freud had to a hundred years ago. What we need is to meet other disciplines in a two-way dialogue that allows an enlivening cross-fertilisation. Psychoanalysis has much to contribute, but we need to offer our contributions in such a way that what we have to give might be received more easily. On the other hand, we have much to learn from other fields of knowledge—as Freud did. This demands an open and self-questioning disposition and the relinquishment of any temptation to evangelise.

By interdisciplinary exchange, I mean giving up the attempt to demonstrate or to teach, to impose our truths on others, and convert them to our beliefs. This involves something nearer to the ordinary sense of the word "dialogue": listening to the others; watching the way they tackle problems similar to our own; looking for convergences and divergences between different fields of knowledge; being ready to question our established truths. Freud was a good example for us at many of these levels.[1]

* * *

In summary, I have described three paradigms concerning artistic creativity and aesthetic experience (centred on sublimation, reparation, and thought provoking), and four approaches to the understanding of a work of art (Leonardo, *Gradiva*, countertransference, and interdisciplinary dialogue). In fact, any psychoanalytical essay on art represents a particular combination of these two axes of description. Thus, it would be possible to imagine a grid where the various combinations between the different paradigms and the different approaches would intersect in such a way that any psychoanalytical paper could be located within it. For instance, the sublimatory and the reparative paradigms are often associated with the *Gradiva* approach. However, other combinations are more problematic: for instance, the thought-provoking paradigm is more at odds with the Leonardo approach, whereas it is cogent with the interdisciplinary approach.

I will attempt now to test these different paradigms and approaches to artistic activity through their applications to two works of a highly influential artist of the twentieth century who has deeply shaped contemporary art: Marcel Duchamp. The principal aim of this exercise will be to try to show, through a practical example, some of the advantages and drawbacks of the different vertex.

On two works of Marcel Duchamp (1887–1968)

I will consider two of the most famous works of Marcel Duchamp: *The Bride Stripped Bare by Her Bachelors, Even* (1915–1923, Figure 1) and *Given: 1. Waterfall 2. The Illuminating Gas* (1946–1966, see Figures 2 and 3). A meaningful feature shared by these two works is the fact that both of them stand as carefully meditated works that occupied Duchamp during long years at the beginning and the end of his life as an artist.

The Bride has been considered, together with the ready-mades, as the fullest expression of Duchamp's radical and provocative artistic position (Cros, 2006; Housez, 2006; Lebel, 1959). This work, also named *The Large Glass* because of the support on which it was made and its important size (277 × 175.8 cm), is composed of two separate parts. The lower one is reserved for the bachelors and the upper one for the bride. In contrast with the explicitly sexual tone conveyed by its title, the formal treatment is extremely austere, mechanical, and even devitalised, evoking scientific and industrial devices through a technical design almost devoid of colour.[2]

The Bride seen from the Leonardo, the Gradiva, and the countertransference approaches

How are we to understand this ambiguous, disconcerting, and unsettling work? We might look at it from the point of view of the Leonardo approach, which is searching to connect the work of art with what we know about the life of the artist and what we speculate about his unconscious conflicts.

At this level, we are puzzled by the multiplicity of possibilities. Held (1973) suggested a most daring hypothesis, arguing that Duchamp suffered from obsessional neurosis. For him, Duchamp's work may be envisaged as an attempt to control pregenital impulses of an anal and voyeuristic nature. From this view, the defensive process, dominated by reaction formation and intellectualisation, led

Figure 4.1. The Bride Stripped Bare by Her Bachelors, Even (1915–1923).

Duchamp to sterility and inhibition, represented by his abandonment of art.[3]

In a more recent trend of thinking, it has been suggested that *The Bride* expresses Duchamp's complex relationships to women, a relationship made of a troubling mix of promiscuity and indifference.

Some commentators have pondered about Duchamp's supposed unspoken, painful, and chilling feelings towards his deaf mother, whom he described as distant, placid, and indifferent. This hypothesis might be sustained by the supposition that, while pregnant with Marcel, his "neurasthenic"[4] mother would have been longing for a baby girl who would replace the little three-year-old Madeleine, who had died seven months before (Seigel, 1995). A link might be made here with the fact that Duchamp entertained a degree of sexual ambiguity, dressing like a woman and signing some of his works under the name of Rrose Selavy, a name that may be taken (Duchamp being very fond of homophonic word play) as "Eros, c'est la vie".

At a slightly different level, it has been suggested that *The Bride* expresses Duchamp's incestuous feelings towards his sister, Suzanne, to whom he was deeply attached and who got married shortly before the start of this work (Held, 1973). The a-grammatical character of the last word of its title, *La mariée mise à nu par ses célibataires, même* would sustain this interpretation if we think of the homophony between *même* and *m'aime*. Duchamp being fond of language puns, the title might be translated as *The Bride Stripped Bare by Her Bachelors Loves Me*. Thus, an Oedipal configuration might be identified, his sister Suzanne standing as a displacement of Duchamp's distant mother. In this line of thought, the mechanical and glacial formal treatment might convey both the mother's acute bereavement at the time of her pregnancy with Marcel and his birth, and Marcel's aggressive feelings towards this frozen mother.

In this same line of thought, but taking a different starting point, we might recall that Duchamp started thinking of *The Bride* immediately after the refusal of the Salon des Independents of his *Nude Descending a Staircase*, a work which combines a Cubist formal treatment with the specific futurist preoccupation with motion and which was to bring him immense popularity across the Atlantic a few years later (Housez, 2006). Speaking of this refusal, which was inflicted with the complicity of his admired and beloved brothers, Duchamp said, "It gave me a turn ... I said: all right, since it's like that, there is no question of joining a group—I'm going to count on no one but myself, alone" (Cabanne, 1971, p. 31). In the light of his brothers being of a Cubist allegiance, the new technical treatment used by Duchamp could be interpreted as representing his fight to acquire the most promising "malic"[5] mould in order to allow him the possession of the idealised *Bride* each of the bachelors was striving for. Thus, *The Large Glass* might express Duchamp's need to deal with narcissistic fantasies of self-sufficiency and autarchy.

We might equally well consider *The Bride* according to Freud's second approach, the one developed in his work on Jensen's *Gradiva*. That is, we might try to identify the (universal) unconscious fantasies conveyed by a particular work of art instead of the author's unconscious.

In this line of thought, we might speculate about the sort of relationship between men and women that the *Bride* conveys. Thus, it has been suggested that *The Large Glass* represents a wishful scene doomed to no final satisfactory encounter, the bride and the bachelors remaining apart forever (Seigel, 1995). Another author (Cros, 2006) sees in the upper side, which contains some visceral-like images, a representation of female orgasm, whereas the lower side, much more mechanical, would suggest onanist fantasies. It would be equally possible to understand *The Large Glass* as a metaphorical representation of an omnipotent bisexual corporal machine, or, perhaps, muse on the sharp contrast between an explicit sexual theme and its mechanical formal treatment. And so on.

The third approach, which draws on countertransference, highlights the subjective character of the spectator's personal appropriation of a work of art and gives legitimacy to his various creative potential readings. As Green put it, "The interpretation of the text . . . is, ultimately, the interpretation that (the analyst) must give to himself about the effects of the text on his own unconscious" (Green, 1992, p. 20). There is not one pre-existing truth contained either in the unconscious of the author or in the unconscious of the work; what matters is what the interpreter does with it. In fact, this approach meets Duchamp's famous aphorism: "It's the spectators who make the pictures". It also agrees with a much older comment, the one from Freud suggesting that "so many readings of [a work of art] are possible" (Freud, 1914b, p. 215).

In summary, the important question here is to consider the particular re-creations that *The Bride* can arouse in a particular beholder, that is, the way in which each spectator allows herself to be touched by it. The possibilities are countless. Taking one example (Abella, 2007), it might be possible to draw on the ascetic attitude underlying Duchamp's aesthetic programme. The selected fact would be, here,

Duchamp's insistence on the need to "contradict his own taste" and his personal inclination, and this to such an extent as to refuse the pleasures of the "physically agreeable and the attractive", the "appeal to the senses", which he scornfully labels the "retinal shudder". In contrast to the "animal expression", to the "disgusting" physicality of painting, Duchamp champions the "beauty of indifference" and fosters what he calls "dry aesthetics". He, therefore, argues for a position that promotes "intellectual expression" and the beauty of thought alone. Art must evolve in the realm of the "grey matter"; the creative act is an act of thought. What matters is the idea alone; its material execution is superfluous.

This ascetic, frugal, and simultaneously omnipotent position mirrors the typical fantasy of anorexia, that is, of triumphing over the physical, sexual, and instinctual body, a source of needs and desires (and, thus, of dependency) in order to take refuge in the narcissistic, autarchic omnipotence of thought alone. In this vein, Duchamp's ascetic artistic programme might be considered as congruent with an anorectic phantasy.

Given . . . seen from the Leonardo, the Gradiva, and the countertransference approaches

Let us turn now to *Given: 1. Waterfall 2. The Illuminating Gas* (1946–1966). This very strange posthumously exhibited work may be seen as a disconcerting and even shocking last touch to Duchamp's work, which shattered its preceding appearance of coherence and unity. Its destabilising effect was multiplied by the fact that for over twenty years Duchamp had worked on it in absolute secrecy, while loudly claiming to be a "defrocked" artist who had definitely abandoned painting. In the spirit of a peep-show, two tiny holes bored in an old, very worn wooden door (Figure 2) allow the view of an alarming scene: a stripped female body lying on her back in a position where we cannot see her face, her swollen legs spread wide apart, her genitals denuded of pubic hair and reduced to an incision. Her hand holds an Auer lamp against the background of a landscape atmospherically reminiscent of those from the Renaissance, for example, the one in the *Mona Lisa* (see Figure 3).

Two aspects are striking in this work: on the one hand, its disturbing subject and, on the other hand, even more importantly, the fact

Figure 4.2. Given: 1. The Waterfall, 1946–1966.

that it appears as a refutation of the very kernel of Duchamp's preceding doctrine. In fact, this unclassifiable, kitsch, and disgusting artistic proposition suggests voyeuristic and perverse—mostly sadistic—fantasies far removed from the "beauty of indifference" hitherto so laboriously sought after by Duchamp. The major innovation lies here in the fact that the provocation targets neither bourgeois values nor the artistic establishment, but precisely Duchamp's followers themselves, those who believed in his artistic programmatic credo.

Following the Leonardo approach, it has been noticed that Duchamp began the preparatory works of *Given* during his love affair, in his late fifties, with Maria Martins, one of the few women with whom he was deeply in love and the first to whom he was ready to get engaged. Some years later, he finally met a kindred spirit and a

Figure 4.3. Given 2. The Illuminating Gas, 1946–1966.

loving companion in his second wife, Teeny, and it was during their marriage, and with her complicity and help, that Duchamp accomplished this work. Thus, *Given* might express the "defrosting" of Duchamp's indifference and coldness, which brought him back to the disturbing complexity of engagement, life, and love.

Using the *Gradiva* approach, much has been said about the troubling nakedness of this entirely depilated and faceless woman, holding an Auer lamp and offering herself in a position of total abandonment. The thorough control Duchamp exercises on the viewer, who is forced to look from a unique and well-established perspective, through the holes in the door, has also been noted. Two possibilities open up here: if we think that this work contains an unconscious (probably universal) fantasy that our aim is to decipher, we are referring strictly to the *Gradiva* approach. On the other hand, if the commentator emphasises the particular way in which the work affects her, if she thinks in terms of her personal re-creation, she is placing her comment inside the countertransference approach. Aggressive, sadistic, and voyeuristic fantasies have been suggested as well as symbolic meanings (the lamp, etc.), which I leave to the reader's imagination to develop.

Finally, it would be possible to place in dialectic opposition these two works: the disturbing physicality of *Given* against the mechanical and de-eroticised formal treatment of *The Bride*. The over-explicit immediacy of *Given* stands against the distant hermeticism of *The Bride*. In consequence, the question could be: might this posthumous work, *Given*, be seen as the return of the physicality previously repressed and denied in Duchamp's "official" work? Put otherwise, the disruptive and perverse suggestions of *Given* could be seen as the equivalent of a hidden retinal binge following, and in contrast to, the asceticism of the anorectic-like preceding period? If so, we could say that this last and most disturbing artistic proposition brings ambivalence and conflict into Duchamp's work, thus adding depth and a lively complexity to his provocative and refreshing, but often very categorical, devitalized, and rigid, statements.

The wish to respect the psychic function of art

Thus, we come to the questions posed at the beginning of this chapter: what are the advantages and the pitfalls of the different psychoanalytical approaches to art? Indeed, the major risk of the Leonardo approach is wild interpretation. Some of the links suggested between Duchamp's work and both his biography and his supposed unconscious conflicts might be totally or partially right. Equally, they might be wrong. As for the second approach, its most important danger remains the use of a work of art as a support for the projection of the interpreter's theories or personal fantasies, the difference being that the projection is made not on to the author but on to the work. The countertransference approach runs the same risk, its comparative strength drawing from the fact that, given that its conclusions are explicitly presented as legitimate subjective re-creations of a given work of art, the question of their truth is not to be challenged. Thus, the different readings of Duchamp's work illustrate, through the large range of heterogeneous hypotheses that have been suggested, the rich but subjective and projective value of any interpretation.

In fact, some of the different readings of a piece of art might be highly creative. Moreover, each of them probably contains a kernel of truth. In the last pages of *Totem and Taboo* (Freud, 1912–1913, pp. 160–161), Freud suggested a distinction among different sorts of reality that is useful on this point. Three different types of reality can be differentiated: a "factual reality", which refers to what really "did" happen in the past, a "historical reality", which applies to what was felt during childhood (that which existed in the mind in the past, thus including the distortions introduced by subjectivity), and, finally, a "psychical reality", which pertains to what is presently "felt" (the actual presentation of the internal world). In as much as we acknowledge these different levels of reality, and provided that we explicitly state which of these realities we are constructing (or reconstructing) in our interpretation of a work of art, we can venture an audacious hypothesis.

Nevertheless, beyond the thorny problem of truth lies a still more fundamental problem. At this point, the question is: at what level and in which way are our contributions to art useful? What do they add to our understanding of art? Still more importantly, do they enhance the psychological function we attribute to art? Do they enrich or, at least, allow, a significant aesthetic experience? Or, on the contrary, while being creative, useful, and true at one level (for instance, illustrating and supporting a theoretical development), might their final result be, at another level, to impinge upon and impoverish the fundamental value of individual aesthetic experience (as we would think of it from a psychoanalytical point of view)?

A similar question has been posed concerning the contributions of other disciplines to art. Thus, French sociologist Bourdieu (1992), in his essay on Flaubert's *L'éducation sentimentale*, defends the legitimacy and the interest of a specifically sociological approach of a literary piece. The fundamental difference lies in the fact that sociologist values are not betrayed *by* the application of sociology to art. That which might be seen, from a sociologist point of view, as the major contribution of art is not contradicted or annihilated by the actual application of sociology to literature. On the contrary, we might fear this could be the case concerning certain applications of psychoanalysis to art.

In order to support my idea, I need to turn to what have been considered the psychological functions of art: sublimation for Freud, reparation for Segal, thought provoking in a more recent trend stemming from some of Bion's contributions. Coming back to Duchamp, we might imagine that, following Freud, the spectators might have the possibility to live out and sublimate a large range of fantasies, both narcissistic ones (of an autarchic, destructive, or anorectic nature) and sexual ones (mainly of a perverse nature).

Segal's paradigm is more difficult to apply, given that Duchamp explicitly refuses the notion of formal beauty. We might, nevertheless, find it useful if we replace the reparative effect of formal beauty *inside the work of art* by the reparative function of beauty offered *by its context*: the destruction and the ugliness expressed in Duchamp's work is compensated, made tolerable, and repaired by its inclusion in the reassuring, beautiful, and respectful frame of a museum or an art gallery.

The third paradigm, which emphasises the promotion of fresh personal thinking, appears, from my point of view, deeply relevant. Through their disconcerting and shocking presentation, Duchamp's works foster personal thinking in a highly effective and often unforgettable way. This aim is, moreover, deeply congruent with Duchamp's maxim, "It is the viewers who make the pictures", and with the important trend in contemporary art that pursues the most personal appropriation of every kind of experience and, therefore, is wary of the effects of seduction and indoctrination.

However, and this is my central point, in order to allow a work of sublimation, reparation, or thought provoking, the psychoanalytical commentator should respect the conditions needed for a real and authentic personal aesthetic experience. In my opinion, the personal appropriation of a work of art in a meaningful way demands a degree of intimacy and privacy for the sublimatory, reparative, or thought-provoking experience to occur. This experience of personal appropriation might be impinged upon by the obstructing presence of other people's thoughts taking up too much room in one's own mind. In other words, the psychoanalytical commentator might need to respect the solitude and the silence this demands. Hence, we might need to avoid saturating, colonising, and sterilising a work of art through the injection of our personal fantasies or theories.

Conclusions and a plea for interdisciplinary dialogue

Currently, the Leonardo approach has been almost entirely abandoned. On the contrary, an important number of papers are published following the *Gradiva* and the countertransference approach. What psychoanalytical commentators find in them lies at different levels: sometimes the work of art supplies a fecund inspiration; at other times, it acts rather as a support allowing the illustration or the development of a theoretical construct. Finally, it can also be (and justifiably so) simply the opportunity to enjoy a pleasant reflection on what Freud called "one of the most attractive subjects to analytic examination" (Freud, 1913j) Quite often, these psychoanalytical comments are intelligent and creative. Thus, they can be considered as legitimate, especially if the author takes pains to specify the sort of reality she is attempting to construct: factual, historical, or psychical. There is, after all, no harm in producing "psychoanalytical novels" if we recognise and present them as such. However, my personal feeling is that through these three approaches, we often learn more about the author's personality or about her theories than about the work of art itself or about its author. Furthermore, in as much as the commentator's goal is the demonstration of a previous theory (as is often the case), the risk, for the commentator, is of learning just what she already knows.[6]

A more recent approach is available that is devoid of some of the pitfalls of the more classical ones: the interdisciplinary dialogue. Applied to Duchamp's work, we might, thus, reflect on some striking convergences between contemporary art and contemporary psychoanalysis, such as the insistence on mental growth and the concern to be wary of the risks of suggestion, seduction, and indoctrination in order to enhance the greatest degree of personal freedom.

Through this avenue, we may aspire to contribute to the understanding of art in a way that is specific to psychoanalysis while trying to learn from other fields of knowledge. This approach is cogent with the thought-provoking paradigm in that it respects the minimum of silence necessary to foster a personal appropriation of culture. Thus, the archaeological model (whose goal is to recover memories or to construct/reconstruct past events or unconscious fantasies) might need to be complemented with what we might call the "mind fitness" paradigm: the one aiming to develop mental muscles in order to enhance thinking and mental growth. That is a paradigm which, I believe, is more attuned to the way in which contemporary psychoanalysis works in the clinical area, while offering broad possibilities to the development of our discipline.

Notes

1. A certain number of issues have been explored, along these lines, by contemporary psychoanalysis. Some of them are: the multi-faceted problems presented by history, memory, and reconstruction; the dialectics between inside–outside, reality–illusion, language–action or individual–society; the consequences of the inevitability of frustration, loss, and death.
2. In the *Notes* which accompany it (Duchamp, 1989, pp. 13–71), we find the description of "the lubricious, fat, bachelor-machine" endowed with "desire-magneto", constituted by the "cemetery of uniforms and liveries" or "matrix of Eros" formed of "nine Malic Moulds" (a neologism derived from male) which, when filled with illuminating gas, will give corresponding malic shapes: the policeman, the cuirassier . . ., the whole thing is connected to the "chocolate grinder" as well as to a chariot, which "should, while reciting its litanies go from A to B and return from B to A, at convulsive speed", which will finally give the "sculpture of drips (points) formed by the splash after having been dazzled by oculist paintings. As for the "bride", "the apotheosis of virginity", she is composed of the "Pendu femelle" (the "Hanged female") connected to her "blossoming": "the Milky Way". She possesses a "life centre", "a motor with quite feeble cylinders . . . the superficial organ of the bride; . . . powered by the love gasoline, a secretion of the bride's sexual glands, and by the electric sparks of the stripping" who transmits her "commands" to the bachelor machine.
3. In 1923, Duchamp, who was not yet forty years old, shocked the artistic *milieu* by announcing his abandonment of artistic activity and his decision to devote himself to what a Breton called "an interminable game of chess".
4. The word belongs to Duchamp.

5. "Malic" is a neologism used by Duchamp for "male".
6. I have myself produced some papers following these approaches, one of them about Duchamp (Abella, 2007). I remember the pleasure I had in writing them and I am grateful for the opportunity they gave me to develop my thinking. Nevertheless, I wonder if they were useful for anyone beside myself. Moreover, I hope they did not impede the reader's individual and personal re-creation of the work of art concerned.

References

Abella, A. (2007). Marcel Duchamp: on the fruitful use of narcissism and destructiveness in contemporary art. *International Journal of Psychoanalysis*, *88*: 1039–1059.

Abella, A. (2008). Christian Boltanski: un artiste contemporain vu et pensé par une psychanalyste. *Revue Française Psychanalyse*, *4*: 1113–1136.

Abella, A. (2010). Contemporary art and Hanna Segal's thinking on aesthetics. *International Journal of Psychoanalysis*, *91*(1): 163–181.

Abella, A. (2012). John Cage and W. R. Bion: an exercise in interdisciplinary dialogue. *International Journal of Psychoanalysis*, *93*(3): 473–487.

Baudry, F. (1984). An essay on method in applied psychoanalysis. *Psychoanalytic Quarterly*, *53*: 551–581.

Bourdieu, P. (1992). *Les règles de l'art. Genèse et structure du champ littéraire*. Paris: Seuil.

Esman, A. H. (1998). What is "applied" in applied psychoanalysis. *International Journal of Psychoanalysis*, *79*: 741–752.

Cabanne, P. (1971). *Dialogues with Marcel Duchamp*, R. Padgett (Trans.). New York: Thames & Hudson.

Cros, C. (2006). *Marcel Duchamp*. London: Reaktion Books.

Duchamp, M. (1989). *The Writings of Marcel Duchamp*, M. Sanouillet & E. Peterson (Eds.). New York: Da Capo Press.

Freud, S. (1905d). *Three Essays on the Theory of Sexuality*. S.E., *7*: 130–243. London: Hogarth.

Freud, S. (1907a). Delusions and dreams in Jensen's *Gradiva*. S.E., *9*: 3–93. London: Hogarth.

Freud, S. (1908e). Creative writers and day-dreaming. S.E., *9*: 141–152. London: Hogarth.

Freud, S. (1910c). *Leonardo da Vinci and a Memory of His Childhood*. S.E., *11*: 57–135. London: Hogarth.

Freud, S. (1912–1913). *Totem and Taboo*. S.E., *13*: 1–162. London: Hogarth.

Freud, S. (1913j). The claims of psychoanalysis to scientific interest. *S.E.*, *13*: 165–190. London: Hogarth.

Freud, S. (1914b). *The Moses of Michelangelo*. *S.E.*, *13*: 211–238. London: Hogarth.

Green, A. (1992). *La déliaison* [Unbinding]. Paris: Les Belles Lettres.

Held, R. (1973). *L'oeil du psychanalyste* [The psychoanalyst's eye]. Paris: Petite Bibliothèque Payot.

Housez, J. (2006). *Marcel Duchamp*. Paris: Grasset.

Lebel, R. (1959). *Sur Marcel Duchamp* [On Marcel Duchamp] Paris: Trianon.

Paskaukas, R. A. (Ed.) (1993). *The Complete Correspondence of Sigmund Freud and Ernest Jones, 1908–1939*. Cambridge, MA: Belknap Press of Harvard University Press.

Segal, H. (1952). A psycho-analytical approach to aesthetics. *International Journal of Psychoanalysis*, *33*: 196–207.

Segal, H. (1991). Art and the depressive position. In: *Dream, Phantasy and Art* (pp. 66–78). New York: Routledge.

Seigel, J. (1995). *The Private Worlds of Marcel Duchamp. Desire, Liberation and the Self in Modern Culture*. Berkeley, CA: University of California Press.

CHAPTER FIVE

From a source to a fountain, or from the sublime to the uncanny

Carlos Weisse

The general idea in this chapter is to build a bridge, to try to understand the cultural, historical, and subjective changes that have taken place to enable the expression of completely different aesthetics and dissimilar conceptions of art in two works, the titles of which have a similar meaning: *The Source* by Ingres, and *The Fountain* by Marcel Duchamp. Our work involves a field of intersection between aesthetics and psychoanalysis that allows us to articulate concepts and terms of both disciplines and to intuit a certain group of transformations that might guide us in this change "from one source to another".

Parallel to the names, in the two works we find the theoretical meaning of the term "source", which we shall fathom: the works of Freud and the works of Lacan are also sources that nourish conceptual developments articulated by this word. On the basis of these two theories, we come to the concept of the source of the drive, a fundamental concept for the understanding of artistic work and activity in relation to one of its vicissitudes, essential in art. I refer to sublimation.

In Freud, there is an aesthetic organised around the core of sublimation, and, in Lacan, a number of aesthetics more or less closely related to this concept: an aesthetic of the void, an aesthetic of anamorphosis, and an aesthetic of the letter. I shall centre this text on the development of the concept of sublimation and its corresponding concept in Lacan, the aesthetic of the void, and the anamorphic aesthetic in its application to both works of art. I emphasise that my intention is not to apply psychoanalysis to art, but the opposite: to value knowledge that art might contribute to psychoanalysis.

Sublimation

The Freudian concept of sublimation consists in drive activity without the intervention of repression: therefore, it implies satisfaction different from sexual satisfaction. How, then, may we explain this satisfaction? Drive discharge is possible by virtue of an enabling object. This object is a "lure" that needs to have certain characteristics, referred to as an erotic or fetishist condition by which this object may be placed in a series with the lost object, the primordial Other that we refer to as *Das Ding*. Discharge of sexual excitation is produced when an object is an effective lure to evoke *Das Ding*, but is sufficiently distant to be differentiated from the incestuous object. If this distance becomes dangerously small, repression intervenes and, consequently, the return of the repressed is expressed by a compromise formation that constitutes a symptom; this is to say that the drive, forbidden by repression, is transformed into a partial discharge that is a symptomatic substitute formation. This is the neurotic vicissitude of the drive.

In sublimation, there is no fixation to the prohibited object; the object encountered by the drive cathexis is the edge of the hole left by the lost object (*Das Ding*). What follows is a trajectory or a detour around this hole; however, this edge consists of unrepressed signifiers, that is to say, those to which the drive is not fixated but that are, in some way, mobile and interchangeable, constituting signifiers of a new, invented symbolic language.[1] These signifiers are diverse objects that contribute to the constitution of a work, symbolic objects to which the drive does not fixate but are outlined by it. For this reason, a change of aim is established simultaneously with a change of object, which has symbolic characteristics.

In Seminar VII, Lacan (1998) theorises on a distinction between two moments in Freudian theory; one is the moment of formations of the unconscious, the unconscious as a language and its signifying operations; the other is the Freud of the death drive and repetition, the field beyond the pleasure principle, of *jouissance* and the real. In this way, he separates the register of the symbolic, which tallies with the pleasure principle, from the beyond of this principle, the register of the real, excentric in relation to the symbolic and equivalent to the Freudian id.

The real of the drive field thereby comes close to the real[2] of *Das Ding*. Therefore, we need to differentiate the id of the unconscious, accentuation of the primitive and primordial quality, from the id as the privileged field of *Das Ding*. In this perspective, the symbolic order is defined as a defence organisation against the Thing. The vortex of the Thing is internal–external to the subject exthymic, outside the symbolic, outside images, outside of meaning, but also immanent to the subject in the paradoxical form of an excluded interior. The Thing is that which is behind the subject.

The Thing has two fundamental faces: from the signifying perspective, the Thing is a void to the extent that it eludes any possible representation and is not representable. However, from the perspective of *jouissance*, the Thing is an incandescent zone, an excess that subjugates the subject to obscure repetition. *Das Ding* is, therefore, an unrepresentable void on the one hand and, on the other hand, a vortex that pulls in, a zone full of *jouissance*, an abyss that swallows up, in relation to which the symbolic order acquires the form of a defence more originary than repression by virtue of the separating action of language on human reality.

Artistic sublimation occupies the void of *Das Ding* through a multiplicity of symbolic–imaginary objects. This helps us to understand Lacan's definition of sublimation: *to raise the object to the dignity of the Thing*. Art's imaginary object acquires a symbolic dimension in the empty place (symbolised) of the real of the Thing.

However, drives cannot be fully sublimated and every drive carries a certain amount of fixation linked to pre-genitality and its erotogenic zones; this limit cannot be overcome: a demand of some amount of direct satisfaction. Therefore, the complex problem of sublimation implies an unstable tension between fixation and plasticity, between the real and the symbolic that is never resolved. Therefore, we have two distinct economies of substitution: the economy of the signifier, which constitutes the symptomatic compromise, and the economy of sublimation, based on a change of aim and object. The vicissitudes of the drive are played out at these two drive poles with the source at one end and the object at the other. The aim is in relation to the object, whereas the source works in relation to the real. We believe that this unmovable persistence of the source is related to the drive's need of direct satisfaction, which, unlike fixation to the object, depends on object libido and whose phantasmatic repression generates the neurotic vicissitude of the drive. Therefore, it is object libido that may be sublimated.

Freud considers that sublimation is related to recognition of the social Other and its social value. There is even a contemporary theory that the validation of art becomes effective institutionally. However, sublimation does not imply elevation, refinement, delicacy, beauty, etc. Social value is expressed through highly variable aesthetic values as demonstrated by the history of art. Aesthetics are historical and children of their time. This is an interesting point of contact between the drive and value, although the point of contact is not expressed in harmony, but just the opposite: there is a rigorous temporal gap between what could be called an established aesthetic, or values that have become ideals, and the drive dimension in the sense of an aesthetic of rupture.

The aesthetics of rupture, great changes of aesthetic paradigms, break away from values established as ideals when these values become condensers of power. What we could call drive aesthetics in non-conformist and confrontational art becomes an interesting field of study to observe the relation of tension between drive, sublimation, and culture. Sublimation is both an articulator and a separator of drive and culture.

Sublimation is not a neutralisation of drive, but drive satisfaction without repression; in fact, sublimation places in evidence the structure of drive: it is in relation to the real of the Thing and not to the imaginary dimension of the object. This relation to the Thing is a relation of defence, but the defence of sublimation is a very special defence, not a neurotic defence based on idealisation–repression. Raising the object to the dignity of the Thing rejects idealisation and is constituted as a symbolic way to re-encounter the real.

In the artistic object, a world opens and the social function of sublimation situates the system of art as a system of signifiers: the drive as rotation around a void or rotation around a point of exthymous point constituted by object a.[3] The drive does not close in on an object, but goes around it infinite times; this means that the drive is always inhibited in its aim. Sublimation is a way to bring the Thing into the present without being destroyed by it. The presentification of the Thing may take place in the presence or absence of the art object. This is to say, either through representation, transfiguration, or absence in this work. In strict truth, every representation is a transfiguration of the object. In absence, its direct absence or the absence of its usefulness is proposed. For this reason, art is symbolic treatment of the real, ultimately analogous to the practice of psychoanalysis.

The Source, *by Ingres*

We shall begin with *The Source*, painted by Ingres when he was seventy-six years of age, in 1856. It represents a girl standing full face and holding up a jar of water. The pose appears to be natural and sensual, but how credible is the naturalness suggested by the figure? For example, the jar is held in an artificial and uncomfortable position, although the pose seems natural and simple. Then why is it composed this way? First, to show the girl, the jar, and the flowing water completely. Each element is aligned with the next on a plane, thereby rejecting a realistic pose while presenting it as such.

The right arm forms a frame for the head in a daring composition, and the form and function of the jar generate associations that we shall enumerate. The shape of the jar is an inverted replica of the girl's head as well as a very clear uterine form. Both head and jar are tilted to the left and there is correspondence between the girl's hair and the flowing water, since they seem to spring together and in parallel. There is also a deep contrast between the empty surface of the jar, with its open mouth from which water springs freely, and the girl's beautiful features, her mouth slightly open and the glimpse of the tip of her tongue.

In the lower part of the painting, at the left of the picture, a natural well flows from the rocks, its foam swirling at the girl's feet, one of which is standing solidly and the other barely touches the froth with her toes; this standing on the foam immediately connects to the theme of the birth of Venus.

The birth of Venus,[4] the goddess of love, originates from the genitals of Uranus, severed by his son, Cronus: the semen thereby spilt

84   ART IN PSYCHOANALYSIS

Figure 5.1.   The Source by Ingres.

forms the sea-foam from which Venus is born. There is a striking contrast between this Venus by Ingres and Botticelli's Venus: in the latter, the goddess covers her breasts with her right hand and the vulva by grasping her long tresses and using them as a veil, whereas in the former, the arms, as they hold the jar, leave these zones open to view.

On another level of the painting, the jar is pure openness, whereas the girl's vulva is closed by the partial crossing of her right leg resolved by her knees held together; in relation to the theme, it is a metaphor of femininity and beauty repeated as a contrast between the virgin and the mother on the one hand, and the whore on the other. It is clear that the girl is a source that replicates the natural source.

Therefore, beauty exists as a veil over the uncanny, since it shows an appeased void contemplated with delight in the work by Ingres. Does this veil of beauty that shows us a beautiful void perhaps present the work of sublimation? The suggestive name *Source* can only evoke the drive, the source of drive, the place of encounter with the Other and with the orifices of the body: mouth, anus, vulva, and penis: sources of bodily excitement, edges of holes where fluids, milk, faeces, urine, and semen run through. Lacan adds the edges of eyelids and ears.

The meaning of a source involves a liquid that wells or springs forth; there is an active element and a passive element that receives what flows out. In this picture, the active and passive elements exchange their functions. The container also becomes a source. This transformation from passive to active brings us to the concept of the source of drive: the natural orifices are first passive receptors, but then become charged actively with drive energy and, in turn, become a source.

Appeasement can be observed in this work, since all the allusions to the castration of the Other (the presence of foam, the vulva, and the jar) are treated through beauty and the symbolic, which provides pleasure; for this reason it becomes a product valued by the social, a detour around the void through the symbolic. This is an aesthetic defined as a symbolic practice orientated towards treating the excess of the real. This is to say that the beautiful is not limited to formal harmony, but extends to the preservation of a certain distance from the obscene and from the real; it is a defence against the real, not a neurotic defence, but the defence of the symbolic in the face of the real.

The gaze

Now we shall take up another aspect of analysis that considers the contributions of psychoanalysis in relation to pictures and objects of art from the viewpoint of the scoptic field of the gaze[5] as object *a*. This represents Lacan's second aesthetic, which Recalcati et al. (2011) call the anamorphic aesthetic through a new paradigm of *jouissance*. In other terms, art is not an organisation to skirt the edges of the real, as in the first aesthetic, but instead enables an encounter with the real.

In his Seminar 11 (The four fundamental concepts of psychoanalysis) (2007), more precisely in Chapter Nine, Lacan analyses: What is a picture? The relation between painting and the scopic field. He drew two triangular systems to illustrate what a picture is. This schema is based on two partly overlapping triangles with their vertices facing each other. On the left vertex, he places the gaze, and on the right, the subject of representation. On the line of intersection, he places the screen function.

This schema presents the doubling of, on the one hand, the eye, the organ that sees and captures the visible and representable world, designated "subject of representation"; on the other hand, "the gaze" that transforms me into a picture or petrifies me like the gaze of Medusa, the gaze of an envious eye, an evil eye that appears as an unsettling spot, that is to say, as the uncanny. It is also a dazzling, blinding light, the pure incarnation of light from which I may protect myself by the screen function. With it, the gaze may be hidden, which implies a certain appeasement, one of the functions of art.

This is more an aesthetic of the encounter with the traumatic real than an organisation of the void; this is the appearance of the scene of the blot function, which produces a break with the familiar and relates to the Freudian concept of the uncanny, beyond the category of the beautiful.

Lacan considers that the picture function divides the waters in terms of what art is and what it is not. A work of art needs to be able to produce an encounter: not an encounter with the subject apprehending the work, but an encounter with the work which catches, moves, and stings the subject; this does not involve the subject falling into anxiety: what is caught is the eye. This entrapment contains the aesthetic experience of appeasement, which conceals the Gaze. This is the Apollonian effect of art: something is given to the eye as nourishment.

The picture function is the frame of representation in which the blot appears when representation becomes rarefied and exposes the subject to the Gaze of the Other, a Gaze that comes from outside and subverts the classical idea of the subject as an artifice of representation. The subject does not look; it is the Other that looks, and before this Other the subject is like denuded life, an object of the Other. The blot is, therefore, a cancellation of the object of representation.

Therefore, a work of art exists when there is an encounter with the blot, when the Gaze makes a hole in the purely representative frame of the work's semantic organisation. Something about the representation touches the point of the uncanny in the subject and the subject then becomes a blot.

The picture forces the subject to emerge traumatically by evoking this limit where the subject is captured. This anamorphic aesthetic takes us beyond the aesthetic of the void to a place where the work organises the void of the Thing. In the anamorphic aesthetic, it is the work itself that obliges the real to emerge as an excess lodged in its very heart. It is a question of deconstructing the frame of representation to enable an encounter with the real or with the discontinuity of the real, death, the unrepresentable real of the Thing. Therefore, it is a question of formal deconstruction and reconstruction, of leaving and returning, disgregation and recomposition. There is no symbolism; the Blot is not awaiting signification.

Human beings know how to place the screen in front of the Gaze. In this case, the place of mediation is the screen. The screen re-establishes things on the perceptive plane. The pictorial work is the screen in front of the gaze. The painting as *trompe l'oeil* announces its nature as an articulation of the imaginary and the symbolic. If the Gaze came into view, what might it reveal? Dirty water? Excrements? Vomit? Something in the order of a latrine or public toilet and disgust when looking at it? For this reason, the picture acts not only on the field of representation. It has other aims and effects. In this direction, the picture appeases the Gaze: the person looking at a painting must always set aside the Gaze. This appeasement is presented in its *trompe l'oeil* aspect, an aspect that is a "gaze-tamer", as Lacan puts it.

What does this mean? The picture announces the essence of appearance; it is a veil, a screen, or a covering over the void of the object *a*, in the sense that what it shows also confirms this void. Since this instant of seeing splices the symbolic with the imaginary, it acts as a suture in response to the virulent and aggressive function of the evil eye because it is related to desire and desire, in turn, is related to castration.

The gesture of painting implies that any action represented in a picture is destined to appear as a theatrical scene necessarily produced by this gesture: it is the gesture of "offering to the eye". The Gaze is the opposite of a gesture of "offering to the eye", since the subject is handled as if by remote control. "Offering to the eye" appeases the Gaze by offering the eye nourishment. In so far as the work sets up a scene and appeases the Gaze, it neutralises it; if not, the Gaze perforates and petrifies the subject; it is the evil eye that paralyses and kills life.

The operation of sublimation leaves a residue on the return trip of the drive's trajectory[6] on the edge of the body, as a plus, an excess, or anything that resonates in it. That is to say that art articulates sublimation, the gesture and the offering to the eye, with a direct drive residue represented on the scopic level by the Gaze. We could say that real art is art that succeeds in making the body feel. Artists and poets create new objects that they throw into the world and which live beyond them; on a body surface they write or draw the outline of a new subject.

The Fountain, by Duchamp

Kant distinguishes the aesthetic category of the beautiful and compares it to the category of the sublime in his *Critique of Judgement*, a work that reached its highest expression in the Romantic period. Kantian reflection concerning the sentiment of the sublime is based on new feelings in relation to nature and the landscape. Although Freudian sublimation does not overlap the Kantian concept of the sublime, it includes it as a case within the general category of sublimation. Freud considers that the beautiful enters the concept of sublimation, since it emphasises the formal beauty of the work.

Trías proposes the following in relation to the sentiment of the sublime:

> The immediate reaction to the spectacle is painful: subjects feel they are in a state of suspension before this object that exceeds and surpasses them. They feel it is a threat to their integration. This is followed by an initial reflection on their insignificance and impotence before this immeasurable object. However, their painful anxiety and vertigo are fought off and defeated by a second reflection, assumed and mixed with the first, in which the subjects rise above the consciousness of their *physical* insignificance to a reflection on their

moral superiority. This is possible because the immeasurable object stirs in the subjects, physically and sentiently, an idea of Reason. (2006, p. 23)

The infinite object renders the idea of infinitude sentient, by which Kant considers that subjects may access rational and moral consciousness of their superiority in relation to nature, although this consciousness, since it is presented chaotically and anarchically, evokes an idea of the infinite. Consequently, the feeling of the sublime has an ambiguous character between pain and pleasure. If the subject is to access aesthetic *jouissance*, the object must be contemplated from a distance, in "disinterested" contemplation; in this way, the subject overcomes fear and anxiety through a feeling of pleasure in connection with this fear and anxiety, which gives the experience great intensity.

Thus, Kant transcends the limits of the beautiful and introduces the sublime. This limit coincides with what veils the gaze and prevents it from appearing behind the screen, either in its function as *trompe l'oeil* or as the direct, concrete appearance of the void.

However, another category is also proposed, which we attribute to part of contemporary art: the appearance of the uncanny, a Freudian category *par excellence*, referring to what should remain hidden but yet appears: the familiar that is repressed returns on the scoptic level through the demonic.

At this point, we complete the arch thrown across the change of aesthetic paradigm. At one pole, beauty, harmony of form and colour, symbolic features wisely structured in delicious modulation; however, the work is more than all this, since it is a way to organise the void through the mediation of beauty. At the other pole, we find Duchamp's *Fountain*, sarcasm thrown into the eyes, converted into a work of art by humour and distance, by the transposition from factory to museum, by the insolence of the gesture that squirts imaginary urine into the eyes, a real giving of shit to be seen. Duchamp was also making fun of himself. "You'll soon find beauty in it," he laughed.

A ready-made is a commonly used object that a minimal intervention by the artist—a signature, a date, the presentation to an exhibition—and especially, a decontextualisation and recontextualisation, transforms into a work of art. It is the artist's decision that makes the useful industrial object—a bicycle wheel, bottle case, or urinal—into a work of art, an artistic object.

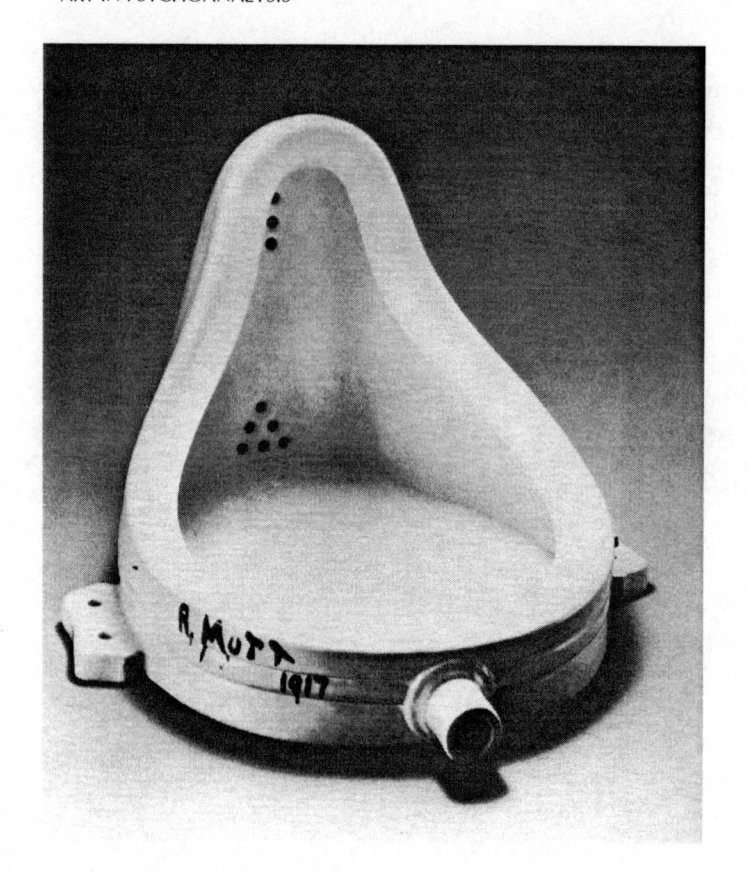

Figure 5.2. *The Fountain* by Marcel Duchamp (1917).

In this particular case of a ready-made, the uncanny category is given not by the operation of encounter with the object as a common industrial object, but by the operation of turning around the urinal that converts it from a receptacle of urine into a source that spurts urine into the eyes: imaginarily, the observer "is pissed upon" by the object.

The change of paradigm

Duchamp changes the parameters of art from the act of seeing to the act of thinking and, therefore, he leaves the idea free of any virtuosity in the form. This is his criticism of art whose use of objects based on their beauty had concealed the true image. Therefore, it was a question of awakening thought beyond the image. Duchamp's idea is to manifest the idea of the work as a container of truth.

Now the question is why such an extreme change took place in relation to the conception of art from one source to the other in the time lapse between1856 and 1917. *The Fountain* by Duchamp is actually a product of serialised industry, a simple urinal that goes from a shop window to a hall for artistic exhibitions with only two modifications: (1) the signature and date, R. Mutt 1917, and (2) the inversion of the artefact's position that converts it from a recipient for urine with its corresponding drain into a source of urine, by virtue of this new position.

Do we perhaps see in this process something of the appearance of the Gaze in this change of one source for another? From the veil the *trompe l'oeil* was concealing from the real in the beautiful girl at the source by Ingres to the appearance of a sarcastic and fundamental act in the formulation of twentieth-century art, what we believe we are seeing is the appearance of the Gaze or the appearance of the uncanny as an aesthetic category. The painting by Ingres alluded to castration (of Uranus in this case)[7] through the interposed veil of beauty, a distance guaranteed by its mythological character. In the work by Duchamp, castration appears almost in the presence of the urinal, since the act of urination can only occur with a flaccid penis, which we could place at the opposite end from phallic turgidity, inherent to detumescence. The source of water has become the source of urine; the veil has grown so thin that only decontextualisation and recontextualisation create distance from the object (urinal) through the signature and the inversion.

At what moment in history does this transmutation of the source appear, and in relation to what artistic movement? It is the Dadaist movement that was born in the Café Voltaire. Dada, or Dadaism, was an anti-art movement that emerged in Zurich in 1916, characterised by provocative gestures and manifestations in which the intention was to destroy all conventions concerning art by creating a rebellion against the established order. Through art as a human activity, it was beginning to become evident that the only human progress was techno-scientific progress; however, far from solving the problem of humanity, it made the world an increasingly sinister, unjust, more unsafe, and toxic place. The human condition became degraded as much as the planet, but also, information on this process is instantaneous: there is no veil, no screen of beauty to hide the horror. Therefore, everything is "offered to the eye" obscenely; we could say that traditional beauty is at the service of deceptive advertising and that its former function of distance is at present replaced by irony, sarcasm, and humour. In this sense, art has become uncanny and has exceeded its sublime state as described by Kant. At that moment at the height of Romanticism and German idealism, the spectacle of the infinite and the exotic involved rapture and respect for natural forces, and awareness of human insignificance, whose tool was especially reason, turned potential technological domination into an expectation.

We think that sublime art has led to modern art, in which the void becomes evident and tangible: something that, at a previous stage, was expressed as *trompe l'oeil* and acted as a screen becomes visible. The about-face between the two paradigms coincides with the fall of the subject centred on reason. The desiring dimension concealed behind the conscious subject becomes more evident when the void participates in the work by outlining it aesthetically. On the other hand, uncanny art that takes *The Fountain* by Duchamp as its origin, literally as a source, corresponds to the emergence of the Gaze in the work. The uncanny aspect of the human condition has acquired presentation in contemporary art in the present. It is a machine to show a world with a minimal veil in times when the ersatz (simulation) lulls the mind while poison accumulates in its folds.

Notes

1. In a previous article, "Angustia, duelo y sublimación : relaciones entre el duelo y la pintura de Giorgio de Chirico" ["Anxiety, mourning and sublimation: relations between mourning and painting in Giorgio de Chirico"] published in the *Revista de Psicoanálisis*, 62(3) (September 2005), we describe how the works of de Chirico show, especially in the period of "Italian Piazzas", the relation between a melancholic equivalent, a psychosomatic disturbance, and identification with his father, deceased in his early adolescence. Through the painting of his Piazzas, de Chirico symbolises his dead father through a new language, in the figure of an uncanny statue in the centre of the Piazza or the projection of his shadow

on their grounds as if it were a reworking through of this frozen mourning that is relaunched in the painter's work.
2. The real is one of the three orders by which all psychoanalytic phenomena may be described; the other two are the imaginary and the symbolic order. The real in this sense is what is beyond the symbolic. For example, in the symbolic order presence and absence may be proposed, since this order is constituted by a signifying set that might designate presence or absence. In the real order no absence is possible, the real is always in its place and knows nothing about everything that could remove it.

Whereas the symbolic is a set of discrete, differentiated elements called signifiers, the real in itself is undifferentiated. It is the symbolic that introduces a cut in the real in the process of signification; the real is outside language and signification. The real is also what is logically impossible in the sense of what is impossible to imagine, to represent, symbolise, modalise, or model. This characteristic of the real is what gives it its essentially traumatic quality. The real has ontic existence and implies a material substance, for example, the body. The real is the object of anxiety, the trauma as encounter with this real, with Tyché.

For example, in hallucinations, what cannot be integrated into the symbolic returns from the real: voices, gazes, bodies. The real is extymic; in the strict sense it is both inside and outside in paradoxical tension. Finally, the real is unrecognisable and cannot be assimilated to anything else.
3. *Object a* is the cause of desire, any object that puts desire into movement, especially part objects defined by the drives. The drive does not attempt to obtain the *object a*, but to turn upon it. It is both the object of anxiety and the final irreducible reserve of libido. The analyst needs to position himself or herself as similar to the *object a*, the cause of the analysand's desire. It is also a remnant residue left behind by the introduction of the symbolic in the real. In the four discourses, Lacan places *object a* as a gain of *jouissance*. The *object a* is a semblance of being that is at the centre of the Borromean knot, in the place where the three orders intersect.
4. "Risen from the foam", Aphrodite was born from sea foam near Paphos (Cyprus) after Cronus, during the Titanomachia, cut off the genitals of Uranus with a scythe and threw them into the sea. In his *Theogonia*, Hesiod tells that the genitals were carried by the sea for a long time. White foam sprang up around the severed member and in its midst an adult maiden was born.
5. Lacan separates the gaze from the act of looking. The gaze becomes the object of the act of looking or the object of the sceptic drive, and is not on

the part of the subject, but is the gaze of the Other. There is an antinomic relation between the gaze and the eye; the eye that looks is the subject's, whereas the gaze is on the object's part and the two never coincide. When the subject looks at an object, the object always returns the subject's gaze, but from a viewpoint that the subject cannot see it. This splitting between the eye and the gaze is the division of the subject itself expressed in the field of vision.

6. Lacan maintains that the aim of the drive is not the object as a final destiny but to circle around it, which is to say that its aim is not a mythical aim of complete satisfaction, but to return to its circular path, and the real source of *jouissance* is repetitive movement. Freud defined the drive as a montage composed of four discontinuous elements: thrust, aim, object, and source. It is a cultural and symbolic construct and has nothing to do with the biological except, as Freud said, through anaclisis. For Lacan, the drive circuit is structured by the three grammatical voices: the active voice (seeing); the reflexive voice (seeing oneself); the passive voice (being seen). The first two, seeing and seeing oneself, are auto-erotic, that is to say that the subject is lacking. In the third, being seen, the drive closes its circuit and then a "new subject" appears. Although the third tense is the passive voice, the drive is always essentially active, and for this reason Lacan writes of this third tense not as "being seen", but as "showing oneself". On the drive level, all passivity assumes just the opposite, activity. This drive circuit is the only way the subject has to transgress the pleasure principle.

For Lacan, the drives are always part drives, not in the sense of being parts of a whole (genital), but because they represent sexuality only partly: they have nothing to do with reproduction, but only with *jouissance*. In other terms, all drive is death drive, since it is excessive, repetitive, and ultimately destructive; they are intimately related to desire, originate in the field of the subject opposed to genitality, which is actually on the part of the Other. However, drive is not only another name for desire, but also the partial aspects through which desire is realised, since desire is one and indivisible, whereas the drives are its partial manifestations.

7. Castration is defined by Lacan as the imaginary lack of a symbolic object; it does not refer to the penis or a real organ, but to the imaginary phallus, and denotes the final moment of the Oedipus complex, its dissolution, when the real father intervenes, demonstrating that he has the phallus, and separates the child from his or her attempts to be the phallus. Lacan refers to castration through to different operations: (a) the castration of the

mother, since in the initial time of the Oedipus complex, the mother is considered by both sexes to possess the phallus. In the second time, the imaginary father is seen as depriving her of that phallus; (b) castration of the subject: this is castration proper, a symbolic act that influences an imaginary object; the child must renounce being the mother's phallus, renounce trying to be the mother's object of desire, and renounce a *jouissance* that is never recovered. This is valid both for boys and girls. Both forms of castration, the mother's and the subject's, confront the subject with the choice of accepting or denying it; the assumption of castration has a "normalising" effect on sexual identity. However, in the best of resolutions, the neurotic resolution, the subject still defends him or herself from castration (or from lack) in the Other, repressing consciousness of castration, which prevents the subject from fully assuming his or her own desire. The perverse resort to disavowal of castration, and the psychotic forecloses it as if it had never existed, which leads to the return of castration in the real, for example, hallucinations of dismemberment. Only by assuming it can the subject adopt a position as a man or woman.

References

Lacan, J. (1998). *Seminario 7: La ética del psicoanálisis*. Buenos Aires: Paidós.
Lacan, J. (2007). *Seminario 11: Los cuatro conceptos fundamentales del psicoanálisis*. Buenos Aires: Paidós.
Recalcati, M.-H. B., Wajcman, G., Coccoz, V., Ponce, X. G., & Vinciguerra, R.-P. (2011). *Las Tres Estéticas de Lacan (Psicoanálisis y Arte)*. Buenos Aires: Ediciones del Cifrado.
Trías, E. (2006). *Lo bello y lo siniestro*. Barcelona: Ariel.

CHAPTER SIX

Creative processes in art and psychoanalysis: moving towards an expanded metapsychology

Hector Fiorini

In his postscript to the second edition of his study on Jensen's *Gradiva*, Freud (1907a) proposes a highly ambitious programme for psychoanalytic investigations on poets and their poems. On the one hand, he wants to know which material from impressions and memories the poet has used to create the work and, on the other hand, through what paths and processes this material was incorporated into poetic creation. Compared to the scope of this programme, subsequent enquiries were tentative and fragmentary. His study on "Creative writers and day-dreaming" (1908e) established a relation: an intense experience in the present awakens the poet's memory of a previous experience in childhood from which emanates a wish whose fulfilment is sought in poetic creation. This thinking opened a direction for investigation that was significant because it was a starting point. However, the risk this direction involved was the consideration of childhood experience in its unspecific emotiveness, since any kind of human fact may evoke childhood experiences. The study Deleuze dedicates to the works of Proust (1970) adds a new dimension when it stresses that childhood experience that has become a work was already poetic emotional experience in childhood, tinted by that child's special sensitivity concerning the relations and contents of human experience.

Possibilities and difficulties encountered by psychoanalysis when thinking about art

Mathieu, in his sweeping review of psychoanalytic texts dedicated to art (Anzieu, 1974), draws a critical conclusion. He considers the formulation of Freudian aesthetics improbable in view of the limitations of its meta-psychological foundations. This might explain why its approaches to art have been nebulous and fragmentary. He proposes a different direction, quoting Berge (Berge, Clancier, Ricoeur, & Rubinstein, 1962): *instead of trying to reveal the key to art, psychoanalysis should ask art for assistance to reveal keys to human nature that psychopathology by itself is unable to unveil*. I consider this thought an excellent guideline that deserves our attention in exploring its ultimate dimensions. This reflection evokes a text engraved on a frontispiece of the Department of Philosophy of Harvard University. It states: "What art does to human beings is what art is". This idea was suggested in a thought by Stendhal: "What is real about art is the state it produces in the soul". It is the reality and depth of these effects that we need to investigate.

In "Formulations on the two principles of mental functioning" (1911b), Freud draws a basic distinction between the principles of pleasure and of reality. He is intrigued by the path of the artist, who uses peculiar processes to install different types of reality impossible to reduce to realities included in the former two principles. Freud wisely pinpoints the problem, but does not advance its elucidation. He knows that he needs the wisdom of artists and poets. He resorts to them in several works.

Artists and philosophers thinking about art: other proposals for psychoanalysis

Many artists have investigated their arts, examining their conditions, materials, processes, and results. These investigations have been exhaustive. Their reflections and theories are especially important. Kandinsky (2003) emphasised that art produces a new and real being, different from any previously existing thing. He finds that this existence responds to the action and thrust of a creative principle able to initiate and sustain highly complex and difficult productions. This principle underpins the learning and invention of methods and styles. Artists are describing a third principle of mental functioning. Magritte (1979) speaks of the work's driving spirit, its organisation, development, and aims. Safranski (2001) highlighted the formulation of a creative principle in Nietzsche as the form-giving principle. The latter author underscored the immense "Power of Form", as expressed in the well-chosen title of a work by Rose (1986). In the investigations of art, the question of form acquires special prominence. Albers (2006) puts it expressly: "Art is purpose and vision as demanded by form".

The concept of a creative principle is vital in Bergson and Sartre, in Duchamp, and all the works of Deleuze. In all existentialist philosophy, this thrust constructs projects that buttress the entire organisation of behaviour with ultimate goals, intentional behaviour aimed at the realisation of valued objectives. In his brief essay, *Le Processus Créatif* (1987), Duchamp quotes the poet Eliot, who separates in himself the suffering human being from the creating spirit. The spirit, the carrier of a principle of creation, is able to transmute the passions that are its materials into elements that form the object of a work. It is clear to us that Duchamp, like Eliot, is emphasising the presence of two different systems: the neurotic (with its conflicts of pleasure *vs.* reality and fantasy *vs.* reality) and the creative system in which this creative principle acts as a principle of transformation by virtue of a transmuting mode of operation that could explain the psychic work of sublimation. Beuys (2006) considered that this principle of creation possesses a configuring power, a world-modifying principle. Winnicott (1971) realised that this world-modifying impulse is operating early in life, in children's creative play. Gedo and Goldberg (1973), following theoretical proposals by Eissler, consider it necessary to incorporate a "principle of creation" into Freudian metapsychology.

Kandinsky elaborates his conception of a creative principle that operates by mobilising conjunctions and disjunctions (which establish convergences whose core contains difference and opposition) rather than by generating conflict between antagonists, promoting dissociation, splitting, and other defence operations. The creative principle described by Deleuze (1969, 1995) may be summarised in the logical form of "disjunctive conjunction", whose antecedent was formulated in Hegel's thesis on the co-existence of opposites. Disjunctive conjunction introduces a more complex dynamic into something that is both linked and separated, and lends itself to simultaneity and sudden alternation between convergence and separation (a model illustrated by Borges in one of his most famous short stories, "The garden of forking paths"): the creation of the "limit" in the model developed in the works of Trías (1991, 1999).

For this author, the limit is the place where we find what is different. In this way, he postulates a basic formation for the logic of disjunctive conjunction.

Kandinsky believes that a pictorial spiritual being is born with the work. The what and how of the work are essential. In it, forms of expression become more relevant than contents. The driving force of the work is an "innate hunger to get somewhere else", which expresses the force of an "internal pressure". This driving force and its concrete operations give it the strength of autonomous existence with precision of composition.

Magritte considers that art operates a system with a special nature, since it sustains a gaze that forever goes further, and, in its searching, seems to give our existence a reason: the decision to go towards something other and to see other objects in certain objects. These shifts are joined together in unending chains: a metaphysical position that goes out to meet the mystery, a universe sustained by paradox beyond the vectors of gratification *vs.* frustration or possession *vs.* loss. The work of art is, thereby, orientated towards liberty; it cannot be fenced in any way, and conjugates the possible with the impossible. Magritte highlights the work as a presentation that exceeds the function of representation and does not evoke thought, but is already thought in an image. The enquiry into creative work emphasises the powers of the imaginary, an observation that deserves a central place in psychoanalysis: to investigate what is revealed about our psychic depths by the effects and procedures of art, beyond words, or at least in other languages.

Movements and phases of the creative process

Creative work starts with a stage of exploration, the contact with working material that obscurely suggests that it might be a carrier of possible forms. This is a vague, ambiguous moment, a stage of doubts and bewilderment, with little and unclearly founded hope. Anzieu (1981) has described a withdrawal or retirement from everyday routines associated with this stage. At this point, we evoke Bion, entering "without memory and without desire" as he follows Oriental inspiration. It is the basic position of the meditator and the Zen archer. The mind is opening to experience other forces and dimensions; these stimuli are intriguing. Neruda (1925) finds that at those moments "there is a knock from objects that call and are not answered, ceaseless movement and an unintelligible name" (p. 189). Several authors have emphasised subjective phenomena of self-destitution and of de-identification experienced as a void, albeit an actively sought void. Paz (1956) has devoted many of his investigations to the experience of opening and emptiness that precedes and accompanies the creative literary process.

A stage of transformations follows, when several paths open up for drawing a spectrum of possibilities. By trial, error, and more trial, a more precise version is distilled which the author considers might respond better to a certain nucleus outlined at the beginning. An experience of discovery and encounter; unlike what Freud assumed about the choice of the sexual object (conceived as a re-encounter), the object of art is a carrier of radical novelty, a genuine *encounter*. To create: "to bring something into existence that was not", that was never before, a process that Sartre (1983) postulated on the basis of the production of a clean sweep, a deconstruction able to make many pre-existing elements into "nothing", thereby leaving room for the emergence of new being.

When a stage of culmination is reached, the time has come to assume and deepen the rigour of materialisation and craftsmanship in the newly elaborated organism. In the case of art, this whole process expresses a project that contains the intention of a work and precedes the still uncertain possibility of a work. It brings along all the tools of conceptual and technical learning and all the experience of previous work.

These phases do not follow a linear sequence: there is a circulation, fluctuation, and superposition among them.

We might find relevant concordances between these phases and those developed in a psychoanalytic process. Deconstructions, confusion of the ego, uncertainties, trials, errors, further trials, and sketches of new relations are part of the path towards interpretation and working through. It develops a perspective of understanding of meaning that is reformulated, making way for the emergence of another that might be the opposite. In all these experiences, we find a third system of the psychical that develops processes and operations that are different from those included by Freud in his "Formulations on the two principles" (1911b). To this third system could be given the term "creative psyche" (Fiorini, 2007), a psyche that operates on a principle of transformations that carries and integrates elements organised on the other two principles and is also subject to their attacks.

In effect, there is a play of subjective experiences of anxiety, emptiness, and disorganisation that psychoanalytic clinical work might clarify, understand, and interpret.

The activated creative psyche might encounter the regressive obstacles of a reactivated neurotic psyche. It might also fall into the abysses of a mobilised psychotic psyche, as well. There are struggles between these systems in which it is important to consider which might take a hegemonic role. They often co-exist in a state of tension that is very difficult to resolve (many examples come to mind, such as Kafka and Beckett) and sometimes leads to separable roads between the author and the person, which lead to the vicissitudes of splitting.

Thinking about sublimation: a necessary extension of metapsychology

This point refers to a study by Freud, particularly rich because it opens up readings in relation to drive paths of sublimation. It is *A Childhood Memory of Leonardo Da Vinci* (1910c). Freud finds a vicissitude of the drive of sublimation in the drive to investigate. He differentiates three possible vicissitudes of this investigative drive: (a) neurotic inhibition of thought activity; (b) partial development of thought activity, affected by the sexualisation of thought by the return of the repressed; (c) sublimation of the sexual drive from the outset. In this case, the libido escapes the vicissitude of repression and reinforces a vigorous drive to investigate. Freud understands that different psychical processes operate in this case. We consider that this Freudian hypothesis needs to be projected to its broadest extent. Freud is presenting a thrust of the sublimation drive, whose strength enables it to dominate sexual libido to the point of attracting modes and aims of the sexual drive into its orbit. Freud proposes it in these terms: a hyper-intense drive for knowledge attracts sexual drive forces as reinforcement. The development of this clinical observation requires meta-psychological extensions with regard to the powers of sublimation. Whereas the classical study of neurotic conditions led to the postulation of centralised energy in the order of a sexual drive, the emergence of dominant creative forces (of knowledge, investigation, or artistic creation, as in Leonardo) required the inclusion of the thrust of other drive forces in the origins of this activity of sublimation. This inclusion opens a panorama of a multiplicity of drives beyond the drive dualism eventually sustained by Freud when he introduced the death drive. In our work, we extend the model in order to think about sublimation as drive forces able to form and transform, and to take over drives and formations originarily linked to sexual drives.

The unconscious phantasm and tertiary processes

Creative work might dip into the organisation of the unconscious phantasm. In the phantasm, there is interplay between an order of binary oppositions such as life *vs.* death, phallus *vs.* castration, active *vs.* passive, and possession *vs.* loss. Creative thought introduces a tertiary order into these logical universes. Tertiary processes dissolve the absolutes in these polarities and arrange them in multi-polar organisations: intermediary formations that build bridges by means of resonances between n dimensions that result in the intertwined designs inherent to hyper-complexity. In several works (e.g., 1995, 2003), Green proposed that we think of tertiary processes as those that bind materials of primary and secondary processes. He insisted on assigning them only this function, a binding function. In my conception (Fiorini, 2007, 2009), these tertiary processes are more important, since they establish psychic formations that institute original forms and organise outlines with expanding limits: objects intrinsic to an open work (Eco, 1984). In psychoanalytic clinical work, we also aspire to enable tertiary processes to motorise thought that registers and models the complexity of textures and planes of the psychic, its different temporal registers, the presence of the past in transference, and the presence of the future in projects. The liaison has its originality, as well as the design created by everything grouped and modelled, by virtue of this intertwining. Beuys (2006) stressed that some modes of thinking and talking have the power to sculpture, configure, and reconfigure.

In a struggle against everything that establishes finitude (a necessary condition for the reality principle), the tertiary processes, with their potential mobility and unstable options, support an infinite horizon. They are built on a law of movement with repeated remissions and displaceable centres of gravity. Thus, they draw the map of multiplicities, the raw material of creative functioning. They design and model. The work of art, like the poem, in the words of Paz (1956, p. 253), establishes "a point of intersection, a fixed and vibrant centre where contradictions are ceaselessly cancelled and re-born". For an instant, this centre consents to immobility, then returns to channels of incessant flow.

Tertiary processes also establish a peculiar temporality. The creative process responds to an organisation of becoming that it constructs and carries along. It contains an architecture of assemblages with unpredictable crossings generated by the necessary and chance. In this architecture, different temporalities also intersect: one is sequential from its origin, whereas another anticipates its developments in the form of a "previous future". In his famous *Quartets*, the poet T. S. Eliot (1944) conjugates these two temporalising directions. He expresses that in his end is his beginning, which he places in counterpoint with the opposite: that in his beginning is his end. An idea he reinforces in the notion that the end precedes the beginning or the end is where we start out. We consider that at this point we may return to Freud's thought concerning the phenomenon of retroactivity, his concept of *a posteriori*. However, we expand it by considering that the future of a creative development is inscribed in its present. The present makes its future an effectively gravitating element. The pulse of this aperture to the future beats in the configuration of the space of the possible. We need to highlight the density of this space that conjugates potentials and thrusts. Janet Frame (2010, p. 2), a New Zealand novelist, underscored the pressure of these forces:

> Possibility was not a bag or box that could be closed and sealed; it was a wide open slope that received everything, absolutely everything. You could not choose or decide, or destroy the powerful flow of possibilities.

This author speaks of a system possessing drive thrusts not susceptible to neutralisation or erasure. A creative vital drive is central in the work of Bergson, to which many philosophers have recently returned.

The neurotic psyche and the creative work of psychoanalysis

The neurotic psyche polarises the terms of a contradiction and renders them antagonistic and static, thereby setting up a modality of conflict, whereas the tertiary process builds bridges able to penetrate the static condition of these poles and to create third places that lodge these differences within larger sets that multiply perspectives. An essential quality of tertiary processes is this multiplying capacity of their angles and visual perspectives. Neurosis gives priority to the past, to lack and what has been lost, whereas creative thought prioritises a present that anticipates the future and the future as a development of other possible futures, carrying its desire along with it and no longer lacking, but instead producing. This emerges first in the production of associative material in analysis, a creation that gradually overlaps even the enunciation of nostalgia for what is absent. This creative thought is called upon in the work of interpretation and historicisation. Creative work sustains the experience of analytic relation which involves transference (Freud), a corrective emotional experience (Alexander), empathic intervention that promotes internalisation of the relational pair (Kohut), or the joint creation of an analytic field (Baranger). Neurosis fears chaos and avoids or paralyses it, whereas creative work in psychoanalysis, as well as in art, seeks it out and goes forth to meet it. Together with chance, chaos is material for creative work. Art and psychoanalysis both seek to generate a fabric in which the pulsating movement of life encounters forms (presentations and representations) to lodge it and to open free channels with renewed impetus. Our studies of creative processes have led us to a general definition: *in creative work, a movement finds its form and this form preserves its capacity to be movement*. Freud detected this form that keeps movement alive in the arm of Michelangelo's Moses. We need this capacity for psychoanalytic interpretation: we need for it to be thought that has taken the form of an enunciation, and to sustain the movement of thought that led to interpretation and held it open to its future, which is intrinsic to interminable work.

References

Albers, J. (2006). *Albers and Moholy-Nagy: From the Bauhaus to the New World*. London: Tate.
Anzieu, D. (1974). *Psychanalyse du Génie Créateur*. Paris: Bordas.
Anzieu, D. (1981). *Le Corps de L'Oeuvre. Essais Psychanalytiques sur le Travail Créateur*. Paris: Gallimard.
Berge, A., Clancier, A., Ricoeur, P., & Rubinstein, L. (1962). *Entretiens Sur L'Art et la Psychanalyse*. Paris: Mouton.
Beuys, J. (2006). *Ensayos y Entrevistas*. Madrid: Síntesis.
Deleuze, G. (1969). *Logique du Sens*. Paris: Minuit.
Deleuze, G. (1970). *Proust et les Signes*. Paris: Presses Universitaires de France.
Deleuze, G. (1995). *Pourparlers*. Paris: Minuit.
Duchamp, M. (1987). *Le Processus Créatif*. Paris: L'Échoppe.
Eco, U. (1984). *Obra Abierta*. Barcelona: Ariel. *Opera Aperta*. Casa Editrice Valentino Bompiani, Milan, 1962.
Eliot, T. S. (1944). *Four Quartets*. London: Faber and Faber.
Fiorini, H. (2007). *The Creating Psyche*. Vitoria, Spain: Agruparte.
Fiorini, H. (2009). Commentary on creativity. In: S. Akthar (Ed.), *Good Feelings* (pp. 317–325). London: Karnac.
Frame, J. (2010). Interview, Buenos Aires. *Clarín Cultura* [newspaper culture supplement], 9 October, p. 2.
Freud, S. (1907a). Delusions and dreams in Jensen's *Gradiva*. *S.E.*, 9: 3–95. London: Hogarth.
Freud, S. (1908e). Creative writers and day-dreaming. *S.E.*, 9: 143–153. London: Hogarth.
Freud, S. (1910c). *Leonardo da Vinci and a Memory of his Childhood*. *S.E.*, 11: 59–137. London: Hogarth.
Freud, S. (1911b). Formulations on the two principles of mental functioning. *S.E.*, 12: 215–226. London: Hogarth.
Gedo, J., & Goldberg, A. (1973). *Models of the Mind*. Chicago, IL: University of Chicago Press.
Green, A. (1995). *Propédeutique: La Métapsychologie revisitée*. Paris: Champ Vallon.
Green, A. (2003). *Idées Directrices pour une Psychanalyse Contemporaine. Méconnaissance et Reconnaissance de L'Inconscient*. Paris: PUF.
Kandinsky, V. (2003). *Escritos sobre Arte y Artistas*. Madrid: Síntesis.
Magritte, R. (1979). *Écrits Complets*. Paris: Flammarion.
Neruda, P. (1925). *Residencia en la tierra. Obras Completas*. Buenos Aires: Losada, 1957.

Paz, O. (1956). *El Arco y la Lira*. Mexico: Fondo de Cultura Económica.
Rose, G. (1986). *The Power of Form*. Madison, CT: International Universities Press.
Safranski, R. (2001). *Nietzsche: Biografía de su Pensamiento*. Barcelona: Tusquets.
Sartre, J.-P. (1983). *El Ser y la Nada*. Buenos Aires: Losada.
Trías, E. (1991). *Lógica del Límite*. Barcelona: Destino.
Trías, E. (1999). *La Razón Fronteriza*. Barcelona: Destino.
Winnicott, D. W. (1971). *Playing and Reality*. London: Tavistock.

CHAPTER SEVEN

In between and across*

Andrea Sabbadini

> "Margins, borders, frames, edges, thresholds ...
> Empty spaces, grey areas, anti-chambers, half-way houses, no-man's lands ..."

Intrigued by the power of words to evoke and provoke, to hurt and heal, to embarrass and inspire, I propose for this chapter a topic that, by its ambiguous or even paradoxical nature, seems almost unapproachable. This is because it covers psychological and cultural domains that, while universally observable, only exist in a state of permanent potentiality, or of dynamc impermanence, located as they are *in between* and *across* other, more clearly identifiable, territories. They border on these, and share with them certain features, but, in fact, they do not belong anywhere tangible.

And, if they do not really exist, they must also be beyond words ... I will, nevertheless, try to use my own words to give at least

---

* This chapter is the expanded version of a lecture presented on 22 October 2010 to a conference organised by the "New Directions Program" of the Washington Center for Psychoanalysis.

a flavour of this subject. I shall endeavour to do so by referring to some of its manifestations, arbitrarily selected from different fields.

The theoretical underpinning to my considerations originates in Winnicott's *transitional space*, described by him as a sort of playground or "resting-place for the individual engaged in the perpetual human task of keeping inner and outer reality separate yet inter-related" (Winnicott, 1953, p. 2). This is an area of fantasy, play, and creativity placed somewhere between the self and the external world.

Here, I intend to expand on that original concept in two important directions. The first involves the introduction of the dimension of *time*, to be added to that of *space*, thus focusing our attention not just on the spatial distance (*neither here nor there*) but also on the experience of the temporal interval (*no longer this, but not yet that*) between two events. In other words, as well as speaking of a *transitional space*, it would be useful also to consider the existence of a *transitional time*—one can think here about those moments of dawn and twilight when day and night dissolve into each other. What happens between two events, for instance, after we have offered a patient an interpretation, and before she responds to it? What happens between two states of mind, for instance, passing out and regaining consciousness, rational reasoning and psychotic delusion, feeling contented and getting enraged (and back again)? What happens in the brief moment when, still half-asleep, your hand switches off the alarm clock on the bedside table, while the rest of you emerges from the fantastical surreality of a dream?

My second extension of Winnicott's idea concerns the introduction of the concept of *bridge space–time*, a bridge being a structure spanning an obstacle for the purpose of providing passage over it (Figure 7.1). While the transitional space relates to the potential area between two objects (to use Winnicott's own colourful expression in relation to toddlers, "between the thumb and the teddy bear" (1953, p. 2)) and implies a developmental movement from one towards the other (for example, from a mainly narcissistic investment on one's own body, towards whole object relationships with other human beings), my metaphor of the bridge space–time also implies that, in the process of connecting two separate objects, events or mental states, we can imagine something extending over and above what lies between them (Sabbadini, 2011). A crossing over that may remind us

Figure 7.1. Bridge.

of Coleridge's "suspension of disbelief", that aspect of illusion as necessary to, say, the audience in a concert hall, as it is to psychoanalysts listening to their patients.

A helpful image bridging over both space and time is that of the *journey*, a metaphor for life itself, in the sense of a travelling that almost disregards the departure and arrival points. For the poet Constantine Cavafy, echoing Robert Louis Stevenson's "To travel hopefully is a better thing than to arrive" (1881), what matters is the experience of the voyage itself.

> As you set out for Ithaka
> hope the voyage is a long one,
> full of adventure, full of discovery . . .
> Ithaka gave you the marvelous journey.
> Without her you would not have set out.
> She has nothing left to give you now.
> (Cavafy, 1911)

By carrying people in their journeys from A to B, ships and trains and other assorted vehicles perform an obvious bridging function. Intriguing among them, and invested with almost mythical qualities,

112   ART IN PSYCHOANALYSIS

are those occasional semi-public means of transportation known in all languages as "taxis". Black in London, white in Milan, yellow in New York, they are integral elements, or even symbols, of our urban landscapes. As they flash past us in the streets having just picked up or delivered their customers, taxis are impermanent and anonymous entities. Taxis are self-contained islands, they are bridges, they are ambiguously connotated transitional spaces, womb-like cocoons protecting us from the external world while, at the same time, exposing us to mortal dangers. Iconic containers-on-wheels of fears and desires, of assorted luggage and hopes and dreams, taxis seem to exist only to remind us that, whether happily rolling along a tree-lined avenue or stuck in a traffic jam, we are ultimately alone in our existential journeys (Figure 7.2).

The bridge space–time image seems particularly apt to describe cultural activities. For instance, in the case of cinema, we could say that pictures—as well as linking the filmmaker's fantasies to those of the spectators, and the fantasies of both to objective reality—also imaginatively cross over the everyday experience of the external world, while at the same time placing their very foundations in it.

In considering psychological and cultural phenomena from this perspective, it is helpful to keep in mind the distinction, sometimes almost imperceptible, between what separates different elements and prevents communication between them—such as censorship, brick

Figure 7.2.   Taxi.

walls, checkpoints, fences, and barriers—and what, instead, holds these parts together and facilitates exchange between them: links, interfaces, hinges, joints, and more or less permeable filters. A paradigmatic instance here is the image of a baby in a double bed, peacefully asleep between her parents: joining them together in their love for her, yet also keeping them apart. That same front door in my house has the double function of keeping intruders away and of welcoming friends in (Figure 7.3).

Free associating now to this last image, I recently gave the title "The window and the door" to a chapter I contributed for a book on the representation of virginity in film (Sabbadini, 2010). I emphasised

Figure 7.3. The front door.

there the existence in young people's imagination of a threshold between childhood innocence and adulthood experience, an ambiguous border territory of bodily sensations, interpersonal relationships, emotional commitments, and sexual morality. A girl might experience her genitals as a closed door (at least for the time being) or as an open window of fulfilling opportunities, as a potential link with the external world or as an ambivalently experienced barrier to it. As the latter, it could operate as a protection, or as an obstacle, or as both things at the same time.

Adolescence as a whole, perhaps more so than other life stages, can be viewed in terms of the transitional time it occupies in a person's existence, and, as such, it is marked in many societies by specific *rites of passage* (such as, in the Jewish tradition, the Bar'Mitzvah). It is a time often experienced by young individuals, whose bodies are not yet fully grown, with considerable confusion, as childish needs clash with adult strivings. Italians commonly refer to young people going through this phase as *Né carne, né pesce* ("Neither meat, nor fish").

All sorts of rites of passage—from baptisms to weddings and funerals—can be seen as bridges punctuating other major transitional phases, and helping human beings to deal with the transience itself of their lives. For Freud, in disagreement with the pessimistic poet accompanying him on a walk, what he calls the "transience of all things" actually increases their beauty: he wrote,

> Limitation in the possibility of an enjoyment raises the value of the enjoyment. A flower that blossoms only for a single night does not seem to us on that account less lovely. Nor can I understand any better why the beauty and perfection of a work of art or of an intellectual achievement should lose its worth because of its temporal limitation. (Freud, 1916a, pp. 305–306)

An event universally marked by countless rites of passage was the approaching end of the second millennium. In my speculations about the fantasies attached to that symbolic temporal watershed, I reasoned that there seemed to be something narcissistically gratifying about belonging to a generation that stretched to a third millennia. Living in both—as a giant standing with each foot on a continent—felt special because it gave us the sensation of being part of different and contrasting worlds: the one of the past and the one of the future, the one of the children and the one of the adults, the one of the already dead and the one of those yet to be born. At the same time, though, we were also left with the illusory impression of not belonging to either world, of being in a constant transitional state that would have provided absolution from the responsibility of sharing ideological meanings, of affecting the social and political institutions to which we belonged, of partaking in our own history. We would then have felt suspended, so to speak, in a state of relative immortality—a condition fitting in well with the hardest to die of all our unconscious beliefs (Sabbadini, 1987).

I shall now briefly dwell on the relevance of the ideas outlined above in relation to certain aspects of our psychoanalytic work. I will not even touch here, despite the fact that it is most relevant to our topic, on the notoriously thorny issue of how physiology and psychology relate to one another, as manifested in those phenomena located on the border between them, such as hypochondriacal and psychosomatic conditions, not to mention normal sexuality. All I will say is that the *mysterious leap* between body and mind, which, by the way, was also at the origins of the Freudian theory of conversion hysteria, has not been replaced yet, as far as I know, by any solid bridge . . .

Another controversial issue concerns the diagnosis of *borderline personality disorder*, a label given a variety of definitions by different clinicians. One that I find helpful suggests that borderline patients are those who can operate as neurotics, but use psychotic (i.e., more primitive) defence mechanisms, such as massive denial, splitting, and projective identification. One of my analysands, always in search of a label for her own condition, once almost triumphantly announced, "At long last, I now think I know what I am: *a borderline!*" And after a minute of silent reflection, she added in a sad tone of voice, ". . . the wrong side of it." I could not have found a better definition of her pathology.

A no less complex aspect of psychoanalytic work relevant to my musings concerns the *transference*. I think of it as a meeting point, or, indeed, as a bridge across different temporalities, in so far as it presents itself as the theatre of a paradoxical situation: within and through it we analyse the past in order to give meaning to the present, and, at the same time, we interpret the present in order to recover and reconstruct the past. Transference is also intrinsically associated to *memory* and to its centrality for our emotional life, in as much as memories take place in a transitional time situated where the past is being relived in the present.

A wonderful illustration of the importance of memories, during and beyond our existence, is provided by a Japanese film, *Afterlife* (1998), directed by Hirokazu Kore-eda. As we learn from one of the opening scenes framing an emblematic square of pure light, the setting (on the surface, a rather prosaic, delapidated school) is, in fact, a metaphysical way-station between, or bridge space–time across, life and death. The guests of this institution, all people who have just died, are offered there a few days to select, with the help of responsible members of staff, one and just one meaningful memory from their individual past history, which a nearby studio will then turn into a video that the guests will eventually be taking away in their afterlife (Sabbadini & Stein, 2001).

A *trauma* occurs when the transition from one condition to the next, instead of taking place gradually (something that in musical terms would be described as a slow *crescendo* or *diminuendo*), is sudden and unexpected (*subito fortissimo*): say, when we become victims of an accident, of a violent attack, or of an unpredicted natural catastrophe. In these cases, it is as if the bridge that should have allowed a smooth and safe passage to the next stage had collapsed, and we were then left feeling as if the earth had opened up under our feet. In our clinical work, it is our responsibility to provide a container for our analysands' traumatic experiences, and also to protect them from unnecessary exposure to mini-traumatic situations within the analysis itself: by offering them, for instance, a safe and consistent setting surrounded by rigorous (yet not rigid) boundaries, and by paying tactful attention to the timing of our interventions. Even the provision of a waiting room (notice that the word *waiting* refers to time, and the word *room* to space) can, in this respect, be useful in allowing our patients to experience a more gradual transition from the outside world to the analytic space.

I consider it important, if often also difficult, to interpret what happens in the *space* between the inside and the outside of my consulting room, and in the *time* between a session and what immediately precedes or follows it. An analysand of mine never replied to my *Good mornings* when I met her in the waiting room, or to my *Good-byes* at the end of sessions. For her, doing so would have meant acknowledging the existence of an empty time between our meetings and of a gap between her and me and, therefore, of the existence of a relationship between us. The breaks in her experience of the analytic process—the transitional space–time between the waiting room and the consulting room, between the door and the couch and the door again, between a session and the next—were magically denied by her (Sabbadini, 1989).

As to what takes place *inside* our psychoanalytic rooms, we are familiar with those oscillatory movements, or crossings of the bridge space–time, when patients place themselves (and implicitly their listening analysts) in a discursive modality characterised by a tension between solipsistic monologue and interpersonal dialogue. Or between free associations and silence, the latter being another phenomenon well known to most of us. I think of silence as a *container of words*, as a more or less transparent and fragile membrane, the common expression *to break the silence* clearly referring to such a view. Wordlessness, in analysis as well as everywhere else, can serve multiple functions: it can be a weapon, a shield, or a bridge. It can be a way to avoid saying something unsayable, but also a way to say what no words could ever tell. Behind all quiet moments, we find unconscious fantasies that the silence—like the dream, the joke, the parapraxis, or the symptom—conceals and expresses at the same time (Sabbadini, 1991).

"The most important thing in music", Beethoven once remarked, "is not in the score". In quoting him, Reik (1926) commented that "in psychoanalysis, too, what is spoken is not the most important thing. It appears to us more important to recognize what speech conceals and what silence reveals" (p. 126). What happens, then, *between* words? In the white spaces that separate them on the page, or the infinitesimally brief silences that separate them in the course of a conversation? What do we imagine is on a music score between a note and a rest and the next note? Or what do we hear during a concert, between the end of the vibrations of a note played on the violin, and the beginning of the next one produced by the cello? While there would be no music if a pause became too long, without short intervals of silence there could be no music either.

Analogously, in the visual arts, there could be no meaningful representation of form without shadows and so-called *negative spaces* around and in between shapes; in written language, there could be no meaningful representation of narrative without punctuation. Some of the work of graphic artists, such as M. C. Escher, and of novelists like James Joyce or José Saramago, can be considered as the exception that confirms the rule. In films, too, if we exclude rare instances of

118 ART IN PSYCHOANALYSIS

unedited "real time" productions, the alternation of shots and sequences, skilfully linked or separated through the process of editing, has constituted the main visual form of storytelling throughout the first 120 years of the history of cinema.

Let us remember here that cinema has emerged in the course of the nineteenth century through an organic development: from the first hazy pictures of pioneer photographers such as Louis Daguerre, Fox Talbot, and George Eastman, to the sequences of photographic images by experimental artists Edweard Muybridge (Figure 7.4) and Étienne-Jules Marey, to the films of the Lumière brothers (the first screenings of which, in 1895, made the birth of cinema chronologically coincide with that of psychoanalysis itself). Once come into existence, cinema has undergone, and is still undergoing, a process of multiple transformations, with transitional periods between its different stages, and bridges linking them together: from silent to talkies, from black-and-white to colour, from analogue to digital, from 35 millimetre celluloid to video and then DVD, from 2-D through HD to 3-D. Etcetera.

While cinema was born at the end of the nineteenth century, the *idea* of cinema goes back more than two millennia, when Plato (360 BC) used the "Simile of the Cave" to describe how chained prisoners, unable to move or turn their heads back, would mistakenly believe that the wooden and stone statues carried in front of a fire behind

Figure 7.4. Edweard Muybridge: *The horse in motion* (1878).

them, and whose shadows were thus projected on the cave wall facing them, were real people and not simulacra. "And so in every way", Plato concluded, "they would believe that the shadows of the objects we mentioned were the whole truth" (*The Republic*, p. 241). Baudry (1970), a prominent Lacanian film scholar, also refers to Plato's myth in developing his own views about what he calls the cinema "apparatus", a concept I could relate to that of the bridge space–time in so far as it constitutes a necessary, creative link between the filmmakers' imagination and their filmic products, and between the latter and their audience. Baudry's influential "apparatus theory" emphasised the ideological nature of the mechanics of film representation. In particular, the camera and the editing suite were considered by Baudry and his followers to be key tools in providing ideological points of view to the spectators' gaze, thus making cinema itself an instrumental bridge for the transmission of dominant cultural values.

What spreads out in front of the cinematographer's eyes and separates him from the scene he is in the process of shooting—but, at the same time, also keeps him in contact with it—is another instance of the bridge space–time. A territory which will soon no longer be occupied by the images framed by the camera, but is not yet occupied by the final product to be eventually projected on the screen. Similarly, for the audience collectively immersed in the regressive darkness of the film theatre, this space and time of play and creativity is to be found, following the beam of light which originates in the projection room, between their gaze and the silver screen. Sitting in the cinema armchair, and at the same time placing their minds and hearts inside the film story, the spectators find themselves occupying a productively ambiguous mental space. Furthermore, our metaphorical bridge connects not only the world of external reality with its filmed representation, but also the latter with the reality perceived by the viewers' gaze. A reality, by the way, which is illusory in more than one sense of the word: contrary to our impression, "movies" do not move at all, for they are composed of sequences of twenty-four still frames per second, separated by imperceptibly small gaps. Lights and shadows flicker in the cinema theatre, this no-man's land between spectator and spectacle, this territory as mysterious, fascinating (and also a little frightening) as the setting of the primal scene. A bridge space–time where films can contain our anxieties, nourish our minds, and even transform our lives.

It might be relevant to observe here that there is a similarity between the *film screen* and the *dream screen* as places of both fusion and separation (see Eberwein, 1984). The concept of dream screen was originally developed by Lewin:

> I conceived the idea that dreams contained a special structure which I named the *dream screen*. . . . I thought of the dream as a picture or a projected set of images, and for the reception of these images I predicated a screen, much like the one we see in the artificial night of a dark motion-picture house before the drama has radiated forth from the window of the projection box. (Lewin, 1953, p. 174)

Furthermore, films and dreams seem to share a morphological equivalence in so far as both can be considered to express latent unconscious wishes through their manifest contents, and both use, for the purpose of circumventing repression, similar mechanisms. These include (in films, especially at the editing stage) condensation, displacement, symbolic representation, secondary revision, and distortions of time and space. "Condensation" is particularly relevant here, in so far as one of its functions (in dreams, as elsewhere, such as in symptom formation) is to launch a bridge between two thoughts, words, or people by creating a composite one with features belonging to both. "The construction of collective and composite figures is one of the chief methods by which condensation operates in dreams", writes Freud (1900a, p. 293). And again, "an *intermediate common entity* had been constructed which admitted of multiple determination" (Freud, 1900a, p. 295, my emphasis).

When discussing creativity from a psychoanalytic perspective, sometimes we forget the creative aspects of the psychoanalytic work itself. In the consistent and, therefore, relatively safe space provided by our "studios", our main analytic functions include the most attentive listening, thinking in a state of relaxed concentration, reflecting on the emotional reactions that words and silences evoke in ourselves and our patients, and, occasionally, talking.

Our task involves the creative use of the material brought to us by our patients, in combination with that brought to sessions by our own personal and professional experience. We make links among different aspects of their lives—from different periods in their histories and belonging to different areas in their minds. Through the use of transference interpretations, we make sense of the remembered childhood in terms of the present, and of the here-and-now of the therapeutic relationship in relation to the past. Much psychoanalytic narrative centres around the same themes as much literature and drama (and films, and operas): love and death, conflicts of loyalties, travelling as a metaphor for life, an ambivalent relationship with our bodies and those of others, the pain of being torn between desires and a sense of duty. As psychoanalysts, we are editors involved in the selection, cutting, and pasting together of dissociated fragments, out of which we help re-create old pictures, or create new ones. We build relationships with people whose main problem is an incapacity to sustain them, and make them the focus of our understanding. As if we were musicians, we help our analysands to enrich with sounds the frightening silence of the void they carry inside. Like painters, we bring some colour to the greyness of their depression. Not unlike archaeologists, or biographers, we excavate in order to reconstruct. We try to make rational sense of what feels incomprehensible and mad. We tolerate within ourselves the anxiety of not knowing, and, with our example, we help others to stay with unresolved uncertainties without manically rushing to self-destructive enactments. When we can, we translate the obscure idiom of psychological symptoms and somatisations, of dreams and parapraxes, into a more comprehensible language, in an attempt to integrate disintegrated regions of our analysands' internal worlds.

All this, and much more, is part of our work. The creative side of it. It is also, I think, what makes psychoanalysis both difficult—indeed, as Freud said, "impossible"—and enormously exciting.

The empty canvas before it gets flooded with colour.

The quiet concert hall as the conductor lifts the baton in the air at the beginning of a concert.

The blank page, or computer screen, before words start leaving their marks on it.

I have struggled, or perhaps just played, with another "impossible" task, that of describing the meaning of gaps and intervals between events and between experiences, the transitional space–time separating them, as well as the metaphorical bridges that could join them.

References

Baudry, J.-L. (1970). Ideological effects of the basic cinematographic apparatus. *Film Quarterly*, 28(2): (1974): 39–47.

Cavafy, C. P. (1911). Ithaka. In: *Collected Poems* (pp. 67–70), G. Savidis (Ed.), E. Keeley & P. Sherrard (Trans.). Princeton, NJ: Princeton University Press, 1992.

Eberwein, R. T. (1984). *Film and the Dream Screen: A Sleep and a Forgetting* Princeton, NJ: Princeton University Press.

Freud, S. (1900a). *The Interpretation of Dreams*. S.E., 4. London: Hogarth.

Freud, S. (1916a). On transience. *S.E., 14*: 303–315. London: Hogarth.

Lewin, B. D. (1953). Reconsideration of the dream screen. *Psychoanalytic Quarterly*, 22: 174–199.

Plato (360 BC). *The Republic*, D. Lee (Trans.). Harmondsworth: Penguin Classics, 1955, Part 7, Para 7, pp. 240–248.

Reik, T. (1926). In the beginning is silence. In: *The Inner Experience of a Psychoanalyst* (pp. 121–126). London: George Allen & Unwin, 1949.

Sabbadini, A. (1987). The year 2000: a psychoanalytic perspective on the fantasy of the new millennium. *Free Associations*, 9: 56–71.

Sabbadini, A. (1989). Boundaries of timelessness. Some thoughts about the temporal dimension of the psychoanalytic space. *International Journal of Psychoanalysis*, 70(2): 305–313.

Sabbadini, A. (1991). Listening to silence. *British Journal of Psychotherapy*, 7(4): 406–415.

Sabbadini, A. (2010). The window and the door. In: T. Jeffers McDonald (Ed.), *Virgin Territory. Representing Sexual Inexperience in Film* (pp. 223–237). Detroit, MI: Wayne State University Press.

Sabbadini, A. (2011). Cameras, mirrors and the bridge space. A Winnicottian lens on cinema. *Projections*, 5(1): 17–30.

Sabbadini, A., & Stein, A. (2001). 'Just choose one': memory and time in Kore-eda's *Wandafuru Raifu* (Afterlife). *International Journal of Psychoanalysis*, 82(3): 603–608.

Stevenson, R. L. (1881). Virginibus Puerisque *and Other Papers*. London: Kegan Paul.

Winnicott, D. W. (1953). Transitional objects and transitional phenomena. In: *Playing and Reality* (pp. 1–18). London: Tavistock, 1971.

CHAPTER EIGHT

A fragment of the complex world: resorting to creation in the midst of negation, disavowal, and working through

Dominique Suchet

The name of an artist or a work of art, a literary text, picture, or piece of music might appear in the form of an *Einfall* (idea) during a session. It is suddenly evoked during narration. We shall consider this extraction from a shared cultural world as an effect of the process of becoming conscious that obeys the constraints of conflict with which resistance counters the lifting of repression and insight (Freud, 1914g). The introduction of this other scene, where the return of unconscious material unfolds in its two aspects, representation and affect, introduces a detour and a delay in the analysand's process of insight. It is a different scene, similar to the dream scene; we might see it at first as the manifest part of a creative psychic act in which unconscious representations are presented for analysis. However, the affective charge of these evocations seems only to slow down working through; in this sense, they are akin to the psychic process of negation (Freud, 1925h) in which consciousness of repressed representations is not associated with true acceptance of the repressed, since this acceptance needs to include an effective admission of its affective force. We shall describe how this evocation that confronts us with the beauty of a highly valued cultural work might serve working through, but also how aesthetic emotion might place it in the service of resistance. We shall also see how confrontation with interpretation during a session might take a similar path. (In psychoanalysis, confrontation with the therapist's interpretation means facing a complex world; the analyst's creation is also subject to the laws of an artist's creativity.)

What is at stake, when something becomes conscious, is the process of working through. It is unconscious and takes place by steps. When repression begins to lift, unconscious representations attach themselves to verbal representations and can, thus, reach consciousness, but this never happens directly. Sometimes, it occurs through the disguises which primary processes provide for the return of the repressed. At other times, it takes place with what we are now considering, the extraction of a fragment from the common cultural world, where the return of the repressed unfurls through a diversion on another scene. The introduction of this scene allows the unconscious material to deploy its faces of both representation and affect, but it introduces a detour, and also a delay in the process of insight for the patient. At first, it can be envisaged as the manifest part of a creative psychic act that allows unconscious representations to come up for analysis. Yet, the affects attached to these evocations seem only to slow down the working through, in such a way that this recourse used by the patient finally appears somewhat akin to the process of negation: becoming aware of the repressed representation occurs without a true admission of the repressed—which can be effective only if its affective force itself is recognised.

A clinical situation illustrating this process

A female patient, at the beginning of a session (Suchet, 2008), seeing flowers in the office, thinks of a poet famous for his children's books in which daffodil-flowers are girls, the poet equally renowned for having written, often rewritten from memory, sad books full of anxiety and death when he was in a Nazi concentration camp, where he died (Seghers, 1974). The patient did not express her emotion at the beauty of the flowers, she only mentioned the name of the poet: "You've made a bouquet of daffodils, you were thinking of Desnos!" Then she added the memory of words from one of those sad poems: "J'ai tant rêvé de toi que tu perds toute réalité" ("I have so dreamt of you that you lose all reality"). This recollection is immediately placed in relation to the analytic situation, where the analyst is out of sight. The patient adds that she is reassured by seeing her analyst when she arrives for her session and when she leaves. Once she has become aware in transference of a threat of retaliation, she starts to talk about her ambivalent feeling of Oedipal rivalry. This feeling is exacerbated at this time by her newly acquired perception of the reality of her internal world. With the poet's words, she is able to express how her mother is *truly* in relation to her (a mother who *takes on some reality*, according to the poet's words) and how she can liberate herself from the rival, aggressive, Oedipal mother she carries within her (*that she has long dreamt of*, again according to the poet's words).

The patient has become aware of the gap between different representations of the object. This is the gain resulting from grief over the Oedipal objects once they lose both their violence and their attractive force. This process of working through rests on the displacement of representations towards *the other scene* of the name/object described by the poet. As work goes on in the session, it is taken apart and reveals what was condensed inside it: the contradiction between infantile tenderness (stories for children) and the violence of a barbaric world (poems about resistance against the Nazis).

We could say that the patient resorts to an artistic composition in order to say something that is not yet quite acceptable. This is like a sudden reaction of resistance against the process of becoming conscious. But what the patient might consider an elegant form of expression is, in fact, a creative act, a word throwing a bridge between repression and the lifting of the repressed, when unconscious motions encourage with their contradictory movement, both revealing and concealing the result of psychic elaboration. We could consider this a transference move of seduction, in which the patient entrusts a shared cultural figure with the task of masking expression of the conflict of Oedipal ambivalence. We also see how, in the transference, the unconscious fantasy pushes to repeat the infantile wish. It succeeds by cutting out a piece of the shared cultural world and putting it into the transference scene between analyst and analysand. It diverts it and subordinates it to its wish. Through these deformations inherent to primary processes, such as those dreamwork creates, it re-creates the poet's name/thing for itself.

The repetition of an Oedipal feeling sustained the patient's ambivalence, actualised in the transference by giving the poet's name/thing to express her wish to seduce the analyst and simultaneously reproach her for not giving her (the analysand) what the analyst possessed and was exhibiting (sex-flowers). This was understood in the following session when the patient exclaimed, "There are no more daffodils, it didn't last for long!" The enigmatic and sexual dimension of the representation girl–daffodil/sex-flower that had escaped full comprehension had been diverted on to the poet's name and verse, along with the violence, anxiety, and guilt inherent to becoming conscious of the unconsciously repressed. Quoting was her way to evade an inability to tell her analyst what she felt directly: "Are these flowers for me?", or "Am I a girl or a boy for you?", or "Are you a girl or boy for me?" Discovered by an effect of transference, the piece extracted from a shared cultural world brought the unconscious conflict to perception.

The work of art (literary, pictorial, or musical evocation) is a perceptive support for what has not yet come into the conscious. Its evocation acquires the status of a psychic act that, like a dream, has a manifest aspect and a hidden meaning. From a dynamic point of view, it is "mute poetry", where the riddle of the artist's state of affect and intention, the hidden meaning of the composition, and the affective state of the art lover echo each other mutually. These echoes between various dynamics of the psychic life of the person sensitive to a work of art, the psychic dynamic of working through, and of the creator is the enigma Freud elucidates when he analyses the strong impression or *mise en abyme* that Michelangelo's statue in San Pietro in Vincoli in Rome produced in him.

The psychic activity of the art lover as a paradigm of working through: Freud confronted with Michelangelo's Moses

How often I mounted the steep steps from the unlovely Corso Cavour to the lonely piazza where the deserted church stands and have essayed to support the angry scorn of the hero's glance! Sometimes I have crept cautiously out of the half-gloom of the interior as though I myself belonged to the mob upon whom his eye is turned – the mob which can hold fast no conviction, which neither has faith nor patience, and which rejoices when it has regained its illusory idols. (Freud, 1914b, p. 213)

In a description very much like a dream narration, Freud tells us of his astonishment before the statue commissioned for the tomb of Jules II. A strong impression, as he said, the strongest ever provoked by a work of art, draws him to visit the hero of San Pietro in Vincoli every day that September of 1912, with the explanation to his wife Martha that he intends to write about it some day. His text was written two years later. It is part of the battle he fought against himself, on the one hand identifying with the *rabble*, guilty of being seduced by the illusion of perceptive satisfaction, and, on the other hand, identifying with a Moses controlling his emotion. In this way, he opens his debate on the conflict inherent to the acquisition of culture. How is it possible to keep up the demands of cultural achievement with its share of renouncement of drive satisfaction, while facing the demands of instant and total satisfaction from unconscious fantasy? How can *Gesichkeit*, or the gain of meaning that results from increased representational activity, guarantee sufficient compensation? These questions concern the psychic work of becoming conscious. They also concern the analyst's activity and extend to cultural progress in which psychoanalysis takes part. The research these questions activate takes a detour through the work of art and leads Freud to elaborate a metapsychology of analytic work. This is why Freud lingers there for a long time, contemplating the statue by Michelangelo, apprehending it in his own particular way: he wants to work out how it is that the statue generates an impact. He refuses to let himself be taken in without also learning by what and why.

Thus, a triple *mise en abyme* follows. First, Freud is awed, fascinated, and, blinded by a strong aesthetic impression, identifies with the idolising masses. Then, as an analyst, he understands that his fear of the immobile statue is a perception of what this Moses, sitting there in eternal anger, represents for him. He identifies with Moses refraining from an inevitable outburst, holding on to the Tables of the Law to keep them from breaking and attaining the highest psychic prowess a human being may reach, smothering his own passion for the benefit and in the name of a mission to which he is devoted. Finally, in the third *mise en abyme*, in a movement that foretells the gesture of desacralisation of *Moses and Monotheism* (Freud, 1939a), Freud identifies with Michelangelo, to whom he attributes the intention of creating a Moses superior to the historical Moses through a gesture that is not included in the sacred text. Only an analytic attitude, with its slow decomposition of thoughts, enables him to arrive at the irrepressible feeling that no intellectual or aesthetic comprehension could circumscribe. *Mise en abyme* is characteristic of the *après-coup* temporality that is specific to psychic work (Chervet, 2009). Thus, by seeking out how the forms of Michelangelo's statue affect him, Freud proposes a theory of working through, and also elaborates a model of the analyst's psychic work, of listening and a way of thinking, in an oscillation between regression and progredience.

When he discovers that the representational content of the statue is a psychic conflict, Freud spectacularly puts things into perspective: the strong impression released to the spectator by the work of art is associated with the awakening of the same conflict that is sculpted in marble. This conflict between spirituality and sensoriality, between the work of culture and drive satisfaction, is figured in the work of art, and, through it, the art lover discovers within himself the movement of the conflict expressed by the composition (Letter to Ferenczi, 6 January 1916, Falzeder & Brabant, 1996). He also encounters the artist's psychic conflict as he was creating this work. The composition conveys and transfers the artist's movement of creativity. Having turned away from reality, the artist has found within himself a way to return to reality by giving it back, transformed, to the sensitive world (Freud, 1908e). The art lover, absorbed in a work of art, finds within himself an oscillation between regressive thinking dominated by sensoriality and progredient thinking, with transformation towards representation. And he might, in turn, engage in creative work by extending the work's effect through their use of it, guided by their own unconscious psychic life. They re-discover in themselves an echo of its creator's psychic conflict.

McDougall (McDougall et al., 2008) considers that extreme violence is operating in all creative activity, together with deep anxiety and a great deal of guilt. It is a violent gesture of control over the world. It reveals the creator's psychic movements and infantile desire: love, hate, the binding force of Eros, and the drive of representation, as well as violence against the real that resists: an analogue of parricidal violence. In the regressivity of the analytic situation, the presence of the work of art is like the Trojan Horse of the representation of this inadmissible violence.

Like Moses, who restrains his gesture of wrath and does not break the Tables of the Law, Freud restrains his gesture of reprimand by publishing *The Moses of Michelangelo* anonymously. He recognises it (in a private letter of 12 April 1933) only ten years later as his *non-analytical child* (Freud, 1960), an illegitimate child, a child of love. Of course, we may follow Jones as he explains that Freud wrote *The Moses of Michelangelo* at a time when he confronted intense emotional conflict, since he wrote it simultaneously with his essays "On narcissism: an introduction" (1914c) and "On the history of the psycho-analytic movement" (1914d): that is to say, just when he was clearly airing his disagreements with Jung. Jones considers that Freud was, thereby, indicating how he is surmounting painful emotions provoked by this recent separation. However, we might also consider that this text is not simply a work based on circumstance in response to the questions of Adler and Jung, but that it is also a metapsychological deepening of metapsychology. Here, metapsychology attains the status of a work of art, an act of intimate creation, a product of the struggle against repression (the response to Adler), subject to the unconscious wish (the response to Jung). The essential strength of this text resides in the fact that, for the analyst, it *represents* (*vorstelt*) what the statue *presents* (*dachstelt*): psychic life itself and its violent struggle against the regressive attraction of matter. Like most of Freud's texts, *The Moses of Michelangelo* has a performative aspect; it is an act of enunciation whose reading creates the modification it enounces. This is the way in which analysts might actually be in an analytic relation with Freud's works.

Becoming conscious requires an articulation of representation and affect on the same scene. In the cure, this is the place of transference. Through it, the patient experiencing the event, here and now, is persuaded of the power of what he discovers. Although a work of art might offer a precious detour for certain representations, the associated affect, that is to say, aesthetic emotion, seems to struggle against insight and delay it. This emotion might possibly be the reverse side, hidden by inversion of narcissistic resistance and specific to negation: the absence of a feeling of remembrance, used against acceptance of the recollected experience. These two affective movements serve resistance in a similar way. They encourage a position of disavowal of vicissitudes of drive movements of love and hate. Whatever has reached figuration is frozen, and the fascination with spectacularity tends to oppose both working through and psychic progress.

Psychoanalysis and aesthetics

A mutual debt binds aesthetics to psychoanalysis, a debt that is the source of their conflicting relations. Freud himself has reservations about the relevance of aesthetics and the notion of beauty in psychoanalysis. In *Three Essays on the Theory of Sexuality* (1905d) he finds the roots of aesthetic emotion and the sense of beauty in the world of sexual excitement (note of 1915). Later, concerning Leonardo da Vinci (1910c), he excludes aesthetics as an object of study for psychoanalysis, adding that we can only recognise that the essence of aesthetic realisation is psychoanalytically inaccessible. In *Civilization and its Discontents* (1930a), he declares outright that psychoanalysis has nothing to say about beauty! He seems to distrust the attraction of the aesthetic field as a dangerous opening leading to an applied psychoanalysis in which metapsychology would no longer enlighten art, but instead art might enlighten metapsychology. From that point on, psychoanalysis must avoid drifting towards any psychological or psychopathological interpretation of works of art or creative acts. These reservations about psychoanalytic interference have encouraged hesitation to theorise on sublimation. At times, sublimation is nothing less than the highest destiny of part drives, whereas at other times it is present from the outset, the very foundation of psychic life, present in unconscious fantasies (*fantasme*) and representations that constitute its inchoactive form (Séchaud, 2005). This difficulty is not dispelled by reading *The Moses of Michelangelo*. Far from dissociating aesthetics from the analyst's field of concern, and in spite of his description of this danger, Freud places the effect of aesthetics at the heart of analytic work. First of all, it is strong aesthetic emotion that activates the representational process, and then he reminds us that since the beginning of his research he has always used works of art to underpin scientific progress. The tragedy of Sophocles and Shakespearean text support the elaboration of the Oedipal theory and the universality of the Oedipus complex. Thus, he presents literary fiction and psychoanalytic fiction as two ways to explore a world to be discovered: the unconscious. Also, did he not write to Fliess (21 September 1899) to explain how dissatisfied he was with his laborious composition of *The Interpretation of Dreams*, and that because he has "within [himself] a certain sense of form, *a way of considering beauty as a sort of perfection* [he considers that the] lack of form [of his manuscript] is an indication that he does not completely master the subject" (Masson, 1985, p. 371, my italics).

Aesthetics and their effect are a source of conflict for Freud; it remains a problem to find a place for them in metapsychology. The aesthetic effect is inserted in the associative process of the session in the same conflict between regression towards sensoriality and the appeal to representation. The evocation of a work of art is a moment of shared creativity whose difficulty resides in the high degree of empathy it generates. This evocation delineates a crossroads where representations and also sensations are shared and mixed between analyst and patient. The signal of this inevitable risk is aesthetic emotion, intimately linked to creativity, a universal experience of the human mind. We cannot imagine avoiding this mixing of aesthetic experience with sensitive or sensorial experience. De M'Uzan (1978) considers this danger zone the *chimera*, capable single-handedly of sustaining Freud's reticence in regard to aesthetics, beauty, and form.

A clinical sequence illustrates the way a patient might use aesthetic emotion during a session

At the beginning of his analysis, this patient was battling against destructive movements of his psychic and physical life. His therapy could be classified as difficult, considering that all its aspects seemed strange and doubtful to him. Fédida (1995) named the analytic situation as the *Site of the Foreigner*, to indicate that it has no other source but the foreignness (*unheimlich*) of transference. It is also a *site of the foreigner* radically "other", since it has no other topic than the one designed by listening to the dynamic of unconscious psychic life. But, for my patient, "strangeness" meant hostile and violent. He incriminated timetables, the availability and unavailability of the analyst, vacations, payment, and punctuality, thereby expressing in transference the chaos of his psychic life. In these conditions he saw only the confirmation and extension of his fate; a life of fear and tragedy. Death, illness, and repeated misfortunes transmitted from generation to generation shaped a narcissistic neurosis of destiny that he considered undoubtedly exceptional. The narcissistic cathectisation of these unfortunate events is the sanctuary of fixed childhood images of each of his parents, each different from the other, both statues in grandiose misery. He had no childhood recollections because he was an orphan, he said. Nevertheless, he managed to find some striking childhood memories in the form of two parallel histories with each of his parents. His recollections separate his father and his mother: on the one hand, memories of an absent father, and, on the other hand, those of a failing mother. The fixity of the images left no room for Oedipal scenarios of ambivalence. No love, no hate, one heard only misfortune and protests against fate. In this context, the analysis he had just started and, nevertheless, continued regularly and worked hard on, was, he believed, fated to fail like everything else. I consider that his analysis is exactly this, transference working in this repetition, and that such a tragic conviction can only be concealing unaltered childhood hopes and desires that nourish it. Conviction holds the analyst's attention as she tracks down the effect of transference, working towards the transformation of repetition into remembering.

Following a dream in which he saw himself "sitting against a wall with his sick son", he realised that his pessimism was repeating his father's wait-and-see attitude towards the future: "Nothing good could come out of it, nothing good could happen with him." I emphasised *"it* as in fate? *him* the son?", and interpreted his ambivalence in wanting, for love, to satisfy his waiting for the beloved object with a failure that would hurt it. The patient remained silent at first, and then said, "Yes, perhaps." Then he remembered that when the ambulance came to take his mother away, he had said to himself, as if taking an oath: "I am a victim for life." Deeply moved, he was silent. He opened the following session by declaring, after a silence, "It has nothing to do with what one [sic] discussed yesterday, but what you said made me think that I am interested in nothing apart from my sleep, my suffering, my money ... why don't I think about other things, why don't I like other things? Why do I take no interest in beautiful things, paintings for example ... just like here," he said, accompanying his words with a gesture. Aesthetic emotion is inscribed in the line of hallucinatory wish fulfilment and a common and shared experience with the analyst. It is the hope of maintaining a link and of deferring the elaboration of a melancholic identification with the lost object. In this sense, as disavowal, it is serving resistance. However, for this patient, it is also a reminder of the accompanying presence of this moving feeling in his personal psychic mode of insight. In session, it accompanies economic modifications of working through.

I remembered that at the beginning of his analysis the first founding event in his transference cathexis appeared in the form of an aesthetic emotion. During a long, lonely journey by car, he was taken aback by a landscape, a lovely sunset, and by a wave of intense emotion associated with memories of other journeys by car when he was a child, sitting in the back, and could see the sun, the road, and his parents together side by side in front of him. His sadness that day had been expressed with words said during the session at the same time as the image and the emotion: "I will never see them again. I wanted to tell you that." Aesthetic emotion is manifested at a moment of release of rediscovered childhood traces, a moment when transference cathexis is accepted by the conscious, when the regressivity of the specific psychic activity of analytic work is tolerated.

Resistance to the complex world

When the patient chooses objects belonging to the analyst as a support for the expression of inaccessible aesthetic emotion, is he not repeating infantile disappointment with idealised parental images? In this way, he is repeating disappointment over the loss of a primary object or, more precisely, disappointment regarding the inevitable loss of a link with the initial objects joined in a fantasy of a primal scene paradigmatic of fantasies of seduction and castration (Lavie, 1992). This is the negation version of resorting to aesthetic evocation. In this transference movement, the patient indicates how he stopped on the way to mourning these objects and to identification, and how he rediscovers the wish to appropriate and control characteristics of the object, or of the object's object. Resorting to perception of a world from which he feels excluded and which he wishes to appropriate was preferable to perceiving the distress of loss of idealness. This appropriation was dictated by envy, perhaps set off by an interpretation given too soon or too directly. Thus, instead of using negation to aid insight of the repressed by accepting the representation, the use of aesthetic evocation is regressive and reduced to its affective force, placed in the service of disavowal. Whereas with negation the repressed is accepted through a disjunction of affect and representation, aesthetic emotion binds representation to affect quite tightly. It is an imperfect negation that has simply displaced the affect. Beauty gives a feeling of elation by counter-cathecting aggressivity and as an idealisation of eroticism.

Meltzer (1984) took up the works of Bion on the caesura of birth and presents the hypothesis of the newborn baby's first aesthetic experience when its existing sensory organs, stimulated but restricted to inactivity in the womb, are suddenly free to function. I bear in mind that Meltzer's theory differs from Bion's, or Klein's psychogenetic conception that considers the infant's immaturity, when he considers that a human being, no matter when, has an emotional experience of the world's impact. The impact of the "beauty of the world" is a shock-wave for a world that is too simple, affected by its confrontation with a complex world. This aesthetic emotion, source of epistemophilic drives, orientates the newborn's later investigations of the object, investigation that Meltzer sums up in a single question: "Is it just as beautiful inside?" Here, we find Freud's posture emphasising that the sense arrives because of beauty is a vicissitude of sexual excitement and that the epistemophilic drive merely takes over the child's sexual investigations. This encounter with the world's beauty is a sexual encounter. The (maternal) world seduces the budding psyche and provokes its "driveness". Laplanche (1992) has insisted on the function of the world's seduction and considers that the drive source is in the implanting in the subject of enigmatic messages emanating from the object. However, we must remember that the object arrives when it is lost, and, thus, the world's beauty is its ephemeral fate (Freud, 1916a). According to Meltzer, the impact of the beauty of the world and its corresponding elusiveness simultaneously provokes curiosity and depression. The question "Is it as beautiful inside?" is the essence of the depressive position. Thus, he inverts the Kleinian proposition by presenting a regressively cathected paranoid–schizoid position that is defensive and protective of depression. The loss of the object is at the source of representational thought, the source of unconscious fantasy and of psychic creativity. It is at the source of language. This is what Freud discovered in 1898 when he analysed a problem with memory in regard to aesthetic emotion, when the figure and the name of the artist who painted the fresco at Orvieto erased each other. If he remembered one, the other was driven away. He discovered how consciousness and mnemic traces exclude each other, long before he conceptualised it in his "A note upon the "mystic writing-pad" (1925a). We never escape this attraction of the simple world of the memory of the bond with our primary objects in opposition to the complex world of the progress of consciousness.

Thus designated, the complex world is the world of the life of the mind, where signification (*Gesichkeit*) transforms sensoriality (*Sensichkeit*). Confrontation with the enigmatic and sexual world circumscribes *après-coup* a world in which sensoriality was lost as soon as it appeared. The significance of the enigmatic and sexual world makes the first relation to the object and to the world a relation to language: part of it is transferred to language, not only verbal language, but all languages. Considering that psychic life originates in the *contretemps* of language, when the arrival of the enigmatic and sexual world of language and signification brings about a "before" (the paradise always already lost of the simple world of sensoriality), we must consequently be alert to the function of spoken words in psychic life. It is this function that carries the world inside it by creating the world through repression. Creative expression inherits it and the "talking cure" is founded on it by opening the space for words of free association and by giving interpretation its power to transform.

The analyst's interpretation

In the session, the analyst's interpretation is a piece of the complex world colliding with the analysand's thinking. Whereas the patient's thought is regressively orientated by transference towards hallucinatory satisfaction of the repetition of infantile wishes, interpretation is an enunciation that sets off an explosive confrontation with the message of an other, replete with still unknown meaning. The encounter with new verbal links lifts repression, followed by a process of working through. This process takes a laborious road that Freud has often described in his technical papers. Defensive recourse to aesthetic emotion occurring on the way throws light on the conflict between becoming conscious and the force of repression.

The analysand is confronted with interpretation, which produces a disorganising effect on the patient's world. At first, the patient disavows it. Then a "No, that's not it" acquires value as acceptance of the repressed when it is followed immediately by an association that confirms it indirectly (Freud, 1925a). In this sense, its effect is similar to aesthetic evocation, with its function of negation in the service of resistance, where it is still a bastion, but already defeated. The analyst's interpretation confronts the patient's simple and infantile world with a piece of the complex, enigmatic, and sexual world.

I shall not follow post-Kleinian theories that consider that the force of resistance through repetition comes from a conservative ego that would always wish to go on with familiar experiences. In these theories, the unconscious always aims to push towards new experiences. However, I suggest that the conservative force originates in the force of repetition of the unconscious realisation of infantile sexual desire. This leads us to bring repression back to the foreground and to consider that drives and their representations are not dammed up, as the Kleinians propose, but, instead, repressed. They are always moved in the unconscious by a force towards realisation of their satisfaction.

During therapy in psychoanalysis, confrontation with the therapist's interpretation means facing a "complex world". It is not simply an emotional shock, but also a sexual trauma. The fact that this trauma moves through a confrontation with the difference between worlds reminds us that human psychic life is organised by castration and that it is confrontation with a difference, anatomical difference, between the sexes that ensures psychic life. Difference is the vector for the affect and representation of what is sexual (Suchet, 2012). Interpretation is a demonstration of the therapist's psychic creativity and *dreaming thought* (Gantheret, 2007) swinging between regressivity and progredience. It is the analyst's work of art. For the analysand, this is doubly violent. An interpretation provides meaning by revealing a gap with latent meaning and also provides the movement of its creation, the analyst's creation, subject to the laws of an artist's creativity.

Interpretation is like an aesthetic evocation in the core of the session. Like a statue appearing out of the dim light of a church, interpretation might cause a *strong impression*, and lead to a conflict between a gain in signification and a loss of the satisfaction ensured by sensoriality via the repetition compulsion of unconscious fantasy. It reveals this satisfaction.

In the cure, this slow process is never certain. Resistance alternates between repression and working through, between progress and negation. Yet, progress is never certain, since the forms of resistance are not, either, because they might also serve progress. For example, when aesthetic evocation functioning as negation allows access to still repressed representations, or when aesthetic emotion serving disavowal reveals its links with psychic creativity; a piece of the complex world resting on the internalisation of the complex, enigmatic, and sexual world of language.

References

Chervet, B. (2009). L'après-coup, la tentative d'inscrire ce qui tend à disparaître, L'Après-Coup. *Revue Française de Psychanalyse*, 5: 1361–1441.
De M'Uzan, M. (1978). La bouche de l'inconscient. *Nouvelle Revue de Psychanalyse*, XVII: 89–98.
Falzeder, E., & Brabant, E. (Eds.) (1996). *The Correspondence of Sigmund Freud and Sandor Ferenczi, Volume 2: 1914–1919*. Cambridge, MA: Harvard University Press.
Fédida, P. (1995). *Le Site de l'Étranger*. Paris: PUF.
Freud, S. (1898). The psychical mechanism of forgetfulness. *S.E.*, 3: 287–297. London: Hogarth.
Freud, S. (1905d). *Three Essays on the Theory of Sexuality. S.E.*, 7: 125–245. London: Hogarth.
Freud, S. (1908e). Creative writers and day-dreaming. *S.E.*, 9: 143–153. London: Hogarth.
Freud, S. (1910c). *Leonardo Da Vinci and a Memory of his Childhood. S.E.*, 11: 59–137. London: Hogarth.
Freud, S. (1914b). *The Moses of Michelangelo. S.E.*, 13: 211–238. London: Hogarth.
Freud, S. (1914c). On narcissism: an introduction. *S.E.*, 14: 73–102. London: Hogarth.
Freud, S. (1914d). On the history of the psycho-analytic movement. *S.E.*, 14: 3–66. London: Hogarth.
Freud, S. (1914g). Remembering, repeating and working-through. *S.E.*, 12: 145–156: London: Hogarth.
Freud, S. (1916a). On transience. *S.E.*, 14: 303–315: London: Hogarth.
Freud, S. (1925a). A note upon the "mystic writing-pad". *S.E.*, 19: 227–232. London: Hogarth.
Freud, S. (1925h). Negation. *S.E.*, 19: 235–239. London: Hogarth.
Freud, S. (1930a). *Civilization and Its Discontents. S.E.*, 21: 59–145. London: Hogarth.
Freud, S. (1939a). *Moses and Monotheism. S.E.*, 23: 3–137. London: Hogarth.
Freud, S. (1960). Lettre à Edouardo Weiss le 12 Avril 1933. In: *Correspondance 1873–1939*. Paris: Gallimard.

Gantheret, F. (2007). Le royaume intermédiaire psychanalyse, littérature, autour de J. B. Pontalis. Paris: Gallimard, Folio Essais.

Laplanche, J. (1992). *La Révolution Copernicienne Inachevée*. Aubier.

Lavie, J. C. (1992). Excellence paradigmatique de la scène primitive. *Nouvelle Revue de Psychoanalyse, 46*: 11–23.

Masson, J. M. (Ed.) (1985). *The Complete Letters of Sigmund Freud to Wilhelm Fliess, 1887–1904*. Cambridge, MA: Harvard University Press.

McDougall, J., André, J., de M'Uzan, M., Marinov, V., Porret, P., Schneider, M., & Suchet, D. (2008). *L'artiste et le psychanalyste*. Paris: PUF.

Meltzer, D. (1984). Le conflit esthétique: son rôle dans le processus de développement psychique. *Bulletin du Groupe d'Études et de Recherches Psychanalytiques pour le Développement de l'Enfant et du Nourrisson, 2*: 1–15.

Séchaud, E. (2005). Perdre, sublimer... *Revue Française de Psychanalyse, 69*(5): 1309–1379.

Seghers, P. (1974). *La résistance et ses poètes, France 1940–1945*. Paris: Seghers.

Suchet, D. (2008). De l'invité à la relique, Le créateur et l'œuvre d'art défaits par la régressivité de la séance d'analyse. In: J. McDougall, J. André, M. de M'Uzan, V. Marinov, P. Porret, M. Schneider, & D. Suchet, *L'artiste et le psychanalyste* (pp. 129–148). Paris: PUF.

Suchet, D. (2012). Opposition au déclin du complexe d'Oedipe. In: *Le Fil d'Oedipe* (pp. 11–29). Paris: PUF, L'Annuel de l'APF.

CHAPTER NINE

Living creatively: the concept of a sound-minded individual and the healing phenomena

José Outeiral

"Health is much more difficult to deal with than disease"

(Winnicott, quoted in Phillips, 1988)

The purpose of this text is to invite readers to a period of sober reflection on the clinical and theoretical thinking of Winnicott and other Middle Group authors, all from the British Psychoanalytical Association, on (1) the matter of creativity being closely connected with health, and (2) the possibility of living creatively using the healing phenomena (Winnicott, 1954). In other words, countless situations of environmental failure are frozen; however, they are defrosted by several different healing phenomena present in day-to-day life, such as friendship, special care provided during a bout of sickness, and poetry, among many other emotional events. Thus, this text's main statement aims to discuss how living creatively sets in motion the healing phenomena and uses creativity also to set in motion the healing mechanisms.

Winnicott wrote that whatever we intend to "take" from him, we have to take from chaos. I believe he referred to the "unconscious", to the local, and maybe we can say "more creative and intelligent" of us, but, going beyond Freud's thinking, he explored creativity in going on being, in the articulation between nature and nurture, between the individual's "nature" and "environmental" care. The complementary series of things that form personality (personality = constitution + childhood experiences + current situation), as set out by Freud, is revisited by Winnicott, who considered the relationship between baby and environment.

In his singular writing, paradoxically simple and, at the same time, complex and deep, Winnicott offers extremely important concepts, which are accepted today by a considerable part of the psychoanalytic community. Winnicott's writings are an invitation to a *squiggle game*, an open system[1] in which he invites us to find, from ideas he introduces, something similar to a network where threads are woven together and form complex patterns of clinical experiences and theoretical concepts. His thinking, it is worth remembering, is based on the English empiricist tradition in which theory comes from experience. Winnicott's theoretical and clinical texts, as he suggests, are to be "used" by the reader, as he construes the word "use". "Use" means to take in order to guide your clinical work and life. Therefore, there will be creative and spontaneous elements and new conceptions, sometimes full of surprises, quests, paradigms, and *non-sense* . . . this is how it is. It is important not to try to "understand everything" in each and every work and, only then, move forward. It is necessary to do what the Beatles (of whom Winnicott was a huge fan) said: "Let it be" and move on.

This kind of communication, written between the lines, allowed André Green to devise his important "negative" concept, when comparing texts from 1951 and 1971, from Winnicott's "Transitional objects and transitional phenomena" (1953) and the suppressions, by this chapter's author, in the last part of this essay. Many of Winnicott's concepts, as he warned, are to be taken from "chaos" unveiled or created by the reader.

In this chapter, I want specifically to discuss the healing phenomena. If I am not mistaken, Winnicott explicitly mentioned them once, in his paper "Metapsychological and clinical aspects of regression within the psycho-analytical set-up", read before the British Psychoanalytical Society in 1954. Winnicott wrote that patients may recover spontaneously from psychosis, and, therefore, psychosis is closely related to health, since many situations of failure that have been frozen are reached and unfrozen by healing phenomena in everyday life, including friendship, care received during illness, poetry, etc.

My first contact with this concept was through a remark by Raquel Zak de Goldstein, from the Argentine Psychoanalytic Association, while discussing Winnicott's works. In fact, I have "incorporated" the concept as if I had read it countless times in different articles written by Winnicott, which actually never happened, because to my knowledge, and I found it to be true many years later, he had written it before, in the above-mentioned text, in 1954; but this is typical of Winnicott's ideas and the "discoveries" (elements he proposes) to which he leads us.

Specific reference is made to the text where this concept was written and I realised I had no idea where it came from, although it was very clear in my mind. It was hidden inside me. Raquel Zak de Goldstein has suggested an article by Mannoni, "La parte del juego" (1978). The author quotes Winnicott's text, but only as an article written in 1954 that describes the phenomenon. However, it was not difficult to find it in one of the three articles Winnicott wrote in 1954, although the "healing phenomena" are not listed in the index of any of Winnicott's books, in the English editions, or in Abram and Newman's dictionaries on his works. I am sure that I had read it a dozen times but could not remember the concept was there, "hidden", waiting to be "found", or, as Winnicott described it, hiding is a joy but not being found a disaster. I "found it" after it had remained hidden (from me) for so many years.

Mannoni (1978), comments on Winnicott's Freudian tradition and refers to sources where the English analyst might have taken from works by psychoanalysis's founder, where his most important conceptions are found. Mannoni starts by discussing the healing phenomena as a function close to healing, drawing a distinction between the verbs *to cure* (cure in the sense of something that comes from the outside, cure by means of a medication, for instance) and *to heal*, in the sense of a process that comes from the inside, close to the concept of healing. For the curious mind, I recommend Mannoni's article. Thus, the healing phenomena, as I see it, are related to two of Winnicott's concepts: living creatively and the concept of a soundminded individual.

So, let's see.

The concept of a sound-minded individual

Winnicott writes (1967) that the flight into sanity is not health, but that we are truly poor if we are simply sane. But what does "sane" mean?

Freud, in a broader sense, considers the individual as "sound of mind" when the person is capable of loving and working; Winnicott adds to this concept the capacity to live creatively.

Phillips (2005) helps us to understand this concept with his comments on the English word "sane", from the Latin *sanus* and the French *sain*, first used in the seventeenth century and included in one of Shakespeare's plays, *Hamlet*. In this text, the English bard used the word "sane" only once in the entire play, whereas he used the word "mad" more than two hundred times and the word "madness" thirty-five times, as Winnicott quoted and I use now, showing that this condition is still in force nowadays.

Shakespeare started to introduce modern criteria to better understand mental states, foreshadowing Descartes, Kant, and other thinkers, and properly and significantly placing Polonius's comment on young Hamlet that there was method in his madness; to determine whether it is sane or mad, we need methods, as set forth by the Cartesian concept. The advent of psychoanalysis, at the end of the nineteenth century, revolutionises this way of thinking.[2]

The relation between a person's mental state and a magical comprehension system, such as possession, starts to yield to reasoning and science with modernity and the Age of Enlightenment; in many of his texts, Shakespeare explored this matter. For him, often, "mad" is an individual who has some reasoning inside, which gives meaning to the text and holds the other's interest: was Hamlet "mad" or not? In my opinion, and I know this is not original, I believe this is a paradox and, as such, and as suggested by Winnicott, it must often be tolerated, not resolved. This paradox is an important theme in Winnicott's thinking.

To believe that the Communion wine is Christ's blood and the wafer is Christ's body is close to the beliefs of primitive tribes, children, and mad people, but if we are in a Christian ritual, in a system of shared beliefs, we understand that it is merely symbolic; therefore, the "sound-of-mind" state depends on several factors, from time and space to the individual's maturation process. Psychoanalysis helps us to understand the existing (and suppressed) madness of the "sane" man, as Freudianly described by André Green.

Winnicott also considers, as one of his challenging opinions, in the text "Creativity and its origins" (1971), that certain individuals fall ill owing to excessive fantasies and unrealities and others, not a few, owing to excessive linking with reality. For him, in certain situations, psychical normality is a symptomatic expression, which hides very primitive mental states and structures. Some defensive organisations, such as the "false self", borderline structures, psychosomatic illness, or schizoid states, might refer to this symptomatic normality.

In his text (1971), Winnicott wrote that people firmly anchored in objectively perceived reality are ill from lack of contact with their subjective world and a creative approach to facts.

Regarding Winnicott's way of thinking, many developments came from many different authors, but, to make a long story short, McDougall (1992), in her book, *Plea for a Measure of Abnormality*, uses and develops the concept of "normopath", Bollas (1987) takes this up with his concept of "normotic" illness, and Phillips (2005) in his book *Going Sane*, contextualises the matter in his "symptomatic normality", and describes madness as a normal state for certain individuals. Winnicott considers that to be normal (or healthy), it is not enough to be sane.

Winnicott, at the age of seventy-one, defines the idea of a healthy individual related to the conception of a sound-minded one, taking us from early emotional development through the facilitating environment (or good-enough mother, or even the commonly devoted mother) to the concept we are now discussing. He thought in terms of three areas in life:[3] (a) life in our world, with interpersonal relationships and what he calls "utilization of the non-human environment"; (b) "inner life", or personal psychical reality; (c) the area of creative living.

Winnicott is thorough when he describes health as a valid and effective life and a rich, creative personality for which the cultural area, or creative living, is its most precious contribution.

Therefore, being alive is not synonymous with health, and health alone does not imply sanity; to be sane is—and this is very important—to live creatively.

Creative living

When developing the idea of creative living, Winnicott (1971) described it as coming after being and doing and being done to, but primarily as being.

Where is this area of living creatively, the third space, resting area and formlessness, of cultural experience? For Winnicott, it is not part of inner reality or outer reality, but, rather, a paradox, an area of mutuality, shared experience, juxtaposition of the psychical space of mother and baby; it is not located, however, in the baby or the mother. This third space is the location of cultural experience, creative living, and the spontaneous gesture. It is the space of objects and transitional phenomena (1971). This way of thinking reveals that in creativity there is no subjugation, no compliance, but instead, freedom, transformation, and sanity.

Winnicott wrote, in *The Family and Individual Development* (1965), that real growth eventually takes the child to an adult sense of responsibility, especially to provide security for the children of the next generation. He sees this in the work of artists, who constantly create new forms and, more than anyone else, remind us of the eternal and lifelong conflict between our impulses and a sense of security.

How does "living creatively" emerge?

In "Creativity and its origins" (1971), he believes it is necessary for a "good-enough mother" to let her baby evolve from the pleasure principle to the reality principle (either in the sense of, or beyond, primary identification (Freud, 1923b). This mother starts with an almost complete adaptation to the baby's needs and, as time goes by, she gradually adapts less, along with the baby's increasing capacity to deal with her failure. A "good-enough mother", thus, provides the baby with illusion ("illusion area"), so that the baby believes itself to be the "creator" of the breast and that the mother—the breast—is subject to the baby's magic spell. This omnipotence is a necessary moment for the baby during this illusion, and not an experience, and let us not forget that the word comes from *ludere*, that is, "play with". This experience of illusion is created at first by the mother, who must also gradually disappoint her baby; therefore, illusion starts with the perception—by the baby—that there is something else, something that is *not-me*, prior to separation anxiety, prior to perception of the object (m/other, the object-mother), as a way to endure this emotional experience the mother and the baby create, while juxtaposing both emotional experiences, the potential space or creativity space, of objects and transitional phenomena. Winnicott helps us to further develop the idea of the pure feminine element connected with "being", and the pure masculine element, connected with "doing". The origin of creativity is linked to the pure feminine element, to "being". We find in these ideas some considerations about the origin of creativity and creative living.

Winnicott wrote (1971) that the infant creates the breast, in a different language, time and again, out of the baby's capacity to love, or, we could say, with need. A subjective phenomenon that we call the mother's breast develops in the infant and, at the right time, the mother puts the real breast exactly where the baby is ready to create it. Therefore, human beings are concerned from birth onwards with the problem of the relation between what is perceived objectively and what is subjectively conceived, and, in solving this problem, there is no health for the person who has not received a good enough start from the mother. She allows the infant an intermediate area between primary creativity and objective perception, based on reality testing. Transitional phenomena are early stages of the use of illusion, necessary for the idea of a relationship with an object perceived by others as external to the subject ("Transitional objects and transitional phenomena", 1953).

Winnicott discusses the moment of primary creativity, a step further for Freud's creativity theory based on the ability to sublimate, since it places this emotional phenomenon in the first stages of life and at the centre of the mother–baby relationship.

Abram, in his dictionary of Winnicott's use of words (1996), explains that for Winnicott, primary creativity is an innate drive to health, a concept inextricably linked to several of his major topics: (a) the need of illusion at the start of life, in relation to the mother, leading to omnipotence; (b) the mother's ability to respond to the baby's spontaneous gesture, facilitating the development of a sense of self emerging from the true self; (c) the role of primary aggression and the infant's need of an object (object-mother and environment-mother) that will survive this ruthless love.

Newman (1995) describes Winnicott's concept of living creatively as the capacity, paradoxically developed with parents at first, not to be annihilated by compliance, always able to see the world afresh.

This means seeing the same street with new eyes each time, a question of depth. At first, the baby is allowed its quota of omnipotence and paradoxically to experience actually having created the world.

The healing phenomena

It will not be a surprise to the reader that it is difficult to translate the term *healing phenomena*: there is a difference between the verb *to cure* and the verb *to heal*, as mentioned above. Healing—it is worth repeating—implies a natural cure, the restoration of damaged living tissue (Mannoni, 1978), which comes from "inside".

Our life[4] is the result of positive and negative experiences. Winnicott wrote that mental health professionals dedicate a lot of their time to studying aspects related to illness, but we do not always spend the same amount of time studying health.

But "What are the healing phenomena?" the reader asks.

They are, so to speak, a set of experiences that bring us to Freud's concept of the aetiological equation or complemental series, where he states that personality is the result of three factors: constitution, childhood experiences, and current situation. In fact, aiming at greater precision, they are mainly the precipitate of very early care, especially sensorial experiences, from the time of the "thing representation" (*Dingvorstellung*), which constitutes what Winnicott called "cataloguing". These experiences might also be present at a later stage, with figurability, representation, or symbolic expression, at the time of the "word representation" (*Wortvorstellung*) and, in this case, they come, in general, as "shielding memories" or "memory forgeries". Friendship, care, acknowledgement, falling in love, and aesthetic experiences are all important parts of these healing phenomena.

Healing phenomena will be triggered and move forward towards health whenever there is a facilitating environment, creative living, or whenever creative living is resumed, referring to primary creativity as described by Winnicott, "after defrosting traumatic experiences", as in Freud, or "cumulative traumas", as described by Masud Khan, from *Beyond the Pleasure Principle* (1920g) by the creator of psychoanalysis, when the mother fails as a "protective shield".

It would be naïve, or even stupid, to say that psychoanalysis, a creation of the Age of Enlightenment at the end of the nineteenth century, "saved" mankind from pain and suffering, from "day-to-day miseries", as described by Freud, and also from neurosis.[5] The human species is approximately 50,000 years old, which is also arguable; that is, we would have nearly two or three thousand generations of ancestors behind us, which we call cultural life (Cook, 2003). In a split second, in the existence of the universe, Homo sapiens tried to ease its suffering, using more or less its ability to establish creative living, a precipitation of heritage (nature) and care (nurture), and from this the potential for physical and psychical development, which Winnicott called the *true self*: to "go on" with life, to live in society, to have some control over instinctive life. Nevertheless, splitting is necessary to create a *false self*, from an adapting self, as preferred by Masud Khan, to protect the true self.

This *true self*, protected by the *false self* (a highly organised defence), has a precipitation of positive experiences and the potential to face traumatic experiences. As explained by Winnicott, they might be friendships, special care provided during a bout of illness, poetry, and to these examples we could add an array of cultural experiences, such as religion, the fine arts, and many other creations of humanity.

Our memories, connected to the "word representation", are made by means of representations, figurability, and symbolism, and we may evoke them through conscious (secondary process) or unconscious (primary process) operations, for instance, and they will be "memory forgeries" or "shielding memories". Not exactly factual, as in external reality, but as our psychical apparatus allows us to grasp these experiences, it is able to store and "evoke" them. The concept of repression is of paramount importance in this formulation. There is also another kind of memory, no less important, described by Winnicott: cataloguing. These are memories that go back to the "word representation" from extremely archaic, sensorial, and care-giving experiences. Both these memories, when positive, are the root of health and creative living and are given, for example, through a spontaneous gesture.

Immediately after traumatic events, these *healing phenomena* are set in motion, in view of the individual's positive experiences and the existence of creative living.

The friendship, for instance, between Freud and Fliess was possibly a *healing phenomenon* set in motion for Freud, as far as we can consider it the analysis of the creator of psychoanalysis, including transferential phenomena.

Frida Kahlo's paintings, most of them self-portraits, were a way for the Mexican artist to alleviate her immense physical and psychical suffering, as were her sculptures for Camille Claudel, with which she tried to work through her emotional difficulties. The same happens, as far as we know, when a child draws or plays; yes, I am just giving an example when I say that a child drawing or playing, that is, in a spontaneous gesture, allows the working through of conflicts, which is nothing new. The therapeutic consultation developed by Winnicott starts out from this fact: in other words, we can set in motion existing healing phenomena, active or potential, in the individual through the establishment of a mutual relationship and a reliable setting, which convey hope.

Summing up, my intention is to discuss topics that I consider very simple, as follows: (a) we have mnemic registers of positive and negative experiences; (b) positive experiences form a precipitation that allows creative living and spontaneous gesture; (c) these experiences refer to primary identification; (d) these experiences (basically, sensorial or care-giving registers) come from very early stages, particularly "cataloguing"; (e) sound-minded individuals are persons who, to a greater or lesser extent, add this creative living to their life; (f) creative living enables the use, when necessary, of the healing phenomena, originating in positive experiences (cultural life, friendships, memories of care-giving, poetry, etc.); (g) these healing phenomena are more related to the verb *to heal* (natural cure) than to the verb *to cure* (from the outside, medications, medical procedures, etc.); (h) healing phenomena are set in motion in a facilitating environment, as a reliable *setting* (*placement*) that provides mutuality and hope.

Therefore, the critical statement of this text is that living creatively sets in motion healing phenomena, precipitated by positive mnemic experiences. This task takes us beyond the concept of health as the ability to love and work, introducing the idea that creative living gives us the opportunity to find happiness and a life worth living, a life to be lived creatively.

Notes

1. "It is interesting to divide thinkers into those who erect a closed system of ideas, and those whose conceptualizations are essentially open.

Winnicott is decidedly of the latter variety. At its best, his writing is an invitation to the reader to go beyond what he has written, to play with it. Some of his most characteristic formulations are put in such a compressed and laconic way that they require the active engagement of the reader's imagination in order to be understood" (Spurling, 1991, p. 60).
2. Foucault, with his normalisation concept, helps us to reconsider the matter of health. In *Surveiller et Punir* (Discipline and Punish) (1987), he comments on the normalisation of society as a medicalisation of individuals' lives.
3. Winnicott has an important theory on spaces; not only the space of illusion and potential space, but also a true cartography or geography of the individual, of the person's "inner world" and relation with the environment.
4. I could not agree more with Ivan Izquierdo, a neuroscientist who studies memory and a good friend of mine, when he says that we are what we remember . . .
5. I believe, as do several other authors, such as Walter Benjamin, that the city of modernity is the cultural broth of the neuroses.

References

Abram, J. (1996). *The Language of Winnicott. A Dictionary of Winnicott's Use of Words*. London: Karnac.

Bollas, C. (1987). *The Shadow of the Object*. New York: Free Association Books.

Cook, M. (2003). *A Brief History of the Human Race*. New York: Norton.

Foucault, M. (1987). *Surveiller et Punir. Naissance de la Prision*. Paris: Gallimard.

Freud, S. (1920g). *Beyond the Pleasure Principle. S.E., 18*: 7–64. London: Hogarth.

Freud, S. (1923b). *The Ego and the Id. S.E., 19*: 3–66. London: Hogarth.

Mannoni, O. (1978). La parte del juego. In: *Donald W. Winnicott*. Buenos Aires: Trieb. Accessed at: http://raquelzdeg.tripod.com/es_amae.htm

McDougall, J. (1992). *Plea for a Measure of Abnormality*. New York: Brunner/Mazel.

Newman, A. (1995). *Non-compliance in Winnicott's Words*. New York: New York University Press.

Phillips, A. (1988). *Winnicott*. Cambridge, MA: Harvard University Press.

Phillips, A. (2005). *Going Sane*. London: Penguin.
Spurling, L. (1991). Winnicott and the mother's face. In: *Winnicott Studies: The Journal of the Squiggle* Foundation (pp. 60–65), No. 6. London: Karnac.
Winnicott, D. W. (1953). Transitional objects and transitional phenomena. *International Journal of Psychoanalysis, 34*: 89–97.
Winnicott, D. W. (1954). Metapsychological and clinical aspects of regression within the psycho-analytical set-up. In: *Through Paediatrics to Psycho-analysis* (pp. 284–291). London: Hogarth Press, 1975.
Winnicott, D. W. (1965). *The Family and Individual Development*. London: Tavistock.
Winnicott, D. W. (1967). The concept of a healthy individual. In: C. Winnicott, R. Shepherd, & M. Davis (Eds.), *D. W. Winnicott: Home Is Where We Start From: Essays by a Psychoanalyst* (pp. 21–39). New York: Penguin, 1975.
Winnicott, D. W. (1971). Creativity and its origins. In: *Playing and Reality* (pp. 87–114). London: Tavistock.

CHAPTER TEN

To heal or create, to create and heal: in search of their author

Murielle Gagnebin

*Creation of a work, creation of a being:
the birth of the "chimera"[1]*

The aim is to demonstrate that psychoanalysis is at once a work of healing and a work of culture. Although healing by analysis may be articulated in terms of what Freud refers to as *Kulturarbeit* in his *New Introductory Lectures* (1933a), and later "the advance in intellectuality" (*Geistigkeit*) (1939a p. 111) in *Moses and Monotheism*, and although *Kulturarbeit* is generally defined as an "individual–collective" transformative work of human reality, I shall introduce yet another factor.

Greatly indebted as I am in my clinical work to the now classic theories of Michel de M'Uzan, I shall bring into play the "chimera" and his "paradoxical system"[2] (de M'Uzan, 1977, 1994, 2005) as crucial pieces in this endeavour. I shall, therefore, concern myself with a rather specific moment in treatment when some patients diversely express a certain amount of fear: not a fear generated by some external object, or stimulated by some imago, but a fear quite simply of analysis, a fear of the analytic phenomenon *itself*. The early stages of treatment generally take place quite happily; the patient has set about recounting his past with varying degrees of curiosity or talent, has expressed affect and emotion towards persons close to him, has reconstructed poles of interest and envisaged a number of obstacles to their achievement, at times seeking help while expressing some anxiety about their hypothetical eventualities. The patient has endured agonies of silence. In short, the patient, at some length, has for us swept through the spectrum of inhibitions and symptoms, discovering the treasures of childhood sexuality—the latter swiftly implicated as the driving force of the former. The patient has also more or less rapidly grasped the various modes of free association and has even enjoyed its pleasures. What is more, the patient has confronted the fantastical dramaturgy of dreams, the fabulous nature of their recounting and their sometimes destabilising interpretations. All this has taken time.

The patient has also gradually become aware that multiple accounts of his past form, in fact, a *fable*. Hence, far from hoping for some sudden lifting of infantile amnesia as a release from his ills, he has moved towards what Viderman (1970), after de M'Uzan, has called *construction* in analysis.

It is at this point that sometimes the cure, which had hitherto enjoyed a very conventional development, seems as if to slip away from the analysand, and—from time to time—the analyst, and now obeys some other, arcane determinism.

Of this new direction taken by the process, we might have some intuition, especially when the mental functioning of the protagonists sometimes adopts archaic modalities roundly characterised by primary identification. A new and baffling grammar of thought emerges then, founded on the sudden, unexpected appearance of strange or even *monstrous* images, of acutely condensed verbal formulations in the analyst, no longer responding to "secondarised" language, but favouring metaphor and metonymy; thought that de M'Uzan describes as "paradoxical".

At this juncture, the regime of analysis changes profoundly and, from a topographical perspective, the crisis develops very clearly in the preconscious, even where it borders on the unconscious. Discourse proceeds by diatax, and condensation rules. We should not be surprised to see the patient affected by the onset of phenomena pertaining to depersonalisation, albeit more often than not in a minor mode. And the change in question hints at increasingly labile identity.

It is, therefore, not uncommon at this point for the patient to begin to experience fear. Such distress in the face of what I shall call the "work of an other" has more than one consequence.

That analysis may be considered analogous to a creation seems to me to merit some attention.

Now it is time to appeal to artistic creation in order to examine this particular moment as it is expressed in treatment. Consequently, we will be exploring the singular instant when the work, having gradually acquired the qualities and status of an *Ego-Alter* (Gagnebin, 2011), begins to exist by itself.

Therefore, I situate myself before the work of art as if I had forgotten the history of the work, the artist, and his times, that is to say, in opposition to any psychobiography or pathography. In a sense, I take Bion's advice to forget the patient's history each time the patient arrives. This, for me, is a question of receiving perceptions coming from the work in order to metabolise them (cf. Bion's alpha function in the presence of raw sensory material, free of associations). Essentially this means to propose being "in reverie" with and around the work. My free associations "in appearance" form something like another virtual work, a kind of "second skin", to use Bick's terminology (1968). This second skin contains excitations stirred in us by face-to-face encounter with the work while, for a time, we have become analogues of the creator of the work, always considered its first active spectator.

This means that the principal aim of any work of art is truly economic and cathartic. It also means that the place or position afforded the symbolising and transformative capabilities of creators, "led as if in spite of themselves", is imperative. Furthermore, it means that these capacities treat their subjective suffering and propel them towards "subjectification", since artists, through the creation of their work, seek the creation of their own being. In analysis, this is when we encounter the construction of the "chimera" and, in works of art, the "pacifying" or "disruptive" manifestations of the *Ego-Alter*. The latter is a maker of strangeness (*étrangeté*) and powerful economic modifications.

The life of the work, therefore, develops much deeper than the channels of sublimation, analogous to the cure which emerges with its own modality eluding analysand and analyst as if guided by a third person, proof at this profoundly modulating moment of its authenticity.

But who is this "third person", this *Ego-Alter*?

Suggested metapsychological models presiding over the construction of a work

Is a model a dream, a "directed perception" (Gagnebin, 1992), a "watchful waiting" (Minazzoli, 1990, p. 97), or perhaps a fiction and, hence, a construction?

Responding to a certain logic of life, that is to say, within the "life of forms" (Focillon, 1943), the construction—in the Freudian sense—of a work (artistic, philosophical, or ideological) is undoubtedly related to the "uncertain" (*l'incertain*)[3], where what is vague, or even improbable, plays a determining role: determining in the sense that various queries are expressed and transport, along with commonly posited creative ardour (psychic) bruises, anxiety and, at times, sudden sterility. This also means that the "uncertain" is worked on within highly and richly organised systems. Throughout "Constructions in analysis" (Freud, 1937d), does Freud not seek to demonstrate that analytic construction is also at times a work of deduction? Constructions and deductions are adept at forming a constellation. This constellation, inevitably threatened equally with eclipse by brilliant flares or by "black holes", magnets apt to fuel new hypotheses, their development bearing the indelible mark of those preceding them, is, thus, matter in constant fusion, evolving over and over again.

In his 1937 text, Freud repeatedly insists that every construction, every fiction, *acts* on the patient, who reorganises, in light of this, a new model, which pours in (Freud, 1937d). For this reason, in the construction of hermeneutic models in art, I privilege not the aesthetic but rather the poietic (*poiein*): the philosophical advancement of the science of art that is produced (Valéry, 1937) rather than merely received (*aesthesis*). The poietic accentuates, in terms of the way a work comes into being, the economic and dynamic perspectives of psychoanalysis.

As for the model conceived according to the perspective of an epistemology of the psychoanalytic notion of construction, I prefer to compare it to a fiction rather than a dream. For Freud, dreams always have a content of strict truth, whereas fiction has but one tense; it is metamorphosable because it is always *incomplete* (Freud, 1937d), although it possesses a *sign of the truth*, which Freud stigmatises in the well-known "I never thought of that," uttered by the patient when the intervention–interpretation rings true (Freud, 1937d).

It is to this *"that"* to which I would now like to draw our examination of the question of a model in the ar "That" eludes the artist not because it belongs to his uncc rather, because "that" pertains to an *unconscious of th* structed as an extension both of the Winnicottian transitional object (Winnicott, 1971) and of the transitional subject as suggested by de M'Uzan,[4] clearly exceeding André Green's trans-narcissistic object (Green, 1992). To speak of an unconscious of the work in a literal sense, in other words as an object or a thing, might be disconcerting. Artists, however, use the impersonal when they speak of the quality of their work: "That holds up the wall!"[5], or "That's got some juice in it!" From the mouths of individuals who, incidentally, tend to be very narcissistic, these expressions sustain the legitimacy of likening the work to a being, as provocative as it might seem. Thus, the work of art becomes comparable to a living creature endowed, just like an individual, with a particular "psychic structure" and, like a person, has a destiny and even a fate.

In this way, I have formulated *two* "fictions" for the apprehension of works of art.

In the first, I regard the work of art as being structured *like* a symptom and I search the interplay of drive and defence system set in motion as well as the return of the repressed (Gagnebin, 1987).

From this perspective, the finished work sees the light of the day, is here, and now reveals *the narration of this dream*, the form given it by the author certainly, but an author also *governed* by all the attendant retentions, disguises, and evasions that are the work of an unconscious—still the author's—coming up, nevertheless, against another *force*: one that is progressively born *within* the work itself and produced *by* the work itself.

This perspective equates the work of writing, or production of the work (the poietics or bringing into being of the work), to the action of repression aimed at the creative instinct (drive) *itself* and also to the masked and wily return of the repressed, already so often party to the unique requisites of the work in its formal autonomy.

In the second "fiction", I envisage the work of art through the prism of the Aristotelian causal system revisited by the contributions of psychoanalysis. This I have called my "quaternary metapsychological modelling of creation" (Gagnebin, 1987, pp. 187–189, 1994, pp. 205–215, 1999, pp. 20–138, 2004a, pp. 38–103, 181–203).

Thus, following Aristotle (1973a,b), we might distinguish in a statue, for example, its *material cause*, what the statue is made of: marble, or clay; its *efficient cause*, that which effects the transition from potentiality to action: the gesture, the hammer, or the force of the sculptor; its *formal cause*, that which makes a thing what it is: in this case, its statue essence: Dionysus, for example; last, its *final cause*, the reference for which something is made: this particular Dionysus, with this bunch of red grapes, hewn for the purpose of the cult devoted to him. For Aristotle, each of these causes is *immanent* to matter itself, or, in other terms, *it is matter that summons the sculptor's gesture* and directs his intentions and work. The translation of this system of causation to the psychoanalytic domain seems to me quite conceivable.

A work with great drive capital (Freud, 1911b, 1930a)—the *material cause*—will, thus, abound in features conjuring up various categories of the drive (dirty, viscous, smashed up, raw, cutting, rough, etc.); a work with a powerful *formal cause* (David, 1975) will attest to the successful integration of "internal spectators" (de M'Uzan, 1977, pp. 3–27) unique to each artist. Indeed, artists derive their capacity to link from their ability to conceive of the fundamental union of their parents formed in the primal scene. Hence, a work wrought by an intense formal cause will bring out a tendency towards concatenation (loops, knots, spirals, volutes, etc.), *emboîtement* (*mise-en-abyme* (a "world within a world"), nested forms, etc.) or triangulated relationships attesting to access to the famous Oedipus (since that is what this is about): the decisive moment when children accept the union of their parents and their own solitude. A work marked by the *final cause* (Segal, 1952), the capacity to mourn, will outdo itself in the art of choices, with ellipsis, selection, and renunciation. Last, a work characterised by an *efficient cause* (Gagnebin, 1987, p. 195), ingenious and meticulous, will by no means reify its method: there will be no consecration of pre-genitality. The instincts will never be exposed crudely as such. No: transformed by the stylistic necessities they inspire, they highlight instead the *skill*, *savoir-faire*, and *style*, that is to say, the artist's freedom wrestling with demands of the medium. This is the apotheosis of the drive for mastery having indeed enabled processes of sublimation (Gagnebin, 1996b).

The main thrust of this heuristic model is that the freer the play between these four causes, the stronger the work will be. Any obstacle encumbering any of the causes turns the creation into a *minor* work.

It might, however, occur that a work displaying one or another shortcoming results in an *authentic* work. In this case, the weak point becomes the site of additional action demanded by the work around its gape: a graft.[6] I point out once again that although these *causes* are psychically defined, they are inscribed *within* the work itself, which gradually metamorphoses into a real *person*. Consider Balzac's Frenhofer, who so passionately loved his *Belle Noiseuse*. In so many examples, the work becomes a true *Ego-Alter* of the artist, commanding him to use this or that adjective, or demanding that he paint with such and such a blue, and so on.

These *causes*, each intricated with the others, thus shed light on creative progression and pin down certain specific forms.

These two models permit an intimate *re-staging* of the construction (poiesis) of each work of art and the discovery in each work of the precise moment where the exegete, following the artist and as an attentive spectator, perceives in the work the force of an other that I have quite often been compelled to call *Ego-Alter* (Gagnebin, 2004a, p. 278).[7]

The Ego-Alter and its work, much deeper than sublimation

But whoever would this famous *Ego-Alter* be? I shall take painting as an example, summarising thus: there are works that *lull* the spectator, transmitting soothing rhythms. Equally, there are *unsettling* works that feature confrontation and shock.

Thus, we return to the epistemology of the notion of construction. What does this fiction of the *Ego-Alter* translate and what treason does it commit from the point of view of epistemology? This question amounts to asking about the substance of *any*, and I stress *any, fiction*? Did not Freud say of the psychic apparatus that it was a "fiction"? What is the substance of our models? What are the psychical forces in us that continually construct and reconstruct them for us?

I would venture to argue at this point that we are all relatively moved to act by projection. Projection conceived at first as disavowal of something unbearable (Freud, 1911b) evincing the failure of repression, even the breaking out of the repressed (we are reminded of Freud in his 1937d text: madness that contains a fragment of *historical truth*), but also projection becoming a tool for understanding.[8]

The work of art could thus be considered an epistemological model of the psychoanalytic notion of construction. Is not a work of art the product of a *hermeneutic weaving* between what it offers us to see, hear, and understand and the response it is given in each era depending on the *state of knowledge* of the times and the *psychic contribution* of its receiver (the spectator, listener, reader, etc.).

The in-between and the rule of "comme si, comme ça"[9]

To say that the site of the work of art is the *space in between* returns us to that so very fertile notion of the "chimera" proposed by de M'Uzan (1978). It also brings us back to our initial proposal regarding the epistemological point of view of the psychoanalytic notion of construction which, following Mallarmé, postulates the fictional nature of any method (*"Toute méthode est une fiction"* ("Every method is a fiction"), Mallarmé, 1869, p. 851), in other words, the self-reflexive property of every fiction. In this way, the mode of analytic construction is twofold. One is the "as if" (*comme si*) or "may-be", spelt with a hyphen and inscribed in the order of a hypothesis that shackles us between the contingent and the plausible. The other is the mode of "may be", spelt this time without hyphen, meaning all that is specific to fiction, fable, and dreams, which, through painting, literary writing, film, and music truly actualise the virtual; it indicates not so much a possible realisation as a truly extant being.

The hyphenated "may-be" is the interpretation of the exegete, indeed of the analyst. The second, unhyphenated, follows the intervention–interpretation or exegesis in so far as they unfold a mythical place (*topos*) that functions like an "as if". But how could this do without the efficiency inherent to the deduction involved in every construction (Freud, 1937d) if, as de M'Uzan has maintained since 1993 (de M'Uzan, 1994, p. 170), this "as if" were not understood to be a true "like that" (*comme ça*)?

The rule of *comme si, comme ça*[10] as expressed by de M'Uzan, deft at bringing out the uncertain in order to deduce the feasible, the false to construct the true, produces resonance in the psychoanalyst–exegete with epistemological models of construction in art as an appeal to understand the resemblance (we love only what we see in ourselves, as Freud states in 1930), and to understand it not only in a future perfect mode, but also as a future, an opening, an aperture, interpreted as the desiring *positivity inherent to all incompleteness* (*inachèvement*).

Model, fiction and construction thus place great importance on a beneficial *need to invent*, always to be reconsidered certainly, but without doubt *characteristic to* or the specific property of this *homo faber* that in essence we continue to be.

The lifting of conflicts: reparation or eternal disquiet? From the Alter Ego to the "Ego-Alter"

The French writer, Marcel Proust, repeatedly declared that behind his character Albertine in *A la Recherche du Temps Perdu* were concealed a number of women, just as behind the "bell tower at Méséglise" there were many bell towers, and that it was useless to seek the original image. For this writer, the artist surpasses the man; an essential distinction that would, therefore, be the work's fundamental reason to exist.

Nevertheless, pathography has long resisted—exactly what Freud developed in *Leonardo da Vinci and a Memory of his Childhood* (1910c). Even Klein considered the work the projection of the artist's internal world in the mode of clear and distinct equivalence, or, in other terms, of "symbolic equations": the big fish represents the penis, the magnificent ocean the mother's body, etc. We also know about the role of envy (Klein) and destructiveness (Freud, 1919h) in the work of creation.

By contrast, it is the notion of *conflict*, so present in Freud, in particular in his *Moses of Michelangelo*, which stands out in my mind.

This conflict pits the dimension of the drive against the countercathexis and enables the adroit return of the ever-masked repressed.

For the Freud of *Moses*, the perspective of conflict situates the subject *par excellence* within the economic model. This then raises the question: what forces are present and how are they articulated (the dynamic point of view)? This perspective of conflict above all brings to the fore the basic dimension of repression, defences, ruses, and *a posteriori*, that is to say, of various metabolisms or sublimations and of diversions (cf. the method used by Freud in *The Moses of Michelangelo* (1914b)) where the psychoanalyst, attentive to the silences and the unsaid in the work and its exegetes, practises a consummate art of making *detours* by setting about piecing together the *erased* history of the figure.

A further consequence of divergence concerning the respective roles of destructiveness and conflict is the notion of *reparation* (Segal, 1952) to which, following Melanie Klein and Hanna Segal, many French psychoanalysts have subscribed; notably Chasseguet-Smirgel, with her distinction between reparation of the object and reparation of the subject (Chasseguet-Smirgel, 1971, 1984).

The difference that separates the Kleinian from the Freudian on this point is that, for the Kleinian, it is the figuration of the mother as primary object that is restored: true reconciliation takes place. This is what Meltzer calls the "sermon to the siblings". Whereas for the Freudian, at first, certainly, it is the appropriation of aesthetic sensations connected to matter (colours, their saturation, the work's pattern and rhythm), there is *asymptotic tension* towards the reconstruction of an always insufficiently established primary narcissism. Later on, these qualities are involved in the interplay between forces and counter-forces, emotions and upsetting surprises, always indicating conflict of an Oedipal nature, with its calls to binding, or even to triangulation, and its demands to work through lack and loss.

What is repaired and what tends asymptotically to be repaired are, therefore, in theory, not the same thing at all. This is perhaps the full extent marked by the Kleinian conception of the pre-Oedipal, a somewhat useless notion for the classic Freudian, who makes do with the Oedipus complex as the essential marker of symbolic castration on whose basis everything is constantly rewritten and reinvented.

Hence, attacks on the mother's body, envy at work, and restoration of the mother, on the one hand; on the other, asymptotic restoration of primary narcissism and, of course, the compulsion to access the Oedipus and castration complexes that marks from that moment forward the capacity to mourn: the spectator's imaginary is, thus, variously called upon to situate itself before a work that is Kleinian or a work that is Freudian in nature.

Yet another divergence distinguishes the Kleinian apparatus from the Freudian. Why do we create? The Kleinian will reply that it is to attack and then eventually repair the primary object, the mother.

By contrast, to this same question—why do we create?—the Freudian analyst will reply that there are generally individuals endowed with an unusually strong and demanding sexual constitution that requires a particular treatment of the powerfully mobilised part drives, in this way avoiding their integration into genitality. This is how the construction of a neurosis might have remained imperfectly operative. It is a matter of the problem of sublimation. Consequently, to create is destiny rather than freedom (*"une fatalité et non une liberté"*[11] (de M'Uzan, 2004, pp. 139–141, 2008, pp. 35–46). It is the trace of the way this is mastered that is found in the work, which progressively makes itself into and becomes, as I have said, a figure in its own right, but with the help, as we have seen, of the intervention of a strange being: the *Ego-Alter*.

This is to say that, for the Freudian that I am, the work would have, so to speak, an unconscious of its own and that the style, if the artist's ego, his know-how, and his talent is involved, goes through a series of tests marked first by some profound loss of identity and then by the intervention of what I have called an *Ego-Alter*.

It is time to return to the phenomenon not of creativity, but, rather, of *creation*. Since 1978 (Gagnebin 1974, 1978, 1984, 1987, 1997, 1999, 2004a,b, 2011) our work has continually focused on this question, and it is in the trajectory of this work and thanks to the comments of artists and artist–analysands that the need gradually imposed itself upon me to postulate this *Ego-Alter* that implies a complete reversal of commonly accepted terms. It is no longer a case of "the artist and his work", but, rather, in a fabulous reversal, "the work and its artist". There was a need not only to show the artist's regressive capabilities in the work of engendering, which has been well mapped out by others, but also to push this very regressive faculty further still, to the territories, so rich and so disquieting, of depersonalisation. For it is when the artist, confronting psychotic, persecutory, or even depressive anxieties, breaks through the barrier of his ego, installs in it a "permanent inquietude" (de M'Uzan, 2009) and chooses to reverse Freud's "Where id was, there ego shall be" in de M'Uzan's judicious formula, "Where ego was, there id shall be", it is then that the *Ego-Alter* may appear. The work of art is no longer the manifestation of reparation, or even the site of conflicting vectors; it becomes the vessel of this "permanent inquietude" that is apt to unsettle and agitate; it is one of the domains of the *Ego-Alter*.

Then what is this *Ego-Alter*?

Far from a banal comparison with some *double*, as Freud relates his experience in "A disturbance of memory on the Acropolis" (1936a) (where Romain Rolland functions as his material double, as did a number of other flesh and blood beings in his creative trajectory: Fliess, Jung, and so on), the *Ego-Alter* is nothing like an *alter ego*.

No, the *Ego-Alter* comes from the work *itself*, which establishes its autonomy and *authenticity*. But what is this *Ego-Alter*? What is it made of? Where does it come from? What is its action and what its fate? Does our model of a cruel but necessary creative function hold water? It is these very serious questions that I have attempted here to answer.

A poet–analysand said to me, "I do not choose my words; it is they that compel me." Another analysand—this time a musician—confided to me in more alarming terms, "It's constantly as if I were hearing a broadcast, but there is another one that's scrambled and scrambles everything else." When the *Ego-Alter* appears, it is, therefore, not without risk.

What is most alive in art: the Ego-Alter

Of the *Moses of Michelangelo*, Freud reviews the various necessarily incomplete, even contradictory interpretations of art historians and translators of the Old Testament. This said, faithful to the strange and powerful impact exerted on him by this sculpture, Freud insists, "And yet do not those very endeavours speak for the fact that we feel the need of discovering in it [the work] some *source of power beyond them* [the form and content] alone?" (Freud 1914c, p. 213, my italics), a source that perhaps involves taking into account the Unconscious itself?

I have sought to display this "other source" in all its richness throughout the course of my writing.

Gracq writes,

> The novel ... is only drawn out of nothingness by the constraint of a demanding image imposed on the novelist throughout, an obsession not entirely literary in nature. "Adorable phantom who has seduced me, lift your veil!" pleads the maker of novels—but the silent apparition places a pen in his hand. (Gracq, 1980, p. 167)

The *Ego-Alter* is able to intervene decisively. Its qualities are now known to us: intrusiveness, interference, intransigence, impatience. Its properties, also: adroit at compelling the artist to draw out what is most authentic from himself, able to perturb and, at the same time, to expand the artist's sensoriality, confining him to solitude, confronting him with multiple experiences of contiguity (both soothing and shocking), exposing him to the formless, yet setting before him the hope of the anti-traumatic; the *Ego-Alter*, as peremptory as it is unexpected, now has a face.

In a similar way this being that is unquestionably akin to notions of the "myself-person" (*la personne de moi-même*)[12] and the "paraphrenic twin" (*jumeau paraphrénique*) advanced by de M'Uzan diverges from them none the less (1999, 2005, pp. 15–41). Indeed, that which distinguishes the *Ego-Alter* in relation to these hypotheses is that, although its roots lie deep in the most intimate, it is also a product of the most general, historically as well as culturally. Does it not impose arbitrary or aleatory forms, even when, through this rigour, it paves the way for innovatory figures, often on the edge of the abyss, which I have called the "spectrum of sublimation";[13] thanks to such innovations, art persists by renewing itself. Understandably, then, following de M'Uzan, I consequently consider that a well-conducted analytical session may be likened to a work of art (de M'Uzan, 1977, p. 90, Gagnebin, 1996a, p. 8).

At this point, it might be opportune to return to Freud, who, in the first issue of the *International Journal*, notes that a difficulty of psychoanalysis is that "the ego is not master in its own house"! (Freud, 1917a, p. 143).

According to Phillips, there are certain concepts that test the unconscious. Would not our *Ego-Alter* be one of them, sowing as it does turbulence, division, and questioning?

The analytic cure is certainly not as concrete as a work of art. The latter, on the other hand, with its heavy materiality, impacted by so many struggles and so much risk-taking, offers us its unmediated being-there.

The *Ego-Alter*, thus, appears as the lever to induce sublimation by engaging the process capable of guiding and preserving this neutralised energy so necessary for creation. Without an *Ego-Alter*, there is no authentic work, as I would be willing to defend.

The work might, therefore, even possess a selfish organisation: endowed with its *energy*, it allows itself to become engaged in various endeavours so long as they preserve its privileged status that confers upon the work its unique brilliance and ontological density.

One analysand, referring to the effect of art on her, once told me, "In art there is something that moves me enormously. Art, *that* makes me soar, *that* blows me away!"

May this contribution shine some light on what Freud—and so many others after him—calls the mystery of genius.

I shall entrust the conclusion of this chapter devoted to the interventions of the *Ego-Alter* in the creative process (of works of art and of beings) to two analysands, two artists moreover, to whom this exegete owes so much. The first, melancholic owing to feelings of "dispossession", declares, "My depression is like the feeling of not being able to speak on my own behalf", whereas the second advances, "A new medium is like a new interlocutor!"

The life of the *Ego-Alter* is just beginning . . .

Notes

1. The "chimera" denotes a kind of new organism resulting from the meeting of two unconsciouses: those of analysand and analyst; a monster possessing its own modalities of functioning. The growth of this mythical infant is affected by various influences originating in its creators. Certain of these influences relate to the structure of the analysand, but we must also take into account those that depend upon the analyst, a product of a particular tendency towards primary identification and of tolerance of experiences of depersonalisation (cf. de M'Uzan, 1978, 1994, pp. 33–44).

2. The "paradoxical system" is an original mode of psychic functioning in the analyst, invaded during the session by strange representations, unexpected phrases, abstract formulae, colourful imagery, reveries worked through to varying degrees, and so on. These thoughts, images, and words, which entail a sort of momentary insanity in the analyst, correspond to psychic processes unfolding in the analysand that have not yet been detected. The most fundamental feature of this phenomenon is that it precedes understanding *both* of the material *and* of the phantasies the patient is able to formulate (cf. de M'Uzan, 1977, pp. 164–181).

3. Cf. Focillon's *La Vie des Formes* in his description of *l'incertain* to describe the continual movement of form within the inner life, that is to say, which has not yet been externalised.
4. De M'Uzan, 1999, 2005, p. 22, cf.

> This is a psychical being whose traces, which persist throughout the individual's history, allow both place and nature to be inferred from them. These traces are less evident than those of pre-genital phases of libidinal development, but they are, however, conspicuous at the bursting on to the scene of the figure of the double, in its often evoked representations. (Translated for this edition)

5. From the French "*Ça tient le mur!*" meaning literally, "That holds (up) the wall!" Compare the description given by George Bataille of the anamorphic condition of the paintings on the walls of Lascaux (Biles, 2007, p. 74).
6. An action analogous to what Kant, in distinguishing the anomalous from the abnormal, sees in nature when it comes to its own aid in order to survive (*Selbsthilfe*, self-defence; Kant, 1790; Gagnebin, 1997, pp. 1301–1310).
7. I depart on this point from Marion Milner and her "dream person one would like to give to" (Milner, 1950, p. 154). Milner considers the content of a work of art "an externalisation, through its shapes and lines and colours, of the unique psycho-physical rhythm of the person making it" (p. 191). She goes as far as to wish that the artist may once more find this "all-out body giving of infancy"; this, her "unconscious hankering to return to the blissful surrender [of infancy]", underlines Anna Freud in her foreword. But her notion of rhythm, in her reflection, later boils down simply to "primitive rhythms, such as sucking, free bowel movement, babbling, masturbating" (p. 224), which is not entirely in keeping with current ideas.
8. Freud (1912–1913), and Kahn, for whom figurability is the result of a work that is

> ... the most tormented by desire and by the infantile, the most conflictive of the instincts bound up in it must find the most anodyne expression. This, then, is the plasticity of formal elements, their capacity to create median elements, their ability to commingle, their possible subjection to the constraint of elaborating the sum of impressions into a whole that fixes the selection of the elements. (Kahn, 2001, translated for this edition)

9. Translator's note: literally: "as if, like that", an expression roughly equivalent to the English "so-so", "sort of" or "neither good nor bad".

10. De M'Uzan writes,

> When the analyst interprets the comments of his patient, his dreams, memories, parapraxes and so on, he is willingly affirmative and says, "Things are done *like that (comme ça)*". And yet, he well knows that his "like that" is but an "as if". But nothing happens if this "*as if*" is not at the same time accepted as a genuine *like that*. (De M'Uzan, 1994)

11. Translator's note: *fatalité* in French can also mean "misfortune", "mischance", or even "curse"—an unhappy circumstance of fate.
12. De M'Uzan renders this grammar of interpretation thus:

> ... the patient feels dimly that he is no longer sure of knowing *who* speaks, but from *where* it speaks. ... When there is doubt as to identities and when the words exchanged do not appear to come entirely from one of the protagonists or entirely from the other, or even when they appear to come from both, the interpretation is for the patient as if uttered by his *self-person*, that is to say, by his double; his double that speaks from a transitional place in this area of indecisive individuation that I am tempted to call an *everyman's land*. From there, the interpretation acquires power of conviction, thanks to which it has a better chance of being assimilated. (De M'Uzan, 1994, p. 103, translated for this edition)

References

Aristotle (1973a). Physics. In: R. McKeon (Ed.), *Introduction to Aristotle* (pp. 114–145). Chicago, IL: University of Chicago Press.

Aristotle (1973b). Metaphysics. In: R. McKeon (Ed.), *Introduction to Aristotle* (pp. 268–331). Chicago, IL: University of Chicago Press.

Bick, E. (1968). The experience of the skin in early object-relations. *International Journal of Psychoanalysis*, 49: 484–486. Reprinted in: A. Briggs (Ed.), *Surviving Space: Papers on Infant Observation* (pp. 55–59). London: Karnac, 2002.

Biles, J. (2007). *Ecce Monstrum: Georges Bataille and the Sacrifice of Form*. New York: Fordham University Press.

Chasseguet-Smirgel, J. (1971). *Pour une psychanalyse de l'art et de la créativité* [Towards a psychoanalysis of art and creativity]. Paris: Payot-Rivages.

Chasseguet-Smirgel, J. (1984). *Éthique et esthétique de la perversion* [Ethics and aesthetics of perversion]. Seyssel: Champ Vallon.

David, C. (1975). La bisexualité psychique [Psychical bisexuality]. *Revue Française de Psychanalyse, 39*(5–6): 713–856.

De M'Uzan, M. (1977). *De l'Art à la Mort: Itinéraire psychanalytique* [From Art to Death: A Psychoanalytic Itinerary]. Paris: Gallimard.

De M'Uzan, M. (1978). La bouche de l'inconscient [The mouth of the unconscious]. *Nouvelle Revue de Psychanalyse, 17*: 89–98.

De M'Uzan, M. (1994). *La bouche de l'inconscient. Essais sur l'interprétation.* Paris: Gallimard.

De M'Uzan, M. (1999). Le jumeau paraphrénique, ou aux confins de l'identité [The paraphrenic twin, or at the limits of identity]. *Revue Française de Psychanalyse, 63*(4): 1135–1151.

De M'Uzan, M. (2004). Addiction, problématique identitaire et activité creatrice: le tonus identitaire de base. [Addiction, the problem of identity and creative activity: the basal identity tone]. *Revue Française de Psychanalyse, 68*(2): 591–597.

De M'Uzan, M. (2005). *Aux confins de l'identité* [At the limits of identity]. Paris: Gallimard.

De M'Uzan, M. (2008). *L'artiste et le psychanalyste [The artist and the psychoanalyst].* Paris: Presses Universitaires de France.

De M'Uzan, M. (2009). L'inquiétante étrangeté, ou "Je ne suis pas celle que vous croyez" [The uncanny, or "I am not who you think I am"]. In: *Monographies et débats de Psychanalyse* (pp. 89–98). Paris: Presses Universitaires de France.

Focillon, H. (1943). *The Life of Forms in Art*, G. Kubler (Trans.). New York: MIT Press.

Freud, S. (1910c). *Leonardo da Vinci and a Memory of His Childhood. S.E., 11*: 59–137. London: Hogarth.

Freud, S. (1911b). Formulations on the two principles of mental functioning. *S.E., 12*: 218–226. London: Hogarth.

Freud, S. (1912–1913). *Totem and Taboo. S.E. 13*: 1–161. London: Hogarth.

Freud, S. (1914b). *The Moses of Michelangelo. S.E., 13*: 209–238. London: Hogarth.

Freud, S. (1917a). A difficulty in the path of psycho-analysis. *S.e., 17*: 135–144.

Freud, S. (1923b). *The Ego and the Id. S.E., 19*: 3–66. London: Hogarth.

Freud, S. (1930a). *Civilization and its Discontents. S.E., 21*: 57–145. London: Hogarth.

Freud, S. (1933a). *New Introductory Lectures on Psycho-analysis. S.E., 22*: 3–182. London: Hogarth.

Freud, S. (1936a). A disturbance of memory on the Acropolis. *S.E., 22*: 239–248. London: Hogarth.

Freud, S. (1937d). Constructions in analysis. *S.E.*, *23*: 257–269. 265–266. London: Hogarth.
Freud, S. (1939a). *Moses and Monotheism*. *S.E.*, *23*: 3–137. London: Hogarth.
Gagnebin, M. (1974). *Czapski, la main et l'espace* [Czapski, the hand and space]. Lausanne: L'Age d'Homme.
Gagnebin, M. (1978). *Fascination de la laideur* [The fascination of ugliness]. *La main et le temps* [The hand and time]. Lausanne: L'Age d'Homme.
Gagnebin, M. (1984). *L'irreprésentable ou les silences de l'œuvre* [The unrepresentable or the silences of the work]. Paris: Presses Universitaires de France.
Gagnebin, M. (1987). *Les ensevelis vivants. Des mécanismes psychiques de la création* [Buried alive. Psychic mechanisms of creation]. Seyssel: Champ Vallon.
Gagnebin, M. (1992). *Flaubert et Salammbô. Genèse d'un texte* [Flaubert and Salammbô. Genesis of a text]. Paris: Presses Universitaires de France.
Gagnebin, M. (1994). *Pour une esthètique de la psychanalyse. L'Artiste, stratège de l'Inconscient* [Towards an aesthetics of psychoanalysis. The artist, strategist of the unconscious] (pp. 33–153). Paris: Presses Universitaires de France.
Gagnebin, M. (1996a). *Michel de M'Uzan*. Paris: Presses Universitaires de France.
Gagnebin, M. (1996b). L'Esthétique comme clinique de l'excès. Essai sur D. Lynch [The aesthetic as clinic of the excess: essay on D. Lynch]. *Figures de l'art*, *2*: 271–286.
Gagnebin, M. (1997). Défense et illustration de la notion de greffe "métaphorisante" [Defence and illustration of the concept of the "metaphorising" graft]. *Revue française de psychanalyse*, *LXI*(4): 1301–1310.
Gagnebin, M. (1999). *Du divan à l'écran. Montages cinématographiques, montages interprétatifs* [From the couch to the screen. Cinematic editing, interpretative editing]. Paris: Presses Universitaires de France.
Gagnebin, M. (2004a). *Authenticité du faux* [The authenticity of the false]. Paris: Presses Universitaires de France, pp. 38–103, 181–203.
Gagnebin, M. (2004b). *Pierre Lesieur: une esthétique de l'analogie* [Pierre Lesieur: aesthetics of analogy] Lausanne: Y. F.
Gagnebin, M. (2011). *En deça de la sublimation: l'Ego-Alter* [This side of sublimation: the Ego-Alter] Paris: Presses Universitaires de France.
Gracq, J. (1980). *En Lisant, en Écrivant* [Reading, writing]. Paris: Corti.
Green, A. (1992). The unbinding process. Reprinted in: *On Private Madness* (pp. 331–359). London: Hogarth Press, 1986.
Kahn, L. (2001). L'action de la forme [The action of the form]. *Revue Française de Psychanalyse*, *65*: 983–1056.

Kant, E. (1790). *Critique of the Power of Judgement*. New York: Cambridge University Press.
Mallarmé, S. (1869). *Proses diverses. Œuvres Complètes*. Paris: Pléiade.
Milner, M. (1950). *On Not Being Able to Paint*. London: Taylor & Francis.
Minazzoli, A. (1990). *La première ombre: reflexion sur le miroir et la pensée* [The first shadow: reflections on the mirror and thought]. Paris: Minuit.
Segal, H. (1952). A psychoanalytic approach to aesthetics. *International Journal of Psychoanalysis, 33*: 196–207. Reprinted in: M. Klein, P. Heimann, & R. Money-Kyrle (Eds.), *New Directions in Psychoanalysis* (pp. 384–405). London: Tavistock, 1955 and in *The Work of Hanna Segal*. New York: Jason Aronson, 1981.
Valéry, P. (1937). Première leçon du cours de poétique [First lesson from a course in poetics]. In: J. Hytier (Ed.), *Paul Valéry. Œuvres complètes* (Volume I, pp. 1342–1358). Paris: Pléiade, 1965.
Viderman, S. (1970). *La construction en analyse* [Construction in analysis]. Paris: Denoël.
Winnicott, D. W. (1971). *Playing and Reality*, London: Tavistock.

CHAPTER ELEVEN

The greatest love of all

Gabriela Goldstein

"The Poet makes himself a seer by a long, gigantic and rational *derangement of all the senses*. All forms of love, suffering, and madness. He searches himself. He exhausts all poisons in himself and keeps only their quintessences. Unspeakable torture where he needs all his faith, all his superhuman strength, where he becomes among all men the great patient, the great criminal, the one accursed-and the supreme Scholar!—Because he reaches the unknown! Since he cultivated his soul, rich already, more than any man! He reaches the *unknown*, and when, bewildered, he ends by losing the intelligence of his visions, he has seen them. Let him die as he leaps through unheard of and unnamable things"

(Rimbaud to Paul Demeny, 15 May 1871)

T he relation between Eros and art is a long story involving love and pleasure. Experiences with art provide pleasure because they unfold an erotic dimension that is extended in time and different from the sexual in its aim, in that it adds sublime pleasure. Art as an encounter with the beautiful is a promise of pleasure, a "promise of happiness", as Stendhal (1822) would say. However, this promise, a promise of love, is held within a symbolic frame. Its objects—expropriated from the subjectivity that has constructed them—are cultural objects, and yet they may provoke deep emotions that reach the unthinkable. This is the role of Eros, the Eros that is love and pleasure and displays the complexity of desire.

We could say that there is a kind of love whose paradigm is art. Here, a many-faced Eros reappears to express the conflict inherent in its nature. We should recall here that for the Greeks, Eros represents not only erotic love, but also all creative impulses. Furthermore, according to the Theogonies, it springs from initial chaos together with Gaia and the underworld (Grimal, 1951). Ever since its origin, mythological Eros has manifested its constitutive contradiction[1] just as the Freudian Eros, which is both part of psychic conflict and cohesive force. Thus, the interrelation between love and art concerns the creative binding force where Eros dwells, and traverses not only beauty, but also the uncanny, strangeness, and loss. This journey reveals a new kind of love, the love of art. It is the core of what we call love and pleasure that, by incorporating *jouissance*, transcends it in enigmatic ways.

The experience of the enigmatic in art, as Balzac describes it in "The unknown masterpiece" (1832), evinces the extreme passions, the pathos of emotions involved in the creative process. Based on this short story, which reproduces the vertigo of creation, we discuss three theoretical moments through which Eros circulates like "the red thread". Love is present in the violence of creation in different ways. It exposes the effects of and on the body at work in art, and when it pierces through the ego's shell, it promotes in subjectivity a *de-encapsulation of narcissism* that also produces an awakening to feelings. More specifically, we suggest that the processes involved in creativity and in the experience with art entail a specific type of love. In its many faces and forms, this love shows its links to unconscious psychic processes and cultural phenomena, which necessarily involve an other. Hence, the "function of art" as the greatest love is also involved in the cure.

Aesthetics and psychoanalysis

Starting from psychoanalysis and its relation to aesthetics, we discuss the paths taken by love in art. Standing at the intersection of these two disciplines, we examine their participation in aesthetic experience and, specifically, in the creative process.

The history of the relationship between aesthetics and psychoanalysis is complex and controversial in more ways than one. Freudian psychoanalysis has pointed out its own limitations in regard to the riddles of art. Although Freud states that it "is only rarely that a psycho-analyst feels impelled to investigate the subject of aesthetics" (1919h, p. 219), he himself delves into the "uncanny" in order to unearth what aesthetics as the "science of the beautiful" is unable to explain. With this movement, he inadvertently introduces a new twist in the thinking about beauty, which now constitutes the cornerstone of modern aesthetics; the appearance of the beautiful reveals, in the uncanny, a paradoxical encounter with art. Under certain conditions, this uncanny encounter acquires the status of aesthetic experience (Goldstein, 2005).

Contemporary aesthetics, in turn, recognises its roots in psychoanalysis. Eagleton (1990, p. 263) states that for Freud "human life is aesthetic . . . in so far as it is all about intense bodily sensations". These sensations involve representations; they are not independent of images and fantasies. From Freud's viewpoint, claims Eagleton, art "is continuous with the libidinal processes which go to make up daily life", which is "exceedingly strange", a strangeness related to the discrepancy between representation and affect. The aesthetic is "the detonator of profound discharges which unmask the human subject as fissured and unfinished" (Eagleton, 1990, p. 264). Freud traces the origin of aesthetic beauty to libidinal impulses. For Freud, says Eagleton, "art is . . . a non-neurotic form of substitute satisfaction". Its logic resembles children's tinkering. This logic is associated with the logic of the unconscious, whose highest expression displays the encounter of the two disciplines, as Borges claims when he considers dreaming the oldest aesthetic activity (1980).

Aesthetics and psychoanalysis inscribe *a new regime* that bridges a zone of opposites where trauma and working through, the symbolic realm and the world of the senses, the beautiful and the uncanny, the rational and the sensual coexist in a state of tension with no stable solution. This tension pertains both to the creative and to the aesthetic experience. The latter, categorised as aesthetics of reception by Jauss (1982) and creative experience, considered aesthetics of production by the Frankfurt School, involves a type of encounter with the art object in which the object acquires autonomy. We might say that it is an encounter with the Other in its radical otherness. More precisely, it is an encounter with a forbidden desire, revealing that aesthetics is also a dangerous and ambiguous matter.

This type of experience with art generates a sort of alienating threshold that signals the start of the encounter with the Other, an encounter that uncovers and conceals something uncanny beyond the beautiful. In other words, it is the shock of the encounter with art, with *great works of art*, since they "question us and demand our reaction" (Riemen, cited in Steiner, 2004, p. 34). Such questioning becomes an effect of subjectivity when it occurs as aesthetic experience (that might be akin to analytic experience), and is related to a feeling of strangeness that involves the potential to move into an "intermediate" place. In this place, passions and the remains of a great love come into play, as in the "madness" of creation. This is what Balzac tells us in his exemplary 1832 short story "The unknown masterpiece".

"The unknown masterpiece"

What is the source of the conditions for creation that Freud recognises in his text on Leonardo (1910c) as being inaccessible to psychoanalysis? What is it that produces something that promotes "violent emotions", like those Freud experiences as he contemplates the Moses of Michelangelo (1914b)? Where is "the blood that engenders calm or passion" (Huberman, 2007, p. 186)? And what is it that provokes this surprising effect: that of giving figures such extraordinary life? These are the young artist's questions in Balzac's story.

"The unknown masterpiece" presents an emblematic scene in relation to art: that of the agony and tremendous struggle that unfolds during the creative process. In the midst of this creating madness, passion and a state of alienation are unleashed as well as love, manifested in the strangest ways. This scene also exposes the question of creation, a major problem in painting, which is how to succeed in bringing a work of art *alive*—how to make it "incarnate".

"Do not look too long at that canvas, young man", says Porbus to Poussin when he sees the young painter standing open-mouthed before a painting. "You could fall victim to despair" (Balzac, 2005 [1832], p. 16). With this warning, Porbus alerts Poussin, who seems lost, fascinated by Master Frenhofer's painting of an idealised woman. In this way, Balzac opens his story about the artist's encounter with a work of art and about the passions of the creative process. Not only is this a marvellous encounter with a masterpiece, but also an opportunity to participate in the instant when the painter is transfigured into a creator and when a revelation, a glimpse into art's enigma, takes place. For the fledgling painter, the old man has become superhuman, "a fantastic spirit living in a mysterious world" (Balzac, 2005[1832], p. 17). The narrator describes Poussin's complex feelings:

> Countless vague thoughts awoke within his soul. The effect of this species of fascination upon his mind can no more be described in words than the passionate longing awakened in an exile's heart by the song that recalls his home. (Balzac, 2005[1832], p. 17)

Frenhofer becomes the embodiment of art:

> [Poussin] saw in this supernatural being a complete type of the artist nature, a nature mocking and kindly, barren and prolific, an erratic spirit intrusted with great and manifold powers which she too often abuses ... For Poussin, the enthusiast, the old man, was suddenly transfigured, and became Art incarnate, Art with its mysteries, its vehement passion and its dreams. (Balzac, 2005[1832], p. 17)

In the midst of his drunkenness on the beautiful forms and colours that the old painter has brought to life in his painting, Poussin is immersed in profound admiration, searching for some sign of the divine. Yet, he finds that "besides an almost diabolical expression in the face that met his gaze, there was that indescribable something which has an irresistible attraction for artists" (Balzac, 2005[1832], p. 3). The "indescribable something" (*"je ne sais quois"* in the original) that a science of the beautiful cannot explain and whose quality of seduction drives to madness is sought out frantically—a condition of something vital that makes us vibrate.

The work comes alive. Pygmalion, Orpheus, something divine is sought in this "incarnation" that must remain veiled none the less. "Veil the divine", says Schelling (cited in Freud, 1919h). But this gift of the old master that young Poussin observes with fascination also suggests something diabolical, as we said, in the condition of creation. The diabolical here is related to the "Demons of the Averno", to *that* burning darkness of unconscious wishes. However, it is also a longing for the father, whose substitute is the devil, as Freud (1923d) points out in his study of the demonic neurosis of the tormented painter Haizmann.

In Balzac's story it is a *desire of love*[2] (*désir d'amour*) that appears in the amorous love between the artist and his work. "She loves me", says the mad painter of his hidden masterpiece. This is also a desire of the love of the father, Frenhofer's teacher, Mabuse, who has passed on to him the secret of how to bring a work to life. Yet, the alienated Frenhofer is reluctant to transfer his secret keys to the young painter, Poussin, and does not want to show his work, since he is still searching for an ideal. The passions among the generations of master painters (Mabuse, Frenhofer, Porbus) and the transference of their secrets, witnessed by the young and promising Poussin, seem to be unyielding in their eagerness to awaken the sleeping Venus and produce a sensual experience through the image. None the less, the desperate Frenhofer coveys something about these keys when he explains to the young artist that "the human body is not contained within the limits of line . . . you feel that the air plays round it" (Balzac, 2005[1832], p. 8).

A woman's shape and the depth of the feminine allude to *the function of the body in art*. This body, touched by the eye while it looks, is always somewhere "between too close and too far away" (Huberman, 2007, p. 104). That figure, the dream woman, is a Venus that, as a transcendental subject, is transformed into "excessive work". This state of matters incorporates the alienated artist, who is seeking incarnation in his painting and understands that it is a question of finding "the skin beyond what is flat" (Huberman, 2007, p. 52). For Leonardo da Vinci, such sentiment (*"sense-mental"*) or feeling conveyed by a painting may reproduce the skin's structure (Huberman, 2007).

It is the body and its sensuality that is so difficult to reproduce in an image as a visual experience of the tactile. This *surface* that Anzieu defines from a psychoanalytic perspective as the "skin-ego" shores up all psychic activity and marks the boundary with the outside, establishing an "exchange with the other". The body, "a vital dimension of human reality" (Anzieu, 1997, p. 198), becomes a reality in the work because in its existence "the painting thinks", explains Didi-Huberman.

In this interweaving of signifier–sensation–sentiment, aesthetics may be seen as a "matrix of thought" (Eagleton, 1990). Under these conditions, aesthetics also manifests the enigmatic character of a work of art, which expresses something and conceals it at the same time (Adorno, 1970). It is what is hidden in the "unknown masterpiece" that sustains the drama experienced by the painter Frenhofer, who is unable to uncover either his ideal painting or the conditions for achieving an incarnate painting. However, at last he advances; he almost gives up but finally reveals the secrets of art when he says,

> You do not penetrate far enough into the inmost secrets of the mystery of form; you do not seek with *love enough* and perseverance enough after the form that baffles and eludes you. Beauty is a thing severe and unapproachable, never to be won by a languid lover. (Balzac, 2005[1832], p. 8, my italics)

The violence of creation

The pathos of creation of an artwork also contains a form of violence, as Balzac's story reveals. Something has to be undergone in order to reach the *topos* of creativity—resistances, repressions, demands, and ideals emerge in this path. Something needs to be *forced violently* in order for the artist to gain access to that place. Violence also drives Eros, according to Bataille (1957). We could state, therefore, that artists are violent people, as McDougall (2010) says, since they "dared to defy *order* . . . dared to show the world what [they] created". Their boldness, which reveals the power of the phenomenon of creation, involves the whole person, says de M'Uzan (2010). This author links it to depersonalisation, which explains the erasure of boundaries between subject and object as a separation between the real world and a fantasised, created world. In this *trance*, artists seem to be "alienated individuals", confirms Shafer (cited in McDougall, 2010, p. 15).

Alienated, strange, and violent, artists traverse regions that force them, so to speak, into a voyage of initiation—in some way, into the depths of the unconscious. The search for the incarnate is akin to *touching the sacred, "das heilige", and the forbidden, that is, object "a" (cause of desire), the body of the mother, the idealised and unreachable woman of Balzac's story*. Such passionate movement towards the object that seemingly transcends human will is manifested when Frenhofer, *alienated and in love*, declares before his unknown masterpiece, "She loves me". In this instant, we understand what he is explaining; something coming from the object demands autonomy. The object has become meaningful.

The sensory, bodily dimension the work recovers in the artist and in the spectator exhibits its primal (in Aulagnier's (1968) sense of the term) nature. The latter is connected with the *substance* of "primary creativity", which for Winnicott (1971) refers to a nostalgia for an immediacy that counteracts the distance provided by representation. Beyond sublimation, what is put into play here is also a type of relation with the object of art which recalls something that retrieves a trace of pleasure: an initial "fusion" that, for the same reason, might come to some kind of separation or violence. Nevertheless, the destruction or violence involved in separation implies an imperative to work through "in a scenario that resolves economically, absorbs tensions and integrates them into forms and images" (Anzieu, 1997, p. 37). I would say anxieties, extreme desire, longing, love, and hate in unceasing movement. As this author puts it, fantasies move from a passive condition into the "efficacy of an act".

Creation involves a topological movement that seems regressive but is also progressive: an oscillation between primary and secondary processes that, in the manner of a "tertiary process" (Green, 1983), leads to a new type of in-between binding and to *making a work of art into a new product with cultural value*. Regression then becomes a withdrawal (*"retrait"*, in Derrida's (1978) sense of the term) that "re-traces" a trace, a new trace that transforms repetition and thereby produces difference. This idea of re-tracing a trace, like working through in the repetition of artistic creation, is found in the *fort-da* game, as formulated by Freud in *Beyond the Pleasure Principle* (1920g). However, the *precariousness* of playing and creating includes both loss and the mastery of its extraterritoriality. This process of making an artwork has a constructive logic that incorporates remains of the ineffable, the unrepresentable, and the unintegrated. Thus, the paradox of art is that it is both *a condition of a re-encounter with trauma and also its workingthrough*. As Schneider (2010, p. 47) confirms, art's effect is twofold: "both to anaesthetise the deepest wounds and to re-experience them".

From the perspective of modern aesthetics, the experience of art transcends the appreciation of the senses—what is beautiful and pleasurable—since it is also an experience of the sublime and the uncanny and incorporates, as we mentioned earlier, the notion of trauma. Foster's notion of "traumatic realism" in art as a version of the spectral (Foster, 1996) reflects this view. The *spectral* aspect of the artwork is a *mediated* way to try to evoke the lost spaces of childhood. On another level, it relates to Benjamin's description of the *aura* in the work of art, which he defines as a "unique phenomenon of a distance" (Benjamin, 1968, pp. 222–223).

We find this remote, lost past in what Warburg sees to reappear in the *movement* of tunics in the breeze of Botticelli's *Spring*[3] (Burucúa, 2003). The very remote past revealed in that moment, in that movement of the form, evokes resonances of the primal and the body. Warburg named this movement of the drive, which has to do with the pathos of emotion and passion, *Pathosformeln*.[4] It is dynamic tension asking to remain unresolved—like Winnicott's idea of paradox—in order to preserve the eternal contest between the Dionysian and the Apollonian. According to Rancière (2009, p. 3), such tension is "a particular relation between thought and non-thought, a particular way that thought is present within sensible materiality, meaning within the insignificant", which constitutes the "aesthetic regime of art".

A paradigm emerges: excitation as pleasure and as "negative pleasure" (associated with Kant's "sublime"). There art discovers its value: *the prime of pleasure, always secret, but also its price, which is to include the artist's body*. In the artistic process of creation *one must give something of one's own*. Furthermore, part of the experience undergone during this process is transferred on to the work, like the imperceptible movement of the music that Eros sings in our ear.

It is not simply a question of anxiety, danger, or emptiness, but, rather, of a *vital tension and the movement of hidden passion*. This tension typical of the creative act, following Winnicott (1971), imposes a certain degree of physical participation. We could add that this excitation becomes dance, attack, revenge, caress, endurance, and love, thus rendering figurable something that is pure quantity, an innermost burden. *Psychosexual and psychosomatic, the violence of creation invokes a secret pleasure of the psychic and libidinal order in the work of art, in the individual who produces it, and in its effect on the spectator.*

The body at work, or Eros and the promise of pleasure

The presence of the body in the work of art enables a transforming dimension where the gaze and art intersect again in a new, specific relation. But what does the image represented in art promote?

The image catches the eye and produces resonances that make our body vibrate, awakening it to zones of unsuspected sensuality, as occurs in "screen memories" (Freud, 1899a), which activate an unconscious memory and disguise a forbidden desire. The gaze eroticised by an image leads us to see, examine, and draw aside the screen of representation, which veils the dreams of our secret intimacy. In art, this gaze has a function: to "make visible" something that cannot be seen, such as castration or the forbidden. "What!" exclaims the old painter in Balzac's story, "Rend the veil that has kept my happiness sacred?" (Balzac, 2005[1832], p. 23). This sacred happiness so carefully guarded confirms that Eros and forbidden love are involved.

The image, *capturing the gaze*, is first seduced by the *charms* (*Reiz*) of the represented body, which function as "lures". With the *promise of pleasure*, the gaze directed to the work tends to examine *the whole* work, the totality of the *image represented*; because pleasure is "humankind's original home", as Agamben (1993[1978], p. 104) insists. This examination of the totality of the work is closely related to what Freud explains in his *Three Essays on the Theory of Sexuality* (1905d, p. 156):

> The progressive concealment of the body which goes along with civilization keeps sexual curiosity awake. This curiosity seeks to complete the sexual object by revealing its hidden parts. It can, however, be diverted ('sublimated') in the direction of art, if its interest can be shifted away from the genitals on *to the shape of the body as a whole.*

This delay in looking it over and aiming the gaze at a whole divides the waters, separating fetishism as a perversion from desire and eroticism. The knot between modesty and perverse action—I know it but I still want to look—is the paradox of fetishism, which leads to the option of not ripping the veil covering the crudity of *das Ding*, the thing. The veil represents modesty as a subtle version of the Freudian dams. The dilemma between the desire to look and its rejection becomes visible. In this option, once free of "Adam's fatal curiosity" (Balzac, 1832), sexual curiosity is transformed into knowledge. It is the drive to knowledge that might be promoted by art. It is Eros as pleasure that, by eroticising an integrating experience, brings together the partial drives by means of art's particular alibi, which joins aesthetic and intellectual pleasure. The epistemophilic and scopic drives are thus transformed into a different way of looking that constitutes a different look—*a second look* (Baranger & Baranger, 2008).

The persistence of a dividing line between parts of a totality signals the difference between a fetish and a lure; the lure determines an erotic condition that fosters both the sexual *and* tenderness. Tenderness as a sublimated drive aim, "dulled" sexuality, is tied to the "pacification of the gaze" that Lacan (1973) considers art to provide. In other words, this process that unfolds in our experience with an image promotes erotogenicity, which is displaced—in principle from the visual—on to psychic life and the entire body. The body then responds like a great erotogenic zone.

> This transport toward a sensory zone activates movements in the recipient within the artist, who also participated in the creative process. Such internal movements originate in mythical, prehistoric times and have the evocative power of the senses, the bodily, the lost 'primal' . . . and the natural (not to say, the 'real'). (Goldstein, 2005, p. 117)

Narcissism and de-encapsulation

The encounter with art brings up the question of narcissism and of art's ability to produce the de-encapsulation of narcissism (Goldstein, 2005). Green (1983) considers that narcissism is the material that holds the ego together. Narcissism cements the components of the ego by granting them a precious gift—a formal identity that involves the feeling of existence. We understand, therefore, this intense aspiration to recover the ego's unity by way of narcissism, since as Freud (1914b) tells us, part of the feeling of self is a residue of this childhood narcissism. In art, we find both aspects of narcissism, that is, Eros, which is life and pleasure, and also Thanatos, which is unbinding and death. Such duality may be seen in the dramatic, flashing brilliance of Moreau's paintings, as a perverse shine in Balthus, in the twisting, anaemic bodies of Schiele, or in the fragile density of degraded flesh in the paintings of Lucian Freud.

None the less, this cementing material might also constitute a *narcissistic shell* and offer "one of the fiercest forms of resistance to analysis" (Green, 2001[1983], p. 9). Art provides a specific possibility to de-encapsulate this shell, since each encounter between subjects and art inaugurates a re-encounter with something similar and also different. Art leads us to experience other worlds beyond the one we know. As Balzac (2005[1832], p. 12) describes it through his master painter, "each figure is a world". Adorno confirms that "artworks detach themselves from the empirical world and bring forth another world, one opposed to the empirical world as if this other world too were an autonomous entity" (1997[1970], p. 1), thereby instating a *discrepancy*. Since it marks a difference, such discrepancy between the object and the discrimination of its perceptual–formal identity promotes the de-encapsulation of narcissism. Moreover, the discrepancy between the dreamed idea and what has been created and found recurs endlessly in art.

The object of artistic creation serves as a mediator through identification, whose precursor is art's Platonic mimesis. The image attracts us to it and, in the same movement, ejects us from the narcissism we had recovered for just an instant. This occurs because a new agency emerges from this *first* pleasurable or cathartic identification, revealing a fissure with a subtle difference. It is in this *act—an effect of pleasure with a limit*—that *the narcissistic shell is* pierced. Through art's "mediation" between ego and object libido, narcissism is de-encapsulated. Libido is "tertiated" and the shell *fissured*, becoming permeable to affects, the other, and reality.

Such experience with a work of art prolongs the libido of narcissism as it embraces and incorporates the object of art. Alterity, thereby, operates in a mediated way, as occurs in the work of transference in the analytic field. It is like the aesthetic phenomenon that imposes a particular *function of non-recognition*. This constancy of disavowal throws us, in a *moderate way*, into another repressed or rejected scenario. In this act our petrified bourgeois ego is de-encapsulated. The ego is, above all, a body ego, a great erotogenic zone, and art is the field in which every type of production takes up, tries out, and attempts to recover a great loss—lost unity.

For the love of art[5]

There is a new love whose paradigm is the love of art. It is the Eros of all creating impulses and the core of what we call love, a form of "disinterested" love that transcends *jouissance* by incorporating it. In these conditions, the object of love is what cannot be possessed, devoured, understood in its entirety, or symbolised.

Freud defines Eros:

> The nucleus of what we mean by love naturally consists ... in sexual love with sexual union as its aim. But we do not separate from this – what in any case has a share in the name "love"—on the one hand, self-love, and on the other, love ... for humanity in general ... and also devotion to ... abstract ideas. (Freud, 1921c, p. 90)

For this reason, Freud decides to take *the word love* in a broad sense, as is used by the Apostle Paul in his Epistle to the Corinthians (Freud, 1921c). Freud also refers to the meaning and use given to love by Plato, based on its origin and its link to sexual life. Yet, in its relation to sexuality, Eros involves a temporal and developmental element (Green, 1983), whereas its relation to art is timeless.

Now, at the end of our discussion, we can return to the question formulated at the beginning in view of the concepts discussed and the ways in which, intertwined in the dimension of love, they have acquired new complexity. We also see how creation and aesthetic experience are differentiated and converge as well. Is there a change of meaning, or an interweaving in which a transformation in the subjective world might reappear based on this way of thinking about love? Is there a space where such interweaving might take place?

In this perspective, aesthetic experience involves the configuration of an "unsettling region", as Agamben 1993[1978]) describes it, because there, beyond the analysis of the subject's feelings, the object demands the subject's participation. Consequently, we might think of relations between object and subject not simply as "confrontation", but, instead, as *shared ground*. The hegemony of this intermediate space explains experience *with* the work of art and this *mit* or with, the meeting point, is a legacy of Heidegger's aesthetics (Goldstein, 2005). The idea of beauty for Plato implies the "attraction of the beautiful" to itself and promotes participation (*metexis*). Therefore, aesthetic experience is event and encounter; it is a middle point, a *paradoxical place of encounter* where the subject *is* the object of art itself as a *condition of mediation that enables this encounter in experience* (Goldstein, 2005).

Aesthetic experience is an *experience on the edge* between the forbidden and the permitted. It is the last veil that art does not uncover, where the pleasure ego is summoned and reality suspended. Pleasure evinces its peculiar relation to time. This multi-dimensional pleasure complex is also present in the making of the work of art. It is the possibility of a momentary *suspension*, a "suspended" state that involves a temporary return, not pathological, to "a time when the ego had not yet marked itself off sharply from the external world and from other people" (Freud, 1919h, p. 236). The other becomes the ego, and the ego is alienated in the other. This process reveals the function of alienation and separation between I and not-I when the joy of identification is experienced—the foundational place of our aesthetic condition, as Meltzer and Harris (1988) also view it in *The Apprehension of Beauty*.

Consequently, a modality of *dialectic splitting*, supported by non-pathological aspects of feelings of alienation, takes place. In these conditions, estrangement indicates the start of an encounter with the Other in that place where human cultural creations might be situated. Winnicott (1971) conceptualised this space as a "third zone", a derivative of play, where there is "relief" from tension imposed by the eternal task of connecting internal with external reality. Aesthetic experience is event, shock, and pacification, a condition of mediation that enables, as does creation, access to new knowledge. In Green's words, "Eros, which is the life force, becomes part of Psyche" (Green, 2008[1997], p. 113).

This greatest love of all reappears in aesthetic experience as something that engages us and leads us to pleasurable feelings and to a return to forgotten traces. Our pleasure, in turn, recovers the experience of the body as sensuality and thought. The body incarnate explains an interweaving in which feeling and understanding are interlaced in what Leonardo describes poetically as the skin that lets itself be spoken, which is also woven together by writing (Didi-Huberman, 1985).

Giving shape to affects that form letters in the body explains the desire and narrative of an impossible love. It is because beyond the sayable, as Marx reminds us when he highlights the element of live expression in thought, "language is sensuous nature" (cited in Eagleton, 1990, p. 197). Hence, it reveals a history, the history of the traces of pleasure, which date back to early experiences of satisfaction and of secret pleasure. It is the history of a forbidden love with the truth of everything that has constituted us.

This kind of love is fostered by art and transcends aesthetic pleasure, since its object is a symbolic cultural object. Like great works of art, it is timeless. A never-ending pleasure emerges in aesthetic experience that is "a heterogeneous thing in relation to the experience of quantified, continuous time" (Agamben, 1993[1978], p. 104). Moreover, this love, the greatest love of all, participates in the cure. Traversing anxiety in an ongoing process, it places certain co-ordinates of satisfaction in a different order; it transfigures passions into form and desire, *jouissance* into love. In the intensity of our experience with art and creation, time is suspended and pleasure extended. Under these conditions, art, supported by Eros, shows how, by transcending narcissism, passion, hate, fear, and fate are ultimately transformed into affects felt and thought, and pleasure is recovered—created anew in different ways that explain and reveal the greatest love of all.

Notes

1. Other interpretations present Eros as the child of Aphrodite and Ares, or Poros and Penia. The version of Pausanias in Plato's Banquet refers to two Aphrodites, the heavenly, or Urania, and the Pandemos, or vulgar one, both represented in the diverse forms of love (Grimal, 1951).
2. Barocci, in Didi-Huberman (1985, p. 86)
3. Warburg calls it das Nachleben der Antike (the survival of the past).
4. This refers to art's potential for representation and expression, with which it evokes constitutive "engrams" by virtue of a different type of memory that invites us into an ancient universe conveying the magic of nature, according to Burucúa (2003).
5. Translator's note: In Spanish, to do something "for the love of art" (*por amor al arte*) means to do it for the goodness of one's heart. The author's play on words cannot be translated.

References

Adorno, T. W. (1970). *Aesthetic Theory*. London: Routledge and Kegan Paul, 1997.
Agamben, G. (1978). *Infancy and History*. London: Verso, 1993.
Anzieu, D. (1997). *Crear Destruir*. Madrid: Biblioteca Nueva.
Aulagnier, P. (1968). *The Violence of Interpretation; From Pictogram to Statement*. Philadelphia: Brunner-Routledge, 2001.
Balzac, H. (1832). *The Unknown Masterpiece and Other Stories*. London: J. M. Dent, 1896. Digitalised version in charge of the New York Public Library, USA, 2005.

Baranger, M., & Baranger, W. (2008). The analytic situation as a dynamic field. *International Journal of Psychoanalysis, 89*: 795–826.
Bataille, G. (1957). *Erotism: Death and Sensuality*. San Francisco, CA: City Light, 1986.
Benjamin, W. (1968). The work of art in the age of mechanical reproduction. In: *Illuminations: Essays and Reflections* (pp. 222–223). New York: Schocken Books.
Borges, J. L. (1980). *Siete Noches*. Mexico City: Editorial Meló.
Burucúa, J. E. (2003). *Historia, arte, cultura. De Aby Warburg a Carlo Ginzburg*. Buenos Aires: Fondo de Cultura Económica.
De M'Uzan, M. (2010). El infierno de la creatividad. In: J. McDougall, J. André, M. de M'Uzan, V. Marinov, P. Porret, M. Schneider, & D. Suchet, . *El Artista y el psicoanalista* (pp. 29–37). Buenos Aires: Nueva Visión.
Derrida, J. (1978). The retrait of metaphor. *Enclitic, 2*(2): 5–34.
Didi-Huberman, G. (1985). *La pintura encarnada*. Valencia: Edición Pre-textos, 2007 (co-edited with the Polytechnic University of Valencia).
Didi-Huberman, G. (2007). *La pintura encrnada y la obra maestra desconocida de Honoré de Balzac*. Valencia: Edición Pre-textos (co-edition with the Polytechnic University of Valencia).
Eagleton, T. (1990). *The Ideology of the Aesthetic*. Oxford: Blackwell.
Foster, H. (1996). *The Return of the Real: The Avant-Garde at the End of the Century*. Cambridge, MA: MIT Press.
Freud, S. (1899a). Screen memories. *S.E., 3*: 301–322. London: Hogarth.
Freud, S. (1905d). Three Essays on the Theory of Sexuality. *S.E., 7*: 125–245. London: Hogarth.
Freud, S. (1910c). Leonardo da Vinci and a Memory of his Childhood. *S.E., 11*: 59–137. London: Hogarth.
Freud, S. (1914b). The Moses of Michelangelo. *S.E., 13*: 211–238. London: Hogarth.
Freud, S. (1919h). The "uncanny". *S.E., 17*: 219–256. London: Hogarth.
Freud, S. (1920g). Beyond the Pleasure Principle. *S.E., 18*: 7–64. London: Hogarth.
Freud, S. (1921c). Group Psychology and the Analysis of the Ego. *S.E., 18*: 67–143. London: Hogarth.
Freud, S. (1923d). A seventeenth-century demonological neurosis. *S.E., 19*: 69–107. London: Hogarth.
Goldstein, G. (2005). *La experiencia estética*. Buenos Aires: Del Estante Editorial.
Green, A. (1983). *Life Narcissism, Death Narcissism*. London: Free Association Books, 2001.

Green, A. (1997). *The Chains of Eros: The Sexual in Psychoanalysis*. London: Karnac, 2008.
Grimal, P. (1951). *The Dictionary of Classical Mythology*. Oxford: Blackwell, 2000.
Jauss, H. R. (1982). *Toward an Aesthetic of Reception*. Minneapolis, MI: University of Minnesota Press.
Lacan, J. (1973). *Book XI. The Four Fundamental Concepts of Psychoanalysis*. New York: W. W. Norton, 1978.
McDougall, J. (2010). El artista y el psicoanalista. In: J. McDougall, J. André, M. de M'Uzan, V. Marinov, P. Porret, M. Schneider, & D. Suchet (Eds.), *El Artista y el psicoanalista* (pp. 11–27). Buenos Aires: Nueva Visión.
Meltzer, D., & Harris, M. (1988). *The Apprehension of Beauty: The Role of Aesthetic Conflict in Development, Art and Violence*. Strathtay, Perthshire: Clunie Press.
Rancière, J. (2009). *The Aesthetic Unconscious*. Cambridge: Polity Press, 2009.
Rimbaud, A. (1966). *Complete Works, Selected Letters*. Chicago, IL: University of Chicago Press, 1966, p. 307.
Schneider, M. (2010). Freud y la lucha con el artista. In: J. McDougall, J. André, M. de M'Uzan, V. Marinov, P. Porret, M. Schneider, & D. Suchet,. *El artista y el psicoanalista* (pp. 39–56). Buenos Aires: Nueva Visión.
Steiner, G. (2004). *The Idea of Europe*. Nexus Library Volume IV. Tillburg: Nexus Institute.
Stendhal [Beyle, M.-H.] (1822). *On Love*. London: Hesperus Press, 2010.
Winnicott, D. W. (1971). *Playing and Reality*. London: Tavistock.

INDEX

Abella, A., xxiv, 58, 60, 67, 76
Abram, J., 141, 145, 149
Adorno, T. W., xx, xxiii, xxvi, 177, 182, 185
affect(ive), xxiii, 5, 7, 14, 21–34, 49, 123–124, 126, 129, 133–134, 136, 152, 173, 182, 184–185
 communication, xvii
 opposing, xviii
 primitive, 30
 regulation, 32, 34
 response, 6, 25–26, 33
 rigidity, 43
 transformation, 22
 understanding, 6
Agamben, G., 180, 183, 185
Age of Enlightenment, 142, 146
aggression, xviii, 41, 59, 66, 87, 125, 134
 hostile, xvii
 impulses, 52
 primary, 145
Albers, J., 99, 106
Allison, J., 34–35
Allport, G. W., 35
André, J., 128, 138

Anzieu, D., 98, 100, 106, 176, 178, 185
Argentine Psychoanalytic Association, 141
Aristotle, 1–3, 6, 17–19, 47, 156, 166
Arnett, J., 41, 54
Arnheim, R., 28, 32, 35
Aulagnier, P., xxi, xxvi, 178, 185
autonomy, xix, xxiii, 100, 155, 162, 174, 178, 182

Balzac, H., 157, 172, 174–177, 180, 182, 185
Bar'Mitzvah, 114
Baranger, M., 105, 180, 186
Baranger, W., 105, 180, 186
Bataille, G., 165, 177, 186
Baudry, F., 61–62, 76
Baudry, J.-L., 119, 122
Bell, C., 4–5, 19
Belting, H., 22, 35
Benjamin, W., xxii, xxvi, 149, 179, 186
Berge, A., 98, 106
Bergman, A., 40, 54
Berlin, I., 23, 35
Bernard, E., 10, 19

Beuys, J., xxiv, 99, 103, 106
Beyle, M.-H. *see*: Stendhal
Bick, E., 153, 166
Biles, J., 165–166
Bion, W. R., xxii, xxiv, 35, 60, 73, 101, 134, 153
Blatt, S. W., 34–35
Bloom, H., 50, 54
Bloomsbury, 3–4
Blum, H., xxiii, 40, 54
Bollas, C., 143, 149
Borges, J. L., xxiv, 100, 173, 186
Botticelli, S., 84, 179
Bourdieu, P., 72, 76
Brabant, E., 128, 137
Burucúa, J. E., xxi, xxvi, 179, 185–186

Cabanne, P., 66, 76
Carpenter, R., 4, 19
Casagemas, C., 44, 46, 52
Cavafy, C. P., 111, 122
Cézanne, P., xxiii, 10–11, 18, 25, 42
Chasseguet-Smirgel, J., 160, 166
Chervet, B., 128, 137
Clancier, A., 98, 106
Close, C., 27
Clynes, M., 28, 35
Coccoz, V., 85, 95
Condivi, A., 14, 19
conscious(ness), xvii–xviii, xxi, 18, 21, 88–89, 95, 123–127, 129, 133–135
  also: unconscious(ness)
  awareness, 24
  moral, 89
  perceptual, 30
  pre-, 12, 31, 152
  process, 30–31, 123, 147
  subject, 92
Cook, M., 147, 149
Copernicus, N., 3
countertransference, xvii, 61, 63, 67
  see also: transference
  approach, 62, 64, 68, 71, 74
Cros, C., 64, 67, 76

Damasio, A., 29, 35
David, C., 156, 167
da Vinci, L., 14, 130, 176
de Goldstein, R. Z., 141
Deleuze, G., xxiv, 97, 99, 106

De M'Uzan, M., xxv–xxvi, 128, 131, 137–138, 151–152, 155–156, 158, 161, 163–167, 177, 186
depression, 14, 42, 48, 51–52, 121, 134, 164
  adolescent, 44
  anxieties, 59, 161
  art, 52
  position, 134
  severe, 51
  suicidal, 46
Derrida, J., 48, 54, 178, 186
development(al), xvii–xviii, 24, 30, 53, 62, 99, 101–102, 145, 183
  adolescent, 43
  challenges, 39, 43
  conceptual, 79
  creative, 104
  ego, 21
  emotional, 143
  libidinal, 165
  movement, 110
  organic, 118
  phase, xvii
  physical, 147
  psychical, 147
  psychological, 54
  theoretical, 72, 74
Dewey, J. 24, 35
dialogue, xvii, xxii, xxiii–xxv, 16–17, 48, 50, 63
  affecto-motor, xvi
  interdisciplinary, 61, 63, 74
  interpersonal, 117
  nuanced, xxiii
  two-way, 63
Didi-Huberman, G., xix–xx, xxvi, 176, 184–186
Duchamp, M., xxiv, 64–76, 79, 88–92, 99, 106

Eagleton, T., xxi, xxvi, 173, 176, 184, 186
Eberwein, R. T., 120, 122
Eco, U., 103, 106
ego, xxv, 18, 23, 59, 101, 161, 172, 181–182, 184 *see also*: development
  alter, xxii–xxiii, xxv, 153, 157, 159, 161–164
  conservative, 136
  development, 21

pleasure, 183
skin-, 176
strength, 17
Ehrenzweig, A., 30, 35
Einstein, A., 22, 36
Eliot, T. S., 13, 19, 27, 36, 99, 104, 106
Epicurus, 3
Epstein, D., 26, 36
Eros, xviii, xxiii, xxv, 66, 74, 128,
    171–172, 177, 179–185
Esman, A. H., 61–62, 76

Falzeder, E., 128, 137
fantasy, xvi, 48, 60, 62, 73, 99, 110, 112,
    114, 133, 173, 178 *see also*: sexual,
    unconscious
  excessive, 143
  hysterical, 58
  identifiable, 61
  narcissistic, 67
  Oedipal, xvi
  of anorexia, 68
  onanist, 67
  parricidal, 44, 46
  personal, 71, 74
  perverse, 69
  universal, xvi
  unrealistic, 30
  voyeuristic, 71
Fédida, P., 131, 137
Fiorini, H., xxiv, 102–103, 106
Fisher, C., 24, 31, 36
Focillon, H., 28, 36, 154, 165, 167
Foster, H., xxi, xxvi, 178–179, 186
Foucault, M., 149
Frame, J., 104, 106
Frank-Schwebel, A., 34, 36
Freud, A., 165
Freud, L., 181
Freud, S. (*passim*)
  aesthetic theory, 6, 98
  cited works, xix, xxi, xxvi, 6, 14, 19,
    21, 36, 48, 50, 53–54, 57–58, 62,
    67, 72, 74, 76–77, 97–98, 102, 106,
    114, 120, 122–123, 127–129,
    134–135, 137, 144, 146, 149, 151,
    154, 156–159, 162–163, 165,
    167–168, 173–176, 178, 180–181,
    183–184, 186
  conversion hysteria, 115

creativity theory, 145
detachment of adolescence, 53
hypotheses, 6, 103
metapsychology, 99
parricidal fantasy, 44
Schreber, 50
Friedman, S. M., 31, 36
Fry, R., 4, 13, 19

Gagnebin, M., xxv, 153–157, 161, 163,
    165, 168
Gantheret, F., 136, 138
Gauguin, P., 42
Gedo, J., 40, 54, 99, 106
Gill, M., 23, 37
Gilot, F., 41, 50, 54
Gilson, E., 27–28, 36
Goethe, J. W., xxi, xxvi
Goldberg, A., 99, 106
Golding, J., 11, 19
Goldstein, G., xxv, 173, 181, 183, 186
Gracq, J., 162, 168
Green, A., xxii, xxiv, 67, 77, 103, 107,
    140, 143, 155, 168, 178, 181,
    183–184, 186–187
Grimal, P., 172, 185, 187
Grotstein, J. S., 35–36
guilt, 16, 41, 43, 46, 49–50, 126–128
    see also: unconscious
  profound, 17

Hanly, C., xxiii, 6, 9, 11, 17–18, 20
Harris, M., 184, 187
Harvard University, 98
hate, 3, 128–129, 132, 178, 185 *see also*:
    unconscious
Heidegger, M., xxi, xxvi, 183
Held, R., 64, 66, 77
Hirn, Y., 4, 20
Hofer, M. A., 35–36
Housez, J., 64, 66, 77

intervention, 59, 62, 80, 94, 116, 154,
    158, 161, 163–164
  empathic, 105
  minimal, 89
  trivial, 26

James, W., 22–23, 33, 36
Jauss, H. R., xx, xxvi, 173, 187

Kahn, L., 165, 169
Kandinsky, V., 98–100, 107
Kant, E., xx–xxi, 88–89, 92, 142, 165, 169, 179
Khan, M., xxiv, 146–147
Kris, E., 23, 36

Lacan, J., xxii, 8, 79–81, 85–87, 93–95, 119, 181, 187
Lake, C., 41, 50, 54
Langer, S., 28, 36
Laplanche, J., 134, 138
Lautrec, 42
Lavie, J. C., 133, 138
Lebel, R., 64, 77
Levitin, J. D., 35–36
Lewin, B. D., 120, 122
Livingstone, M., 29, 36

Magritte, R., 99–100, 107
Mahler, M., 40, 54
Mailer, N., 52, 54
Mallarmé, S., 158, 169
Mandelstam, N., 27, 36
Mannoni, O., 141, 146, 149
Marinov, V., 128, 138
Masson, J. M., 131, 138
McDougall, J., 128, 138, 143, 149, 177, 187
melancholia, 42–43, 46, 51, 92, 132, 164
Meltzer, D., 134, 138, 160, 184, 187
Merleau-Ponty, M., 25, 36
metapsychology, xxii, 102, 127, 129–131
    extended, xxiv
    Freudian, 99
Meyer, L. B., 29, 37
Michelangelo, xxii, 13–19, 57, 105, 126–130, 174
Milner, M., 165, 169
Minazzoli, A., 154, 169
Monet, C., xxiii, 7–9, 18, 28
mother, xvi, 32, 66, 85, 95, 125, 144–146, 159–160, 177 see also: Oedipal
    –baby relationship, 145
    barefoot, 44
    castration of, 94–95
    –child engagements, 24
    devoted, 143
    distant, 66
    downcast, 42

environment-, 145
failing, 132
frozen, 66
good-enough, 143–144
    –infant transactions, xvi
neurasthenic, 66
object-, 144–145
motion, 6, 8, 14, 22–26, 28–29, 31–32, 34–35, 66, 139, 147–148, 155
    implicit, 24–26, 30–34
mourning, 43–44, 49, 51, 59, 92–93, 133, 156, 160
Museum of Modern Art, New York, 11, 13

narcissistic, xvi, xviii, 3, 40–41, 49, 68, 155, 172, 181–182, 185 see also: fantasy, object
    cathectisation, 131
    childhood, 181
    components, 58
    gratification, 114
    investment, 110
    mortification, 50
    needs, 41, 53
    neurosis, 131
    primary, 160
    resistance, 129
    wishes, 41
Neruda, P., 101, 107
Nettheim, N., 28, 35
Newman, A., 141, 145, 149
Noy, P., 24, 30, 37

object, 82–83, 85, 87–89, 93–94, 125, 130, 133–134, 144–145, 155, 160, 172, 174, 177–178, 182–183 see also: mother, Oedipal, self
    artistic, 4, 82, 89
    beloved, xviii, 132
    cultural, 72, 184
    enabling, 80
    external, 151
    good, xvii
    imaginary, 95
    infinite, 89
    libido, 82, 182
    loss, xvi, xx, 80, 132, 134
    loved, 59
    narcissistic, xviii, 155

of desire, 95
of representation, 87
part, xvi, 93
primary, xvi, 133, 135, 160
prohibited, 80
relations, xvi, 40, 50, 110, 135
sexual, 101, 180
symbolic, 94
  -imaginary, 81
transitional, xvi, 155
world, 40
objective
  aesthetic forms, 33
  perception, 145
  reality, 112, 143
  valued, 99
Oedipal
  ambivalence, 125, 132
  attachment, 12
  configuration, 66
  conflicts, xvi, 48
  fantasies, xvi
  feeling, 126
  mother, 125
  nature, 160
  object, 125
  pre-, xvi, 160
  rivals, 44, 125
  theory, 130
  victory, 44, 50
Oedipus, 18, 48, 50, 156
  complex, 94–95, 130, 160
Outeiral, J., xxiv

Parker, D. H., 4, 20
Paskaukas, R. A., 57, 77
Paz, O., 101, 104, 107
Penrose, R., 47, 49, 54
Perkins, J., 46, 55
Phidias, 2
Philadelphia Museum of Art, 11
Phillips, A., xxiv, 139, 142–143, 149–150, 163
Picasso, P., xxiii, 11–12, 14, 18, 30, 39–54
  Blue Period, 39, 42–44, 46–49, 51–54
  Rose Period, 52
Pine, F., 40, 54
Plato, xx, 1–3, 5–6, 9, 11, 15–20, 118–119, 122, 182–183, 185

Ponce, X. G., 85, 95
Porret, P., 128, 138
Pratt, C. C., 28, 37
processes, xxiii, 97–98, 102, 156, 172
  see also: psychic, unconscious
  creative, xxi, xxv, 105
  defensive, 1, 11, 18
  libidinal, 173
  primary, 30, 35, 103, 124–125, 178
  reparative, 59
  secondary, xxii–xxiii, 29–31, 35, 103, 178
  tertiary, xxiv, 103–105
projection, 3, 25, 27, 43, 46, 62, 71–72, 92, 157, 159
  neural, 34
projective identification, 115
Prufrock, J. A., 13
psyche, 102, 134
  creative, 102
  human, 3
  neurotic, 102, 105
  psychotic, 102
psychic, 51, 74, 99, 102–103, 127, 132, 154, 158, 165, 179
  accomplishments, 53
  act, 123–124, 126
  activities, 7, 126, 133, 176
  apparatus, 157
  atmosphere, xx
  conflict, 128, 172
  creativity, 134, 136–137
  depths, 100
  development, 147
  dynamic, 126
  elaboration, 125
  entities, 2, 22
  forces, 157
  formations, 103
  function, 71, 164
  intra-, 40
  life, 126, 128–131, 135–136, 181
  normality, 143
  processes, 102, 123, 164, 172
  progress, 129
  reality, 12, 72, 143
  space, 144
  structure, 155
  suffering, 148
  work, 128

Rancière, J., xxi, xxvi, 179, 187
Rappaport, D., 23, 37
Ravin, J., 46, 55
Recalcati, M.-H. B., 85, 95
Reik, T., 117, 122
representations, 47, 105, 125, 129–131, 136, 147, 164–165, 173
  abstract, 18
  repressed, 123, 136
  verbal, 124
repression, xvi, 80–82, 102, 120, 123–125, 129, 135–136, 147, 155, 157, 159, 177
  phantasmic, 82
Richardson, J., 44, 55
Ricoeur, P., 98, 106
Riemen, R., xxiii, xxvi, 174
Rilke, R. M., 25, 37
Rimbaud, A., 171, 187
Robinson, M., 33, 37
Rose, G. J., xxiii, 23, 37, 99, 107
Rosen, C., 29, 37
Ross, N. W., 26, 37
Royal Academy of Art, Madrid, 40
Rubinstein, L., 98, 106

Sabbadini, A., xxiv, 110, 113, 115–117, 122
Safranski, R., 99, 107
Saragnano, G., xx, xxvi
Sartre, J.-P., 11, 20, 99, 101, 107
Schafer, R., 23, 37
Schilder, P., 22–23, 29, 37
Schneider, M., 128, 138, 178, 187
Schore, A. N., 35, 37
Séchaud, E., 130, 138
Segal, H., xxiv, 58–60, 73, 77, 156, 160, 169
Seghers, P., 124, 138
Seigel, J., 66–67, 77
self, xvi–xvii, 24, 29, 33, 42–43, 48, 110, 181
  adapting, 147
  -assertion, 15
  -body, 29
  -contemplation, 3
  -defence, 165
  -definition, 53
  -denial, 16–17
  -destitution, 101
  -destructive, 49, 121
  -esteem, 16, 51
  -evident, 3
  false, 143, 147
  -inflicted, 16
  internalised, 50
  -love, xviii, 183
  -object, xvii
  -person, 166
  -portrait, 11–12, 16–17, 44, 148
  -questioning, 63
  -realisation, 40
  -referential, 49
  -reflexive, 158
  sense of, 145
  -sufficiency, 67
  true, 145, 147
sexual(ity), 14, 16, 68, 94, 102, 136, 171, 181, 183 see also: object
  a-, 14
  activity, 50, 52
  ambiguity, 12, 66
  arousal, 16
  bi-, 52, 67
  childhood, 152
  constitution, 161
  curiosity, xvi, 58, 180
  desire, 58, 136
  dimension, 126
  drive, 102–103
  encounter, 134
  excitation, 80
  excitement, 130, 134
  fantasy, 73
  glands, 75
  hetero-, 5, 17
  homo-, 5, 14–17, 44, 52
  identity, 52, 95
  implications, 41
  impulse, 52
  investigations, 134
  libido, 102
  life, 16, 183
  love, 15, 183
  morality, 114
  normal, 115
  psycho-, 179
  relationship, 15, 44
  satisfaction, 80
  theme, 67

tone, 64
trauma, 136
union, 50, 183
world, 135–137
Shakespeare, W., 13, 18, 20, 130, 142
Sheets-Johnstone, M., 29, 37
Sklarew, B., 24, 37
Sklarew, M., 24, 37
Solomon, M., 35, 37
Spurling, H., 25, 37, 149–150
Stein, A., 116, 122
Steiner, G., xxiv, xxvi, 174, 187
Stendhal, 98, 171, 187
Stevenson, R. L., 111, 122
subject(ive), xx, xxv, 25, 30, 33, 72, 81, 86–89, 92, 94–95, 160, 177, 183 *see also*: conscious
 changes, 79
 character, 67
 construction, xxv
 elements, xxvii
 experience, 34, 102
 model, 32
 phenomenon, 101, 145
 suffering, 153
 transitional, 155
 world, 143, 183
subjectivity, xix, xxiii–xxv, 33, 72, 172, 174
sublimation, xvi, xxiii–xxiv, 5, 9, 14–15, 17–18, 26, 34, 43, 58, 63, 73, 79–83, 85, 88, 92, 99, 102–103, 130, 153, 156–157, 159, 161, 163, 178
 aesthetic, 32
 drive, xvi, 102
 Freudian, 88
Suchet, D., xxiv, 124, 128, 136, 138
symbol(-ic), xvii, xxiii, 42–44, 49, 81–83, 85, 87, 89, 93, 95, 114, 142, 147, 153, 173, 182 *see also*: object
 castration, 160
 characteristic, 80
 construct, 94
 continuity, xx
 dimension, 81
 equations, 159
 expression, 146
 formation, 59
 frame, 172
 -imaginary, 81
 interpretation, xvii
 language, 80
 meaning, 71
 order, 81, 93
 representation, 120

theory, xx, 30, 74, 82, 128, 134, 140, 149, 160 *see also*: Oedipal
 aesthetic, 6
 apparatus, 119
 classical, 4
 creativity, 145
 Freudian, 80, 115
 psychoanalytic, xxv
 simulation, 34
Tolstoy, L. N., 26, 38
Tomkins, S., 28, 38
transference, xvii, 103, 105, 115, 125–126, 129, 131–132, 135, 176, 179, 182
 see also: countertransference
 cathexis, 133
 interpretation, 121
 movement, 133
transferential phenomena, 147
transitional *see also*: object, subject
 period, 52, 118
 phase, 42, 114
 phenomena, 140, 144–145
 place, 166
 space, xvi, xxiv, 110, 112
 -time, 117, 121
 state, 115
 time, xxiv, 110, 114–115
trauma(tic), xviii, xxi, 39, 51, 86–87, 93, 116, 136, 173, 178 *see also*: sexual
 anti-, 163
 childhood, 40
 cumulative, 146
 encounter, xxi
 events, 147
 experience, xvi, 46, 116, 146–147
 past, 46
 realism, 178
 situations, 116
Trías, E., 88, 95, 100, 107

unconscious(ness), xvii–xviii, xxi, 12, 21, 40, 67, 81, 124, 130, 136, 139, 152, 155, 161–165, 172–173, 176–177 *see also*: conscious(ness)
 beliefs, 115

bisexuality, 52
conflict, 39, 62, 64, 71, 126
desire, xx
fantasies, 60, 67, 71, 75, 117, 125, 127, 130, 134, 136
guilt, 44
hate, xviii
love, xviii, 44
material, 123–124
memory, 180
motions, 125
phantasm, 103
possession, 44
process, 21, 30, 147
psychic
   life, 128, 131
   processes, 172
   reality, 12
punishment, 50
realisation, 136
recognition, 32
representation, 123–124
repression, 126
thinking, 61
wishes, 120, 129

Valéry, P., 154, 169
Van Gogh, V., 42
Venus, 83–84, 176
Veron, E., 4, 20
Vico, 23
Viderman, S., 152, 169
Vinciguerra, R.-P., 85, 95
violence, 125–126, 128–129, 131, 136, 177–178
   attack, 116
   emotion, 174
   inadmissible, 128
   of creation, 172, 177, 179

Wajcman, G., 85, 95
Weisse, C., xxiv
Winnicott, D. W., xxii, xxvi, 99, 107, 110, 122, 139–150, 155, 169, 178–179, 184, 187

Zimet, C., 34–35
Zola, E., 9, 20
Zuckerkandl, V., 25, 38